THE
Quilting
ANSWER BOOK

Solutions to Every Problem You'll Ever Face

Answers to Every Question You'll Ever Ask

BARBARA WEILAND TALBERT

Storey Publishing

The mission of Storey Publishing is to serve our customers by
publishing practical information that encourages
personal independence in harmony with the environment.

Edited by Deborah Balmuth and Nancy D. Wood
Art direction and book design by Jessica Armstrong
Text production by Jennifer Jepson Smith

Cover photography by Mars Vilaubi
Quilt featured on cover created by Tala Neathawk
Illustration by Missy Shepler

Indexed by Nancy D. Wood

Printed in China by Regent Publishing Services
10 9 8 7 6 5 4 3

Library of Congress Cataloging-in-Publication Data

Weiland Talbert, Barbara
  The quilting answer book / by Barbara Weiland Talbert.
    p. cm.
  Includes index.
  ISBN 978-1-60342-144-7 (pbk. : alk. paper)
  1. Quilting. I. Title.
TT835.W446 2009
746.46—dc22

                                    2009001478

The biggest thanks goes to my best friend and cheerleader, my husband Stan Talbert, who supports me and my work in countless spoken and unspoken ways. Bless you, love of my life! This book is dedicated to you!

Contents

Acknowledgments

After a lifetime of sewing and quilting and writing about it, I find it difficult to list and thank all those who have supported me on my creative journey. My most special thanks goes to my mother, Eloise S. Weiland, a wonderful quiltmaker in her own right, who taught me to sew. She was always there to support my endeavors in 4-H, the Make It Yourself With Wool Contest, and my education in Textiles and Clothing at Colorado State University.

When Mom took up quiltmaking in the early '80s, I had finished only one quilt. She was a natural at it and I loved watching her skills mature. I'm happy to say I'm the proud owner of the one quilt she designed and then pieced and quilted entirely by hand. After that experience she quickly graduated to machine piecing and quilting, becoming a "topper," a quilter with many finished quilt tops ready to quilt. Mom is an inspiration and certainly contributed to my love for all things sewing- and quilting-related.

In addition to my mother, I owe a huge debt of gratitude to all those quilt-book authors whose work I have been privileged to edit since 1991. So many talented women from the United States and abroad have influenced my life and my quilting with their art and generous spirit. It would take pages to properly thank each one — they know who they are.

Introduction

When I made my first patchwork quilt in 1975, just before the renaissance of American quiltmaking took root in the midst of the 1976 Bicentennial celebrations, I knew nothing about quiltmaking. My first quilt was an adaptation of a quilt printed in black and white in a *Godey's Lady's Book* magazine of the 1860s.

I cut the large triangular patches for the quilt from solid red and solid white polyester/cotton gabardine (heavy) and used cotton plissé prints (lightweight and stretchy) for the two wide borders that framed the patches. The binding and backing were cut from a cotton/polyester polka-dot calico. The batting was a dense matt of polyester fleece, and the resulting quilt was a bit heavy and cumbersome — but it was colorful and warm.

Not knowing how to proceed with hand quilting such a large and heavy quilt after it was assembled, I tied the layers together with navy-blue wool yarn at the corners where the blocks met, row by row. I used the finished quilt on my bed for several years; I made my next quilt about ten years later during my first quiltmaking class.

As I embarked on that first quiltmaking adventure, there were no how-to books, and there were certainly no special tools. Sewing shears, a tape measure, ruler, graph paper, and a pencil, plus my trusty sewing machine, were all I had, plus well-developed dressmaking skills. I knew I could do it — after all it only required fabric and cutting and sewing straight lines — and there was no fitting involved.

Looking back over the years, I wish I had had the tools, materials, and books that are available to quilters today. It would have been helpful to have a basic quiltmaking handbook like this one close to my machine to answer my questions and guide me through the basic steps of quiltmaking. I am so grateful I had the opportunity to write this handbook to help others keep the answers they need at their fingertips, so all of their quiltmaking is successful, educational, and enjoyable.

In the years that have passed since my first quilt was published in a compilation of American needlework projects (*Needlework Nostalgia,* Butterick Publishing), I have taken quilting classes at my local quilt shops and at large quilting venues such as Quilt Festival, held every fall in Houston, Texas (*see* Resources). I've rubbed shoulders and worked with many of the best-known quilters in the country as a quilt-book editor, and I've learned something new from each of them.

I've made many quilts — only one of them following a printed pattern designed by someone else. The others are quilts and quilted projects of my own design or adaptations of vintage quilts in my collection — and some have been published as individual patterns. Like most quiltmakers, I have at least one or two projects in process and many ideas in my head for the next quilt and the next one.

This book contains the questions I have had along with those of many others who love to play with color and fabric to create beautiful quilts for themselves, family, and friends. They are questions you might ask as a beginner or even as a more experienced quiltmaker. Unless you make the same quilt design over and over, you are bound to learn something new with each project you start, and you will likely encounter new problems or challenges to resolve with each one. This book includes basic information that you will refer to often, as well as information that will ultimately become a part of your knowledge base that you use on a daily basis.

Get Started

One of the best ways to begin your own quiltmaking adventure and to get your questions answered is to take a quilting class from the pros at your local quilt shop. Quilting lessons are also available online. If there is a quilt guild in your area, join these quilting enthusiasts, and you're sure to come away from each meeting inspired and educated, refreshed and excited about your projects.

Develop a quilting buddy or two to share your experiences and problem-solve together. Some of the best quilt-book authors work in pairs, each one contributing their own perspective, skills, and methods to come up with more than one way to do the same thing with great success. Most importantly, enjoy yourself and share your quiltmaking skills with your friends. Have fun and keep on quilting with this little handbook at your fingertips. Quilting is good for your soul!

CHAPTER 1

Getting Started

Quiltmaking is one of America's most popular creative sewing pastimes. Quiltmakers use an array of beautiful fabrics, along with special tools and techniques, to create quilts that are both utilitarian and artistic. Like any craft, quiltmaking has its own terminology and techniques. Understanding what makes a quilt a quilt, the styles of quiltmaking possible, and the basic components needed to make patchwork and appliqué blocks — all are important first steps for beginners. More skilled quiltmakers will find this a good refresher course. So, first things first!

Quilt Anatomy 101

Quilts can be as small as a potholder or large enough to cover a bed, a wall, or even the side of a building. Originally utilitarian, today quilts have become an art form all their own. Many are bed coverings, but others are used for wall art, lap quilts, and smaller items such as placemats, table runners, and pillows. Quilted clothing, often called wearable art, is another popular use for the fabrics and techniques you will use as a quiltmaker.

- -

Q What makes a quilt a quilt?

A A quilt is composed of three essential layers plus quilting stitches and edge finishing. The "quilt sandwich" has:

▶ a decorative quilt top composed of pieced or appliquéd blocks (or both)

▶ the filler, called batting

▶ the backing

▶ quilting stitches to hold the layers together: these can be simple straight lines or more decorative stitching; quilts can also be tied together with yarn or thread

▶ binding to finish the outer edges

Variations of this basic sandwich do exist, but the classic three-layer quilt is the basis for discussion in the pages that follow. For the record, this illustration shows a quilt with a straight side-by-side setting, straight-cut inner borders, and outer borders with pieced corner squares.

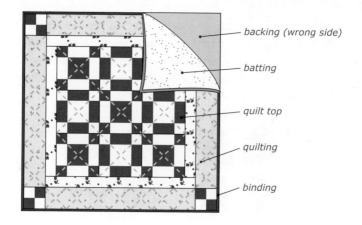

backing (wrong side)

batting

quilt top

quilting

binding

Q **What is a pieced quilt top and how does that differ from an appliquéd quilt?**

A A pieced quilt top is typically made of patchwork blocks — usually squares made of two or more smaller pieces arranged to create an interesting pattern.

An appliquéd quilt is also composed of blocks, but the patterns on the surface of the blocks and borders are made by cutting design shapes (a floral bouquet for example) and then positioning them on the surface of a background block. The pieces may be held in place with invisible handstitches or a variety of machine stitches.

Some pieced tops also feature appliquéd embellishment and some appliquéd quilts may have pieced elements. Most quilts

13

are framed by one or more borders, which can be solid strips of fabric, or border strips composed of patchwork piecing. Some quilts have sashing, sashing squares, corner squares, setting triangles, setting squares, or some combination of these. The required pieces depend on the quilt setting.

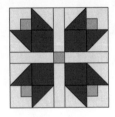

*Tulips All Around
patchwork block*

*Tulip Toss
appliqué block*

Q What is a quilt setting?

A "Setting" refers to the way blocks are arranged in a patchwork or appliquéd quilt. Most quilts are arranged in a straight setting or a diagonal setting (*see* Set Gallery *on pages 210–11*).There are also several variations of each of these two basic settings from which to choose.

SEE ALSO: *Settings and Borders, page 207.*

QUILT STYLES

Quilt design is a personal choice, but it helps to know your options for designing quilts. There are far more quilt types than the ones featured here, but these represent the most common styles. Combined with quilt-setting options (*see page 208*) the possibilities for unique quilt designs are limited only to your personal creativity and aesthetic preferences.

Album block

Album, Friendship, or Memory Quilt. A type of quilt made of blocks sewn by different individuals. These quilts are often created as a gift to commemorate a special occasion and may be signed by the makers with indelible ink or with embroidery. Contemporary memory quilts often include photos printed on specially treated fabric.

Amish-style strip quilt

Amish Quilt. Quilts featuring rich solid colors and large geometric shapes that reflect the simplicity of color and design common to the Amish culture. Jewel-tone colors, plus black, dark purple, and navy blue are typical.

Appliqué Quilt. Quilts featuring blocks and borders created by sewing design motifs to background squares and strips and joining them into quilt tops. They range from primitive to folk art to highly sophisticated and complex designs.

SEE ALSO: *All About Appliqué, page 169.*

(Quilt Styles, *continued*)

Art Quilt. Usually a quilt intended to hang on the wall, but some are postcard size and some are very large. They may be pieced, appliquéd, and/or highly embellished with any of a number of art techniques, including stamping, stenciling, painting, free-form stitching, and 3-D effects, to name a few.

typical Baltimore Album block

Baltimore Album Quilt. Appliquéd quilts featuring blocks with different appliqués in each one (*see page 210*). Appliqués are often quite complex and symbolic; floral designs, baskets, and wreaths are common designs. These quilts were popularized in Baltimore, Maryland, in the mid-1800s, hence the name. Red and green fabrics were popular choices for these designs.

Crazy Quilt block

Crazy Quilt. A quilt made of blocks constructed with irregular pieces or scraps of fabric with no predetermined pattern. The blocks are often heavily embellished with embroidery. They were popular during Victorian times and were made of silks, velvets, and other dressmaking fabrics and trims.

Charm Quilt. A quilt made of small blocks, usually no larger than 5" square, but often only 2" square. In a true charm quilt, no fabric is repeated — every one is different.

Hawaiian Quilt. A wholecloth quilt (*see page 18*) with a large-scale, snowflake-like appliqué, usually a solid color on a white background. Because of the complexity of the design shapes, this type of appliqué is usually done by hand with the needle-turn method (*see page 196*).

Hawaiian appliqué

Honeycomb (hexagon). An overall pattern of small hexagon shapes. These quilts are usually made using English paper piecing and sewn together with hand stitches. This type of piecing results in quilts with uneven outer edges that are finished with a turn-and-stitch technique instead of binding.

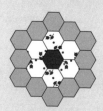

Honeycomb (Grandmother's Flower Garden)

SEE ALSO: *English Paper Piecing, page 161.*

Log Cabin Quilt. A traditional American quilt. The blocks typically have a red center square symbolizing the hearth or a yellow square symbolizing the light in the cabin window. The center is surrounded by the "logs" — strips of fabric added in a clockwise (or counterclockwise) fashion. Blocks are usually composed

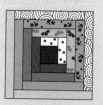

Log Cabin block

with light strips on one half and dark on the other, and are arranged in a number of different ways. Playing with a set of Log Cabin blocks on a design wall (*see page 212*) can yield interesting new patterns.

Medallion Quilt. A quilt with a central block or set of four blocks, often set on point (diagonal setting) surrounded by other quilt elements including additional blocks, sashing, setting triangles, and multiple borders. (*See page 211.*)

Sampler Quilt. Usually a patchwork quilt made of many different block designs sewn from the same group of fabrics. Sampler blocks are often made by beginners to learn piecing skills.

Scrap Quilt. A patchwork quilt made of pieces or blocks cut from scraps. In a "planned scrappy" quilt, the user purchases a group of fabrics to make scrappy blocks for the quilt rather than relying on her collection of scraps from previous projects.

Strip Quilt. Quilts with blocks arranged in horizontal or vertical rows that alternate with plain strips of fabric. Plain strips offer a great background for more elaborate quilting designs. (*See the Amish quilt on page 15.*)

Wholecloth Quilt. A quilt made with one large piece of fabric for the top and another matching one for the backing, with batting in between. (The fabric for the front and back may have piecing seams to make them large enough.) The design relies entirely on intricate quilting designs.

Yo-Yo Quilt. An assembly of small, round puffs of fabric (made from gathered circles) that have been joined edge to edge (*see page 390*).

Q I have a quilt my grandmother made, but there are no quilting stitches, just little tufts of yarn that hold the layers together. Is it really a quilt?

A Technically, yes, if it has the three layers described in the first question in this section. What you have is a tied quilt, often called a comforter. Stitching through the quilt layers with yarn or heavy thread and then tying the ends securely is an easy way to finish a quilt. It is often used for bed coverings or lap quilts for quick results. Once you begin to quilt the layers with stitches and see the decorative results possible with even simple straight stitching, you may never tie a quilt again.

SEE ALSO: *Tying a Quilt, page 340.*

Patchwork Building Blocks

Many patchwork block designs are composed of simple geometric shapes that are easy to cut using rotary cutting methods. Many other shapes, including curved pieces, can be assembled into patchwork blocks, but they may require template cutting and/or specialized piecing techniques. Combine the myriad block design possibilities with the incredible array of beautiful fabrics available, and the quilt-block design possibilities are endless. And when you add appliqué to patchwork blocks, the block design options multiply further.

SEE ALSO: *Rotary Cutting and Strip Piecing, page 87; Templates, Pressing and Piecing, page 107; and Quilter's Math Made Easy, page 395.*

Q What shapes are most often used to create patchwork blocks?

A The basic geometric shapes used to create most patchwork blocks are shown below. These shapes, called patches and hence the name patchwork, can be rotary-cut without using a template, if you prefer, although some may require a specially designed ruler or the use of a cutting guide with the rotary ruler. They can also be marked on the fabric using templates and then cut out with scissors. Combining these shapes to create your own block designs is fun and easy when you understand how to draw blocks on a grid. *(See the next question.)*

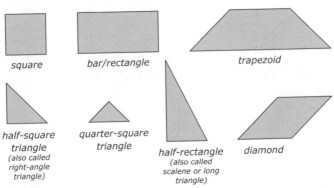

square   bar/rectangle   trapezoid

half-square
triangle
*(also called
right-angle
triangle)*

quarter-square
triangle

half-rectangle
*(also called
scalene or long
triangle)*

diamond

Once cut, the basic geometric patches are joined into patchwork units that are then combined to create patchwork blocks. (Some of them can be made using the strip-piecing method described in chapter 4.)

Common units are shown on the facing page; those that finish as squares are also used as patchwork blocks (names in parentheses). The 4-patch unit can stand on its own, or be combined with other units to create an entirely different patchwork block.

2-patch unit   3-patch unit   2-bar unit   3-bar unit

half-rectangle unit

pieced diamond unit

pieced trapezoid unit

pieced triangle unit (Flying Geese)

4-patch unit (Fourpatch)

9-patch unit (Ninepatch)

quarter-square triangle unit (Hourglass)

half-square triangle unit (Ocean Waves)

4 half-square triangles (Pinwheel)

square with half-square triangles (Square-in-a-Square)

Q What do you mean by designing blocks on a grid?

A Graph paper is a grid. Paper with 4 or 8 squares per inch is necessary if you want to try designing your own blocks using the shapes and units shown on the previous page. (For some designs you may need graph paper with 5 or 10 squares to the inch). Many quilt-block patterns with simple geometric shapes are designed on square grids that can be broken down into equal rows or units. Some of the most commonly used grids for patchwork blocks include the ones shown at the bottom of this page.

In addition, these grids can be filled in such a way that not all units are the same shape, resulting in uneven grids. Because of the patch shapes and sizes, the grid is not as obvious in the finished block, but it is still the underlying framework for the block. The most commonly used uneven grids include uneven Fourpatch, Fivepatch, and Ninepatch grids. The block examples that follow are identified with their grid as well as the pieces or units required to make them. The grid lines are the graph lines underlying them.

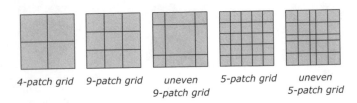

4-patch grid   9-patch grid   uneven   5-patch grid   uneven
                                  9-patch grid   5-patch grid

Putting pieced units and simple patches (unpieced) together to create blocks is the next step. These are only a few of the designs that you can create using the units shown on page 21.

Rail Fence
*2-bar units
(9-patch grid)*

Hopscotch
*4-patch + half-square
triangle units
(4-patch grid)*

The Bobbin
*3-patch + half-
rectangle units
(9-patch grid)*

Broken Dishes
*square + 3-bar +
hourglass
(9-patch grid)*

Diamond Pinwheel
*2-patch + pieced
diamond
(4-patch grid)*

Pinwheel Square
*pinwheel units +
square + rectangles
(uneven 5-patch grid)*

Hen & Chicks
*9-patch in 3-patch
units
(9-patch grid)*

Fair and Square
*squares + rectangles
+ square-in-a-square
(uneven 9-patch grid)*

Spinning Spools
*pieced trapezoid +
rectangles
(4-patch grid)*

Beginner's Luck

When you're excited about learning a new craft, it's easy to get in over your head and end up with an unfinished or unsuccessful project. It's better to start with a simple and easy design, such as a small quilted project like a placemat or table runner, and work up to more challenging designs as you continue to develop your skills.

- -

Q Do you have any tips for success for a beginning quilter?

A Begin by taking an introductory quilting class from your local quilt shop. It's one of the easiest ways to learn the lingo and get professional advice and direction when choosing a quilt pattern appropriate for your skill level. You'll also get help with fabric selection and color planning, two essential keys to a successful project. If you don't have access to a store in your area, there are Web sites that offer instruction for beginners. Here are few basics to keep in mind:

▶ **Make sure you have the basic tools.** *(See page 69.)*

▶ **Start small and simple.** It's really tempting to try to make a complex quilt, but you'll serve your best interests by first making a baby quilt, wall quilt, or small lap quilt.

▶ **Look for patterns with easy blocks.** Start with a few simple patches and straight seams. Larger blocks with fewer pieces are easier than large blocks with lots of small pieces.

▶ **Begin with a limited color palette.** Two- and three-color quilts can be just as interesting and successful as those with more fabrics. (*See page 49.*)

▶ **Use 100 percent cotton designed for quiltmaking.** Buy the best you can afford for your project. Quilter's cottons don't ravel much, are easy-care, and easy to cut and sew.

▶ **Preshrink the fabrics before you begin.** Add a spritz of spray sizing or starch to any fabric that loses a lot of body in the wash and press the fabric before you start cutting.

▶ **Look for a pattern with blocks that don't require templates for the pieces.** Try those with rotary-cut strips, squares, rectangles, and half-square triangles first.

▶ **Read through the directions first.** Be sure you understand the cutting and block construction before you cut.

▶ **Practice stitching accurate ¼-inch-wide seam allowances.** (*See page 124.*)

▶ **Make a practice block.** Learn how it goes together and how to press it.

▶ **Keep a sharp seam ripper handy.** Even experienced quiltmakers use them more often than you might think.

▶ **Follow the pressing directions in the pattern.** If no pressing directions are included, refer to Press It Right (*see page 113*).

▶ **Use thin batting, not thick.** It's easier to handle.

▶ **Don't obsess over errors.** Give yourself credit for your progress and growing bank of quiltmaking skills.

Q There are so many details to keep track of! How will I remember it all?

A The best advice I can offer is to keep a quilting notebook. A three-ring binder is ideal, because it allows you to add and remove materials whenever you like. You can start with a 1" or 2" spine, but you might be surprised how quickly you fill that up. If you think you'll do a lot of quilting, start with a 3" spine, to give you room to grow. Tabbed or numbered dividers can help you organize topics, and clear plastic sheet protectors will give you a place to tuck away odds and ends.

Here is a starter list of some things you might want to keep:

▶ Photographs and articles that inspire you to quilt
▶ Your sketches, plans, and ideas for new projects
▶ Technique directions from quilting classes
▶ Stitching and batting samples
▶ Packaging with directions for new tools and notions
▶ Interesting quilting designs
▶ Notes on tension adjustments
▶ Photos and records of work in progress
▶ Any quilting information that you might want for future reference

Some quilters keep careful written and photographic records of each project they make. Your quilting notebook will not only be an invaluable reference, it can serve as a journal that will capture a lifetime of quilting.

CHAPTER 2

Choosing Fabric

Most quiltmaking projects require cutting fabric into small pieces and then reassembling them to create the decorative quilt top. This is true for all types of patchwork and appliqué quilts. Choosing the fabric for your quilts is an essential part of turning out a beautifully crafted project that will last and last. Quilter-friendly fabric choices abound. Understanding fabric terms as well as the fabric descriptions used in quilt patterns is essential to choosing the best fabrics for the quilt design you are making.

Best Quilting Fabrics

The majority of patchwork and appliqué quilts are made from 100 percent woven cotton, commonly known as quilter's cotton. Other fabrics are sometimes used in combination for special effects and decorative embellishments in the blocks or quilt surface. For art quilts, the choice of fabrics is much broader because these quilts are most often used as wall hangings and care issues are not as pressing as for quilts that will be used and washed.

- -

Q Why is cotton fabric so ideal for quiltmaking?

A Quilter's cotton is relatively lightweight, but opaque and easy to launder. The plain weave is stable, so excess raveling is not a concern. This is particularly important for patchwork with its many piecing seams, and for appliqué with its underlying cut-and-turned edges. Cotton has an excellent memory: when you fold it and firmly finger-press it, the crease remains. That makes it easy to manipulate as you sew the blocks and other pieces together.

Cotton is also soft, drapable, and relatively inexpensive. Cotton shrinks from 1 to 5 percent, but prewashing helps reduce the shrinkage in subsequent washings. The shrinkage is seen as positive by quilters who love the dimpling that occurs around the quilting stitches after a finished quilt is washed.

Q **What about wool? Can I use that for quiltmaking?**

A Yes, but it will be heavier than a cotton quilt, may not require batting, and will require dry cleaning. Wool appliqué quilts are particularly appealing.

- -

Q **How is quilter's cotton sold?**

A Most quilter's cottons are doubled — folded in half lengthwise — and then wrapped around a cardboard bolt that includes information about the fabric on the label at the bolt end. Quilter's cottons range in width from 39" to 45", measured from selvage to selvage (*see page 35*).

Most published quilt patterns are based on 40" or 42" of usable width after preshrinking, and the fabric needed to make the quilt is listed in yards. (See the chart on page 30 for the most common cut sizes, helpful when planning a cutting layout that will waste the least amount of fabric.) The selvages are not usable in quilts, so you will lose at least ½" of the fabric width before or after preshrinking.

If the fabric you want isn't at least 44" wide on the bolt, purchase additional fabric to allow for the variance and potential shrinkage. Some basic colors and prints are available in much wider pieces and are popular for backings on large quilts because they don't require piecing.

- -

Q **What are fat quarters, fat eighths, jelly rolls, and charm packs?**

A Many quilt patterns require minimal yardage of some fabrics, for instance ⅛- and ¼-yard cuts. If these pieces are cut across the fabric width, the result is a narrow 4½"- or 9"-wide strip that is 44" or 45" long. Fat quarters and fat eighths have the same amount of fabric as the straight-cut strips would have, but are cut in larger rectangles that are easier to handle and result in less waste. Most quilt shops sell these pre-cuts individually as well as in coordinated packs.

Charm packs and jelly rolls afford the quilter a great way to acquire lots of different fabrics for scrap quilts. Charm packs contain 5" squares of many different fabrics and are priced according to the number of squares in the pack. Jelly rolls may contain as many as 40 strips of fabric, each 2½" wide (a little over 2¾ yards). Jelly rolls may go by other names, and the total yardage varies. Many patchwork blocks can be made by cutting units from 2½" strips, making them a good choice for creating scrappy quilts (*see page 18*) without the necessity of buying yardage of many different fabrics.

Standard Cut Sizes
Fat quarter = 18" × 22"
Fat eighth = 9" × 22"
Fat sixteenth = 4½" × 22"

Note: When you preshrink fat quarters or eighths, the pieces will be slightly smaller. Preshrinking charm squares and jelly rolls is not practical unless you launder by hand.

Q How do I know I'm buying quality cotton for my quilt? Are there tests I should do?

A Fabric hand (how a fabric feels) and drape (how a fabric hangs) vary from manufacturer to manufacturer. Some are almost silky and drape beautifully. Some feel quite stiff, almost boardy. The quality of the cotton used, the dyes, and the manufacturing processes all affect the fabric hand. Excess dye can bleed onto other fabrics, and excess sizing — which may give a cotton fabric some or all of its body — washes out, changing the fabric hand. If the fabric feels and drapes like a fabric that would be comfortable to wear in a shirt or blouse, is not too stiff or tightly woven, and is 100 percent cotton, it's likely a good choice for your quilt.

- -

Q Are there cotton fabrics to avoid for quiltmaking?

A Fortunately, it's easy to see and feel which fabrics to avoid:

▶ **Loosely woven fabrics.** Fabrics that are unstable, stretch out of shape, and don't have enough body to stand up to the construction techniques will not wear well.

▶ **Fabrics that are noticeably thinner than most.**

▶ **Overly stiff fabrics.** Some fabrics are stiff due to sizing; however, sizing washes out.

▶ **Misprints or poor color saturation.** Missing or incorrectly printed sections may be unusable in your quilt.

▶ **Too much dye.** Rub the fabric layers together and watch for color rub-off, called crocking (*see next question*).

▶ **Fabrics that are obviously off grain.** On printed fabrics, it may be easier to examine the grainline on the wrong side because the color saturation is not as intense. Examine the selvages to see if the design wanders off at an angle. If the threads don't run parallel and perpendicular to the selvage, it's best to avoid the fabric. Grainline imperfections are particularly noticeable and problematic for directional designs.

▶ **Fabric with a noticeably strong odor.** This indicates too much finish, used in an attempt to disguise poor quality.

- -

Q What is color crocking?

A When you rub two layers of fabric together and you can see color come off on your hands or transfer from one fabric to the other, that's *crocking*. When a fabric is wet and the water changes color, the dye is *bleeding* from the fabric into the water — and onto other fabrics, if present, in the same water. Neither one is desirable in fabrics for quilts. If crocking exists, the excess dye will run during the first wash and perhaps during successive washes, and is often redeposited on lighter colors in the quilt.

Q Should I use a solid color or a print for the quilt backing?

A Personally, I prefer prints, as they are more visually interesting and they hide quilting stitch errors. Allover prints with relatively small motifs (patterns) are more "forgiving" of stitching inaccuracies than those with large, widely spaced motifs. Busy prints that cover the fabric surface are also a good choice because the stitches get lost in the busy-ness. Tone-on-tone prints (*see page 47*) make good backings as well.

Fabric Stashing

Most confirmed quiltmakers own a fabric stash — fabrics they've accumulated but have not yet used. Some quilter's call this their fabric library. I call it a quilter's paintbox. Scraps and leftovers are also an important part of the stash, which offer the quiltmaker an array of print and color choices for appliqués and scrappy patchwork blocks.

Q How do I start building a stash of my own?

A Each quiltmaker's paintbox will vary depending on budget, available storage space, personal taste, and quilt-making style. The most important rule to follow when adding a fabric to your stash is that you love it. Buying it just because it's on sale is usually not a good idea. To give you an idea of how to build a collection, here's how I choose fabrics for my stash:

▶ Fat quarters, fat eighths, jelly rolls, and charm packs (*see page 30*) are an economical way to build up a collection of colors and prints for scrappy quilts.

▶ When I see a fabric I absolutely love, I usually buy three or four yards of it. That's enough to include it in a quilt top, use for borders, or to back a smaller quilt.

▶ Whenever possible I buy backing fabrics at end-of-bolt sales.

▶ I have a good selection of 2-yard cuts of mottled tone-on-tone fabrics in a rainbow of colors. These fabrics work beautifully for block backgrounds as well as for borders and bindings. They are also good "blenders"; they help make color transitions in blocks and they offer interesting and realistic shading for appliqués.

▶ I buy white and off-white, tone-on-tone prints in 3-yard cuts so I always have a good selection for block backgrounds.

▶ Since I usually work in bright, clear colors, those are what you'll find most in my stash, as well as anything in the pink family because it's my favorite color.

▶ If I'm following a patchwork quilt pattern, I always buy a little extra (⅛ to ¼ yard, if the required yardage is minimal; ½ to ¾ yard when the fabric requirements are larger). This allows for preshrinking as well as for changing my mind about how I will use the fabric.

Fabric Preparation

Before you cut the pieces for your quilt, it's important to understand how woven fabric is made and how to prepare it for optimum results. When handling fabric and cutting the pieces, paying attention to grainline is essential. Cutting fabrics on the grain will prevent stretching that affects the size of the finished blocks and hence the quilt.

- -

Q **What is fabric grainline?**

A Quilter's cottons and all other woven fabrics are produced on looms strung with a series of lengthwise warp threads, referred to as the *lengthwise grain*. The *crosswise* threads are woven in and out of the lengthwise yarns, back and forth across the loom. At the outer edges, these yarns are packed more closely together (more threads per inch) and they are called *selvages* (self-edges). Because they interlace with more threads per inch at the edges, the selvages are firmer and more closely woven than the rest of the fabric and they don't ravel. Sometimes the selvages shrink more than the rest of the fabric, causing puckering so don't use them in your quilt.

The lengthwise yarns in the fabric are the strongest and have little stretch. The crosswise yarns are usually not as strong, so the fabric has a bit of give or stretch in that direction. If you draw a 45-degree angle from adjacent corners, you'll find the bias grain. This direction has lots of stretch. Placement of the grainline is important when cutting the pieces to ensure that your quilt pieces and blocks do not stretch out of shape while you are sewing.

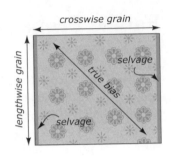

- -

Q How do I follow the grainline when I cut out the pieces for my quilt?

A Most quilt pieces are cut with the outer edges of the patches following the lengthwise or crosswise grain as closely as possible in order to avoid stretching the pieces during sewing. The cutting directions for most quilts will specify the grainline direction — often called "straight of grain" — for the individual pieces with a double-pointed arrow.

If you are using templates (patterns for shaped pieces for quilt blocks), look for the grainline arrows to guide your placement on the fabric for cutting; the arrow should be parallel to the lengthwise or the cross-wise threads in the fabric. It's important to remember that the bias grain stretches and is undesirable along the outer edges of the finished blocks or the finished quilt top.

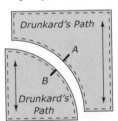

Use grainline arrows for positioning on fabric.

Q When is it okay to cut on the bias?

A Quiltmakers use bias to advantage when cutting some pieces. Binding for the outer edges of a quilt is often cut on the bias for better wear. Bias-cut edges are easier to turn under on some appliqué shapes (*see page 185*).

- -

Q I've heard that some quilters preshrink all quilting fabrics and others never do. Who's right?

A Both! It boils down to personal preference and often to the preferences of those from whom you learn to quilt. While I am firmly in the preshrinking camp, there are different philosophies about this issue. Here are a few things to consider:

▶ Quiltmakers who believe quilts should never be washed say preshrinking isn't necessary.

▶ Quilts that have nonwashable embellishments and fabrics that must be dry-cleaned do not require preshrinking.

▶ Many quilters don't like dry cleaning because of the residual chemicals left in the quilt. So preshrinking and washing is the only option for quilts that will be laundered.

▶ Many quilters prefer working with crisp unwashed fabrics, claiming they are easier to cut and handle without stretching and don't ravel during the cutting and piecing.

▶ Others wash fabrics to control shrinkage and bleeding, then add a light coat of spray starch to fabrics that lose too much body in the wash. Some quiltmakers will immerse fabrics in a starch bath and then press them dry to make the fabrics stiff for easier cutting.

▶ If you're sensitive to chemicals, it's essential to launder cotton fabrics to remove finishing chemicals and dyes.

▶ Those who prefer the look of antique quilts, may pre-shrink the fabric but not the cotton batting (*see page 273*), and then wash the finished quilt to raise the texture for an heirloom look — the puckered, popcornlike surface that characterizes vintage quilts. If you don't preshrink the fabric either, the texture is even more pronounced after the first wash.

▶ Since different fabrics shrink at different rates, preshrink-ing them all first levels the field.

▶ *One rule not to break:* If you preshrink one fabric for your quilt, preshrink them all so there will be no surprises later.

- -

Q Won't the colors bleed or run during preshrinking or subsequent launderings?

A Today's quality quilter's cottons are less likely to bleed and run than those available 30 years ago. If you plan to preshrink your fabric, it's a good idea to check them — espe-cially dark, saturated colors — for colorfastness. Cut small swatches of each fabric for your quilt and machine-baste them to a piece of muslin or light-colored cotton. Wash in warm or hot water with mild detergent and dry in the dryer. Check to see if any of the colors bled into others. If so, separate the offending fabric(s) and wash them again to disperse the excess dyes into the wash water. Test again and if bleeding continues, choose a different fabric or try using a dye fixative (*see the last question on this page*).

- -

Q Okay, so what's the best way to preshrink quilter's cottons?

A If the fabrics pass the bleed test, they can be laundered together — darks with darks, mediums together, and lights with lights, just in case. Wash in warm water with ¼ cup of mild detergent such Orvus Paste or Woolite (with a dye-grabber sheet from the laundry section in the grocery store if desired). Remove the fabric from the washer and give each piece a good shake to fluff it before tossing it into the dryer. Tumble dry on the permanent-press setting until barely damp. Press dry to smooth out wrinkles and then fold neatly for storage.

- -

Q Is there anything I can add to the wash water to set the dyes in my quilting fabrics?

A Retayne is a dye fixative that sets the color in commercially dyed fabrics. When cottons show signs of color bleeding in your colorfastness test (*see page 38*), using this product would be a good idea. After washing the fabric with Retayne, test for colorfastness again. If it still runs, don't use the fabric in a quilt you plan to wash.

Synthrapol is another product that you might want to try. When used as directed, it attracts excess dye in cotton fabrics so the dye is not deposited on other fabrics in the wash.

Note: Some references suggest setting dyes with vinegar or salt, but they do not work as dye fixatives. Vinegar, however, does help remove soap scum, odors, and stains.

Solving Problems

Q I laundered my fabrics to preshrink them, and when I took them out of the dryer they were hopelessly raveled and twisted together. How can I prevent this?

A There are several strategies that will help prevent this problem:

▶ To prevent raveling, serge the raw edges before washing the fabric or use a long, wide zigzag stitch.

▶ For cuts of 1 yard or more, fold the fabric in half crosswise and serge or zigzag the two raw edges together.

▶ To prevent extensive twisting, which causes wrinkles, add a few large terry towels to the dryer.

▶ Divide ⅛- and ¼-yard cuts (as well as fat eighths and fat quarters) into small groups and place them in large, zip-top mesh laundry bags, the kind used for washing lingerie.

▶ Some quilters clip the four corners at a 45-degree angle to prevent raveling.

Q Help! When I washed a recently finished quilt, the dark blue fabric bled onto the light colors. Is there any way to remove the color where it doesn't belong?

A You can try soaking the quilt in Synthrapol, a product designed to attract dyes, following the manufacturer's directions. While the quilt soaks, move it around periodically to disperse any of the dyes that continue to release into the water. If you use a washing machine, use only gentle agitation for this process. Lay out the quilt to dry on a flat surface. If you notice dyes are still running, rinse and dry again. This process is worth a try but there are no guarantees.

- -

Q I didn't preshrink my fabrics, and now my quilt is stained. Would it be safe to wash it?

A That's a tough call. If you can stand to risk damaging the quilt in a laundering mishap, try the delicate cycle, cold water, and use a dye magnet — and good luck!

- -

Q I've discovered that one manufacturer's quilter's cotton is far easier to handle and shrinks less than any others I've tried. I'm really tempted to use only their fabrics in my quilt. Is that a good idea?

A While it would be nice to use fabrics from only one manufacturer in a quilt, that's not very realistic. Quilts are far more exciting when you choose fabrics you love, regardless of manufacturer, to combine in your quilts. Plus, you automatically limit your choices when you stick with only one manufacturer. In addition, the color stories and designs change each season, so next season or next year you may not find anything you like in the line from a particular manufacturer. I think it's better to use fabric from a number of manufacturers to create quilts with character, while you learn how to work around the challenges you may find in some fabrics.

Fabric-Selection Strategies

Choosing fabric for your quilting project is one of the most fun and enjoyable parts of the quiltmaking process. If you are a beginner, you will probably choose a pattern in a book and copy or adapt the color scheme shown. Or, you might take a beginner's class and choose fabrics with the teacher's guidance. As you make more quilts and improve your skills, you will also develop your own style — and the confidence to design your own quilts and choose the fabrics on your own.

- -

Q **There are so many fabrics in the quilt shop, I don't know how to choose. Do you have any suggestions?**

A Most rules are made to be broken but I can share some general fabric selection strategies that work:

1. Begin with a multicolored focus print with three or more colors that you love. This works best in a medium- to

large-scale design motif. Then choose other coordinating and contrasting prints using the focus fabric as your guide. Aim for a mix of light and dark prints. *Note:* You're not required to actually use the focus fabric in your quilt; it can just be the inspiration for the color palette or used for the backing and/or binding.

2. Another factor to take into consideration is variety in scale and print density. A quilt cut entirely from tiny prints or dense prints won't be as interesting as one with prints in different scales. Relative scale (small, medium, and large) is used to define fabric selections in quilt project materials lists. Consider the size of the motifs in relationship to each other.

3. If you are working with a quilt pattern, examine the color choices in the photo that comes with the pattern. Notice the balance of darks and lights; prints, solids, or near solids; print type (for instance: floral, geometric); the size of the motifs (small, medium, large); and the overall color scheme. Is the quilt a complementary, analogous, two-tone, or a tertiary scheme? (*See pages 50–51.*) Even if the fabrics used are not your favorites, use the finished quilt as a guide for your own unique take on the quilt design.

4. If a pattern calls for a solid color, consider substituting a mottled tone-on-tone print or a small allover print that "reads" as a solid. This kind of print can help hide inaccuracies in piecing and in quilting the layers together. The subtle changes in color add movement and textural interest to the quilt that isn't possible with solid colors.

5. This might sound obvious, but choose colors and prints that you like, perhaps the colors you wear or those in your decorating scheme. Choose a group of colors and prints that are different values (*see the next question*), so there is some contrast in the finished quilt.

6. If the colors and prints you've chosen need a little punch, try adding a little black to the color recipe. Another idea: One professional quiltmaker I know says every quilt needs a little yellow, and it doesn't have to be pure yellow or gold — neutrals with a golden cast qualify, too. Of course this may not work at all in some color palettes.

7. Look at the fat-quarter bundles available at your quilt shop for color cues. They are often cut and bundled in color-coordinated groups of print styles, colors, and values that will work well together in a quilt. Use them as a guide to choose yardage for your project.

8. Ask for help in your local quilt shop. Many employees are quiltmakers themselves and can help you choose fabrics for your quilt. At the very least, they can offer a constructive opinion about your selections. If available, take a beginner's class on fabric and color selection.

- -

Q What is the "value" of a fabric and why is it so important?

A Value defines the relative lightness or darkness of a fabric. It's an important factor in fabric selection because using different values creates visual depth and contrast and helps define the patch shapes in the block. Without value differences, the individual patches in your block will all but disappear and you won't be happy with the results.

a range of values

Value is easier to determine when looking at solid colors or small, simple prints on open backgrounds. The more color and detail in a print, the more difficult it may be to define its color value at first. Values also shift in a block, depending on their placement. A medium-value fabric may look light on a very

Pinwheel blocks with different value placements

dark background or look dark when used with a yellow print. Where you place lights and darks within the block can have a marked effect on the final look of the block, as seen above.

Many quilters use a value finder to evaluate the colors they've chosen. You can purchase red and green plastic value finders, or you can make your own by cutting 2" × 6" strips from green and red see-through plastic notebook covers. By viewing warm colors (red, yellow, and orange) and green through a red value finder, you can see the contrast without the distraction of the actual colors. Use the green one for cool colors (red-violet, purple, blue, and blue-green).

Another way to organize values in a group of fabrics is to cut swatches of each one and arrange them side-by-side on a copy machine. The photocopy changes the colors to a gray scale and makes it easier to see the values.

- -

Q How do I know what the fabric terms in materials charts for quilt patterns mean?

A It's important to develop a print vocabulary. Here are some terms and definitions to get you started.

Abstract. Imaginative motifs that are not recognizable as real people, things, or places.

Allover print. The fabric surface is covered with a basic design and there is no up or down direction. The motifs may be "tossed" on a background color or they may be closely packed together so that very little of the background color shows.

Background print. Most quilts require a background fabric, one against which the remaining fabrics in the quilt will shine. Sometimes this is a light neutral or pastel, but it may be a medium or dark color, a print or a solid, or a tone-on-tone print. Small prints on neutral backgrounds are also popular.

Batik. These prints are made with a special wax-resist process, and typically have mottled and dappled surfaces.

Border print. Designs printed in a linear fashion, parallel to the selvages; can be used for borders and binding. Patches can be fussy cut from these for interesting effects (*see page 123*).

Calico. A printed cotton fabric with a diminutive allover pattern, often a floral design.

Conversation/Novelty. These prints depict real things and people, but the design is often humorous, sometimes even cartoony in feeling. Many children's prints fall into this category.

Directional. A print with a design that follows a definite vertical, horizontal, or diagonal direction; many of these prints have an obvious top and bottom.

Ethnic. These prints have motifs and designs specific to a particular identifiable culture, Asian or African for example.

Geometric. This includes plaids and stripes and prints with geometric motifs — dots, spots, squares, and lines, for example.

Realistic/Representational. These prints have motifs that look like what they are, for instance: fruits, vegetables, animals, and tree bark.

Stylized. Natural objects are simplified and repeated on the fabric surface in this print category.

Toile. Typically, they feature large, lifelike, pastoral scenes in a single color (traditionally red, blue, or black) printed on a plain background.

Tone-on-tone. Also called "near solids," prints in this category often look like a solid color from a distance; up close the print may have a mottled pattern printed in a color or range of colors that are similar to but not exactly the same as the background.

- -

FABRIC SELECTION CHECKLIST

After choosing the fabrics for your quilt, use this checklist as a guide to make sure that the combinations will result in a pleasing overall design:

☐ **Focus or theme fabric.** The fabric should exhibit a range of colors that are like the color scheme you have in mind.

☐ **Contrast.** Look for varying values in relationship to each other (lights, mediums, and darks) for depth and definition in the quilt blocks.

☐ **Visual variety.** Vary print scales for interest and to move the eye across and around the quilt.

☐ **Zing.** Throw in an accent color. This could be a small amount of a bright, rich saturated color, or an unexpected color.

Making Decisions

Q So, how do I choose the actual colors and prints for my quilt?

A As you experiment with color and gain quiltmaking experience, the process of choosing fabrics and colors will become far less daunting. Here are a few simple color-planning and fabric-buying strategies that might help:

▶ **Purchase a kit** with a pattern and fabrics for that pattern; you make no decisions on this one, but if you pay attention to what the kit maker chose, you can learn a lot about color interactions.

▶ **Choose a quilt pattern** — an individual one or one from a book of patterns — and follow the color recipe the designer used. You probably won't be able to find the *exact* fabrics and colors used, but you will be able to find fabrics in similar colors, values, and print styles so that you can closely duplicate the look of the quilt you've chosen.

▶ **Use a variety of values** of a single color, which is called a monochromatic color scheme. You can't go wrong with a well-planned monochromatic scheme when you choose a range of lights to darks. You can take the scheme a step further by mixing in one contrasting color for added interest.

▶ **Plan a two-color scheme** by choosing a predominant color (such as red) and a background color (such as cream or white). Then choose red prints in one or more shades (darker tones like burgundy and/or lighter tints such as pink) for the blocks and borders.

▶ **Look for the color registration dots,** small circles of color on the selvage, often with numbers within the circles. These dots reveal the color recipe for that fabric — one dot for each different color in the print. These are a great help when choosing coordinating or complementary colors for your quilt.

▶ **Choose a theme** and fabrics/colors that represent it, for example baby motifs and pastel colors. Look for fabrics that include each of the colors in the theme fabric and choose prints that you think will work with it for various elements in the quilt pattern you are making. Select more fabrics than required at first, so you have a group from which to choose.

▶ **Look at nature** for color cues. Study color combinations in your garden and in scenery to see how colors work with each other.

– –

Q Can I use a color wheel to help me choose colors for my quilt?

A The color wheel offers wonderful guidance because it is a way of seeing the relationships between colors. Begin with the three color schemes below, then move on to more complex color-wheel combos after you've read more about color in one of the books listed in the Resources.

Complementary colors. Colors that lie opposite each other on the color wheel are complements: red and green; orange and blue; red-orange and blue-green; violet and yellow; yellow-green and red-violet. Use a variety of shades of the two complements, for example, like fabrics in a variety of shades of pink (light red) and soft to medium greens.

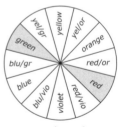

complementary

Analogous colors. Two or three colors that lie next to each other on the color wheel are called analogous. To add some visual punch, add an accent color that is at least two colors away from them on the wheel.

analogous

Tertiary colors. Choose a dominant color for your quilt and then find the other two at equidistant locations on the color wheel, for example: green, violet, and orange. This is also called a tri-tone or triad scheme. Choose one color as the primary and the other two as accent colors to guide your fabric selections.

tertiary

- -

Q **How do I know the fabrics I've chosen in the shop will really work together in my quilt?**

A Try some of my shopping strategies:

▶ Choose more than one fabric for each of the ones you need for the quilt pattern you are following, and then take the bolts to an empty counter where you can fan them out like a big deck of cards to see how they relate to each other. If there isn't enough room to fan them out, stack them so you can look at all of them together, bolt edge to bolt edge.

▶ Walk away with your back to the bolts and turn around for a fresh look. They always look a bit different when viewed from a distance. Some of them pop out as too strong or too soft for the others. Some will not "match" the other similar colors in the selection. Some colors will seem to "moosh" together — which may work in some designs, but perhaps not for the quilt you are making. Some prints that look great up close just "brown out" or disappear into each other from a distance. Prints with metallic accents are sure to look different from a distance. Eliminate the fabrics that obviously don't work with the rest.

▶ Use the squint test: Squinting at fabrics blurs some of the details and helps isolate values and colors that don't work in the mix. After deleting the fabrics that don't work, it's easier to make the final selections from those left from the original group.

▶ Before settling on a final group, make sure that you have chosen fabrics in different values for depth, and different print scales for interest and movement.

▶ Check your selections in natural daylight before finalizing your choices and having the fabrics cut. Lighting can be deceiving.

Q I can't visualize what the fabrics will look like when they are cut up and sewn together. I don't want to do all that work, then be unhappy with the results.

A For new quilters, trial and error is one way to learn what works and what doesn't. To minimize your errors and ensure success, try these solutions:

▶ Work with color-coordinated lines from a single fabric manufacturer; it's one safe way to be sure your fabrics will work together. Eventually you will want to break out of that all-too-confining box, but it's a good way to learn.

▶ Starting with a small quilt project and getting help from a knowledgeable salesperson or quilting teacher is one way to ensure success with fabric selection.

▶ Try cutting window templates for each of the shapes in your block before you head to the quilt shop. If your block pattern doesn't provide full-size templates, make your own (*see* Making Window Templates *on the next page*).

If using templates, place them over the fabrics you are considering. This method really helps you see how cutting into the fabric will break up the print. For example, cutting small patches from a print with the motif widely spaced on the background may not be desirable, as you could end up with patches that are almost all background. Patches like these are apt to "stick out" in the quilt in contrast to those with obvious motifs. You can still use the fabric, but you will need more of it so you can "fussy cut" (*see page 123*) the patches to include the motifs. A window template can help you avoid selection or yardage mistakes.

MAKING WINDOW TEMPLATES

To make your own window template, draw your block of choice to the full finished size on paper (do not include seam allowances). Overlay each shape in the block with template plastic (*see page 82*) and trace each one. If you are tracing printed templates from a book or pattern, trace along the seamlines, *not* the cutting lines. Use an X-acto knife to cut the shape out of the plastic. If you want to mask out the surrounding fabric completely, you can make the windows on index cards or heavyweight paper (for instance, cut them from a file folder). Here's an example of how to break the Pinwheel block into templates.

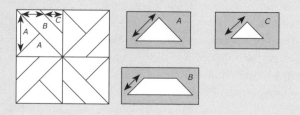

Q **What do I do if I've purchased the fabrics but still have some hesitation about how they will work?**

A Make a sample block or a block paste-up by cutting the required patches without seam allowances and arranging them on a sheet of paper. Secure them with a gluestick. Making a sample block from fabric is actually better because you'll learn how the block goes together.

CHAPTER 3

Batting and Thread

Today, quilt batting choices abound, with new products being introduced regularly to answer quilters' needs for function and aesthetics. Batting adds warmth and depth to the finished quilt. Which batting to use can be based on its thickness (or loft), fiber content, and laundering considerations, all of which are discussed in this chapter.

Thread is another major component of a quilt. You will need thread for hand or machine piecing, for attaching appliqués, for decorative embellishments, and of course, for the quilting that holds the quilt top, batting, and backing layers together. Thread type depends on the end use and desired result.

All About Batting

Once limited to cotton, today's battings are available in polyester, cotton/polyester blends, silk, and wool. Luxury fibers such as cashmere and alpaca are added to other batting fibers. And, you'll find "green" products such as bamboo in some batting-fiber blends. Your choice of batting depends on the finished look and feel you desire for your quilt.

- -

Q What is batting?

A Batting is a blanket of loose fibers, bonded together in some fashion, and used between the front and back of a quilt to add loft (depth or thickness) and warmth to a finished quilt. When stitches are used to anchor all three quilt layers together, this forms the characteristic hills and valleys and tiny puckers in a quilt, adding visual dimension and depth. Batting is available in an array of fiber contents, each one offering its own advantages and disadvantages.

- -

Q How do I choose the best batting for my quilt?

A You'll probably want to try different types of batting on small projects to see how each one behaves and handles. Make quilted-block test samples, then label them and keep them in a quilting notebook for future reference (*see page 26*).

Consider the following questions as you review the qualities of each type of batting (*see the chart on pages 60–61*).

▶ How will the quilt it be used? In a bed quilt, lap quilt, wall quilt, child's quilt, throw pillow, table settings? In a quilted garment, batting with little or no loft is preferred to keep finished garments as soft and supple as possible.

▶ How often, if ever, will the quilt be laundered?

▶ How much shrinkage is okay?

▶ How warm do I want the quilt to be?

▶ Do I want a flat, sculpted look, something with more pouf, or an "antique" look, with obvious shrinkage along the quilting caused by repeated launderings?

▶ Do I have a preference for the fiber content? Do I have any allergies that automatically eliminate some choices?

▶ Do I plan to quilt by hand or machine, or to tie the quilt layers instead?

▶ How much quilting do I want to do? Some battings require less space between rows or quilting motifs in order to keep the batting fibers trapped in the right place.

- -

Q **What do I need to know about the different types of batting?**

A Always read the manufacturer's descriptions, recommendations, and special directions, including the best spacing distance for the quilting stitches. The most commonly available batting types are listed in the chart on pages 60–61. Others are available, combining characteristics of the individual fibers such as cashmere, bamboo, or alpaca, for specific results. To inform your buying decisions, familiarize yourself with the descriptive terms you'll find on batting packaging (below); then see the chart on pages 60–61 for more on different types of batting and their characteristics:

▶ **Loft.** Batting thickness or puffiness. The more loft, the puffier the quilt will be.

▶ **Low-loft** battings are soft, drapable, easy to needle by hand or on the machine; good for a hand-quilted heirloom look; a good showcase for quilting stitches.

▶ **Medium-loft** battings are puffier, warmer, thicker, good for machine or hand quilting.

▶ **High-loft** battings are made of polyester, best for tied quilts; very difficult to machine-quilt; give the look of a down-filled comforter.

▶ **Glazing and bonding.** These are processes used in batting construction that help add stability to the loose fibers so they won't migrate through the surface of the finished quilt, creating "beards" of fiber on the surface.

▶ **Needling.** Putting the needle (hand or machine) through the batting during the quilting process. Synthetic battings are easier to quilt than cotton and require less quilting than cotton and cotton/poly blends. Ease of needling is especially important to hand quilters.

▶ **Needle-punching.** A process in which a set of barbed needles punches the batting to twist and tangle the fibers together. This helps to deter fiber migration and bearding and holds fibers together so quilting stitches may be spaced as far as 2" to 3" apart in cotton battings. Needle-punched batting is flatter than a bonded batting.

▶ **Scrim.** A thin, open fabric layer through which batting fibers are needlepunched to add a layer of stability and help hold the fibers together; may make hand quilting more difficult; battings with scrim are not as supple.

- -

Q How do I decide whether to use cotton or polyester?

A The following quick comparison can help you decide, but does not apply to fiber blends. Blends combine qualities of two or more fibers and are often made to help offset less than desirable qualities and enhance or improve more desirable ones. Read packaging carefully to determine quality and care.

COTTON BATTING	POLYESTER BATTING
▶ Takes longer to dry	▶ Dries faster
▶ Shrinks 1 to 5 percent when washed, unless pretreated	▶ Minimal shrinkage; stands up to regular laundering
▶ Is a little heavier weight	▶ Adds warmth without weight but doesn't breathe as well
▶ Becomes more supple and softens with use and laundering	▶ Has more loft
▶ Gives a flatter, heirloom look to the finished quilt	▶ Strong, durable fibers; more stable
▶ Breathes better; more comfortable in warm, damp climates	▶ Resists mold and mildew
▶ Requires closer stitch spacing than polyester	▶ Easier to quilt
	▶ Bearding may be a problem

BATTING CHARACTERISTICS

	Fiber Content	Care	Needling	Loft
Natural Fibers	**100% Cotton**	Wash	Can be a bit challenging by hand but easy to machine quilt; has no scrim	Low loft — very flat and good for antique, heirloom look
	Wool & cotton blend	Dry-clean or hand-wash; see package directions	Easy; lanolin in wool helps needle glide through layers; often used for tied quilts	Medium to high
	Silk	Dry-clean	Usually easy, but can be sticky	Low
	Cotton flannel	Wash	Easy	Thin
Synthetics & Blends	**80% Cotton/ 20% Poly OR 60% Cotton/ 40% Poly**	Wash	Bonded fibers are easy to needle	Not quite as flat as 100% cotton
	Polyester	Wash	Easy for machine or hand quilting, but as loft increases, more difficult to handle thickness at the machine	Up to 3" thick; bonded not as lofty as needle-punched; bonded keep loft & consistency; good for repeated washings; needle-punched have more blanketlike consistency
	Polyester fleece	Wash	Hand-needling difficult	Relatively low loft; flat

Weight	Advantages	Potential Problems
Medium	Breathes in summer; warm in winter; not as warm as polyester; good insulator; soft and drapable; shrinkage adds heirloom look; more opaque than polyester; launders without pilling or bearding	Shrinkage; preshrink (page 274); waste seeds and particles can break the needle and disperse oil; heavier than polyester
Medium; resilient	Warm and soft; good insulator; breathable; offers warmth without weight; soft and drapable; heirloom look; warm in winter, cool in summer	Bearding (page 64) may be a problem; attracts moths unless moth-proofed; more expensive than cotton or polyester batting
Very light-weight	Luxurious; warm without weight; great for quilted clothing; good insulator; beautiful drape	Expensive; more difficult to find; beards through cotton fabric
Light-weight	Woven and napped; some added warmth	Shrinks; be sure to preshrink (page 273)
Depends on loft	Combines characteristics of both fibers; lightweight warmth; resists fiber migration	See cotton
Various	Warmth without weight; less expensive than other alternatives; very resilient; nonallergenic; unaffected by mold or mildew	Fiber migration & bearding (page 64) in unbonded batting
Medium to heavy	Often thicker, denser, and less flexible than batting; best for craft projects, home dec items, wall quilts	Available by the yard, but width is limited; heavy in a bed quilt

Q What size batting should I buy for my quilt?

A Batting is available in assorted bed and craft sizes shown in the chart below. Buy a piece of batting at least 2" larger than the quilt top on each of the four sides to allow for the natural "shrinkage" that happens when you add quilting stitches.

For large quilts, cut batting up to 4" wider than the quilt-top along each edge. This gives you more room at the edges to hoop a quilt for hand-quilting in the borders. You will trim away the excess after the quilting is completed. Batting by the yard is also available in some shops and online in widths from 45" to 90".

Standard Batting Sizes	
Craft	36" × 45"
Crib	45" × 60"
Twin	72" × 90"
Double	81" × 96"
Queen	90" × 108"
King	120" × 120"

Solving Problems

Q I live in a warm climate and want a really thin batting for my quilt. What can I use?

A Some quilters use a layer of cotton flannel for "summer quilts," but the resulting quilt has little or no loft. When excess weight and warmth are undesirable, Hobbs Thermore Ultra-Thin polyester batting is a good choice for a lightweight quilt as well as for quilted garments. Some quilters split this thin batting into two layers for an even thinner one. This must be done carefully so the resulting batting splits are of even thickness throughout. If the batting surface has been treated to prevent bearding (*see page 64*), then one side of each split will lose that quality and bearding may be a problem. *Note:* Don't try to split a batting that has a scrim layer.

- -

Q I always have leftover batting. Any ideas on how to use them?

A Large batting scraps can be spliced for pieces large enough for small or lap-size quilts or wall hangings. I don't recommend it for bed quilts that will be used and laundered often. Here are two methods for splicing batting:

Straight-edge. Butt the edges and use a catchstitch (shown) to sew the pieces together, edge to edge. Do not pull the stitches tight or a bump may form at the join.

Puzzle-cut. Overlap two pieces by 1". Cut through both layers in a free-form wave. Align the edges and catchstitch together.

straight-edge batting splice

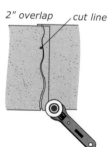

2" overlap — cut line

puzzle-cut batting splice

- -

Q There are fuzzy wisps of batting all over the surface of my finished quilt. What caused this?

A Loose fibers in polyester batting migrate to the surface of the quilt and out through the quilt top and back (fiber migration). Because these fibers are so strong, they don't break off. Instead, they lie in little tufts on the surface of your quilt. This is called bearding. Removing the beards is a tedious job to be done by hand. Don't be tempted to use a razor or a device for removing pills from sweaters. The problem is likely to continue through the life of the quilt.

Use black batting when possible for quilts that are predominantly dark. If your quilt is made of light and dark colors, decide which color batting is best. Look for glazed, bonded, or needle-punched battings (*see page 58*), as these batting construction methods help minimize or eliminate the problem.

Thread Selection

There is no one thread type that is all-purpose. You'll need different threads for sewing the quilt pieces together by hand or machine, as well as for basting the layers together prior to quilting, plus a different type for the actual hand- or machine-quilting stitches. You may need special threads such as rayon and metallic machine embroidery thread for special effects and embellishments.

Q What type of thread should I use for piecing my patchwork blocks?

A Polyester (100 percent) and cotton/poly blend all-purpose sewing thread is what you will find most widely available in quilt and fabric stores. These threads are easy to sew with, wash and wear well, and last over time. And, they are available in a wide range of colors for those who prefer a perfect color match for piecing seams. Cotton and cotton-covered polyester threads are easy to press; if you use 100 percent polyester thread for piecing, press your work at the synthetic setting to avoid damaging the thread.

DON'T SKIMP

To avoid thread breakage, shredding, and knotting when sewing by hand or machine, don't buy threads from the bargain table. Low-quality cotton thread is more likely to create lint that will fill up the bobbin area in the machine and create stitch-quality problems. Don't use old thread either. If you can easily break it off the spool, it will probably break in your quilt when put under stress. Throw it away.

Q Some of my threads have numbers on the label — 50/3, for example. What do they mean?

A Thread diameter is denoted by the first number: the higher the number, the finer the thread. The thread you use for sewing patches and quilt pieces together (piecing the quilt) should blend into the fabric — not stand on top of the seamline — so a 50- or 60-weight thread (often shortened to "50 wt." or "60 wt.") is the best choice. The second number refers to the number of thread strands that have been twisted together to make a stronger thread. Some pointers:

▶ The typical thread size for piecing is 50/3 and the tension on most sewing machines is factory-set for this weight.

▶ For appliqué, 60-weight thread is a nice alternative; since it is finer, it won't be as noticeable along the turned edges.

▶ Embroidery threads, which you might use in the needle for decorative quilting, are typically 30-weight and 40-weight.

▶ Use 60 wt. bobbin thread in the bobbin when quilting with specialty threads or when doing machine embroidery or satin-stitch appliqués. This helps to avoid heavy thread build-up on the back of the quilt top.

— —

Q **Is it necessary to stop and change the top and/or bobbin thread for different colors in a quilt?**

A That would waste both thread and time. For multicolor quilts, use a neutral color: gray, tan, or off-white. For dark colors, a darker neutral is a good choice. For pieced quilts with lots of light colors, choose white, off-white, or a very soft pastel that is close in hue to the colors in the quilt.

When threading my machine for piecing, I often use up the thread on half-filled bobbins in my collection, if the color will blend. It's a great way to use up thread odds and ends.

Q What type of thread is best for appliqué?

A For hand appliqué, choose cotton or all-purpose thread in a color that matches the appliqué color, not the background fabric. Some quilters like using silk thread for hand appliqué as it is soft, fine, and strong, and it all but disappears into the appliqué edge. For machine appliqué, choose the thread based on the method you're using.

- -

Q What thread should I use for quilting?

A Quilters of the past used only cotton sewing thread. Today, special cotton thread is manufactured specifically for hand quilting and another for machine quilting. Ask at your quilt shop for the one appropriate for the quilting method you've chosen. Reserve these threads for quilting; they are not meant for general hand sewing or for attaching appliqués.

Monofilament thread is another option for almost invisible machine-quilting stitches. This fine, somewhat wiry thread is made of polyester or nylon (sometimes labeled polyamide) and is available in "clear" to use on most light and medium colors and multicolor prints, and in "smoke" for darker colors. Some quiltmakers prefer it for machine quilting because it all but disappears into the colors of the quilt fabric; for beginners, this is a bonus as it helps disguise quilt-stitch inconsistencies. It can be used in the needle and the bobbin or in only one of the two.

- -

Q Some of my friends store thread in the freezer. Is that necessary?

A Don't store thread in the refrigerator or the freezer — cold dries it out. Keep thread out of direct sunlight to avoid fading and weakening, and protect it from dust, which can clog up the sewing machine and cause stitch and tension problems. Storing thread in drawers or covered boxes is the best way to protect thread.

Q How do I know if the thread I have on hand is suitable for quilting?

A The thread you use for your quilting projects should be fine and extremely smooth, with no visible slubs or bumps that will get caught in the tension discs, needle, or bobbin area (which can cause thread breakage). If you're not sure about the thread quality, unwind a short length and hold it up to the light. If you see a little fuzz, that's okay, but if there's lots of fuzz or bumps and slubs, don't use it in your project.

Q Can I use glazed or waxed threads for machine-piecing and quilting?

A Never use waxed or glazed threads in your machine. The finish can rub off during the up-and-down stitching motion, which can gum up the tension discs and cause stitching problems. Use these threads for hand quilting only.

CHAPTER 4

Essential Tools

As with any fine craft, the quality of the tools you use for quiltmaking affects the final results. For quiltmaking, there are a few basics you will need to get started and many specialty tools that intermediate and expert quilt-makers wouldn't be without. If you are just beginning to quilt or have limited funds, the essential tools are discussed in the following pages. Other tools will be discussed throughout the book as they pertain to particular technical quiltmaking questions and challenges. Most quiltmaking tools are available at your local quilt shop, from mail-order catalogs, and on numerous quilting Web sites on the Internet.

Getting Started

Ask any quiltmaker and they are bound to have favorite tools that may not be included here. Add to your quilting tool kit as you learn about new products that will help improve or speed your projects.

– –

Q **The array of tools at my quilt shop is pretty over-whelming. Which ones do I need?**

A You don't need them all — at least not all at once. But you do need some basic equipment for your sewing room. Ideally, quilting requires a devoted space (if possible), with room for a sewing machine, a cutting table, an iron, and an ironing board for starters.

Your sewing machine should be your best friend. Keep it properly maintained by having it serviced at least once a year — more often if you quilt and sew regularly. A basic machine with a balanced straight stitch is essential. Other decorative and utility stitches are also helpful, particularly for machine appliqué and quilting, but they are extras. You can make beautiful quilts using the machine straight stitch and some simple hand stitches. Most machine manufacturer's now offer machines designed with special features that appeal to quilters in particular. If you need a new machine, be sure to ask if the machine you are interested in has such features.

Needles and Presser Feet

Q Do I need special sewing-machine needles for quilting?

A Keep a supply of size 75/11 or 80/12 Sharp needles (Top-stitch and Microtex needles are Sharps) on hand for most quilt fabrics and types of stitching. The first number indicates the European numbering system, the second the American. The lower the number, the finer the needle. Use topstitching needles, which have larger eyes, for thicker threads. Threads other than quilting cotton and all-purpose sewing thread with a cotton-covered polyester core may require a specialty needle, such as a needle designed for metallic threads.

- -

Q I have a large supply of Universal needles for my sewing machine. Can I use those for piecing and quilting?

A The point of a Universal needle is slightly rounded in comparison to a Sharp. Universals are good for stitching on most woven and knit fabrics and many quilters use them for piecing and quilting. Stitching patchwork pieces together with a Sharp needle usually yields a slightly straighter stitch on cotton fabrics, which can affect the accuracy of the seams. If you don't have Sharps though, use a Universal needle. Some companies offer quilting needles with specially tapered points that glide through the quilt layers and across seams.

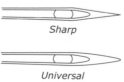

Sharp

Universal

Q How often should I change the sewing machine needle?

A A good rule of thumb is to change needles when you start a new project. Even cotton will snag and run when hit by a slightly burred or slightly dull needle. If you are piecing or quilting a large quilt, you may need to change the needle several times. You'll max out a needle's efficiency in 8 to 10 hours of sewing, but change sooner if necessary.

Q Does needle size make a difference? Which is best for patchwork piecing?

A Use larger needles for thicker threads and finer needles for finer threads. Needle size 80/12 is a good all-purpose size for piecing most quilter's cottons. For fabrics that have a tight weave (batiks and hand-dyed cottons, for example), you may have smoother stitching with a size 70/12 Sharp. Do a test.

Q What about needles for sewing by hand?

A For hand quilting, you will need a package of Betweens, size 7 to 12 (the higher the number the finer and shorter the needle). Shorter needles make shorter stitches, one of the hallmarks of fine hand quilting, but it may take some practice with longer needles first. For appliqué and binding, buy a package of Sharps in assorted sizes.

Q Do I need a special presser foot for piecing and quilting?

A Although you can do machine piecing with a standard presser foot, you may want to purchase a ¼" patchwork foot to help you stitch an accurate ¼" seam allowance — the standard for quiltmaking. You'll use it for other stitching chores, too. An open-toe foot is helpful for machine appliqué (*see page 176*).

A walking foot is essential to prevent layers from shifting when doing machine-assisted quilting. For free-motion machine quilting (*see page 320*), you will need a special darning or embroidery foot, used with the feed dogs disengaged.

¼" patchwork foot

open-toe free-motion embroidery foot

darning foot

walking foot

open-toe foot

SEE ALSO: *Machine-Quilting Basics, pages 304–9.*

Sewing Room Basics

Q What do I need for a table or work surface?

A A counter-height worktable is essential for cutting tasks and quilt-assembly steps prior to quilting. The larger it can be, the better. One alternative is a hollow-core door supported by cabinets, microwave carts, or wire-basket systems at each end.

If you don't have a counter-height area, you can raise a table temporarily by placing the legs on top of juice cans. Leave the juice in the cans or fill empty juice cans with plaster of Paris to add weight for a sturdier table on lifts. Or, you could try bed risers, which are designed to lift beds higher off the floor for more underbed storage.

- -

Q I've heard that different light bulbs can change the way my colors look. What do you recommend?

A Adequate lighting is essential at your sewing machine, pressing area, and cutting table. Use color-corrected bulbs if possible to reduce shadows and keep your color selections in perspective. Decorative and utilitarian sewing lamps in floor and table models are widely available and are a must for sewing at night and when working with dark colors. Small portable models are ideal. Bulbs that emit natural, white, or outdoor lighting are best in a quiltmaking environment.

Pressing Tools

Q How should I set up my iron and ironing board?

A Locate your ironing board close to your sewing machine; pressing as you sew is essential for precision piecing. If that's not possible, purchase a pressing pad to keep on or near the sewing-machine table so that frequent trips to the ironing board aren't necessary. My favorite is a small cutting board with a pressing pad that folds up — great to take to quilt class!

- -

Q I'm thinking about buying a new iron. Are there some features I should consider for quiltmaking?

A A good iron with a steam setting is essential for pressing. Even if you decide *not* to use steam when pressing quilt units (*see page 116*), you still need it to remove wrinkles when preparing fabrics for cutting. Below are some pointers that you may find especially helpful:

▶ Look for a smooth soleplate and enough weight to make a difference. A too-heavy iron can be tiring when you have lots of pressing to do.

▶ Some quilters prefer an iron with a nonstick surface, claiming it is easier to clean and glides more easily than stainless-steel models. If you buy one of these, keep pins out of the way of the soleplate, since the nonstick coating can peel if you scratch the iron.

▶ Most new irons come with an automatic shut-off feature that operates within a certain time period if you forget to turn off the iron.

▶ Some more-expensive irons have freestanding or built-in high-capacity water tanks, which offer the advantage of constant steam.

▶ A small craft iron and ironing pad are handy to have near your sewing machine for press-as-you-sew steps and for appliqué preparation (*see page 189*).

craft iron

SPECIAL CARE FOR YOUR IRON

You might want to invest in a Teflon press cloth or appliqué pressing sheet. These specialty cloths will protect the soleplate of your iron, your ironing board, and your fabric. This is helpful when you are doing fusible appliqué or using fusible web in place of stitches for some finishing and decorative work. Excess web adheres to the press cloth and is easily scraped away before you use the cloth on your next project.

Sheets of parchment paper are a good substitute (look in paper products at the craft store or the baking section of your grocery store). If you use fusible web on transfer sheets, this paper can also be used. Take care when removing parchment from the web and store it in a folder. Discard after using it as a pressing sheet with fusibles.

Cutting Tools

Q Do I need special tools for cutting out quilt pieces?

A A ruler, cutting mat, rotary cutter, and several pairs of scissors comprise the cutting assortment you'll need:

Dressmaker's shears. Bent-handle shears are often essential for cutting appliqués and patches for hand piecing. For wrist safety, consider a spring-loaded version to help prevent carpal tunnel syndrome. Use only for fabric cutting.

dressmaker's shears

Small double-pointed embroidery scissors. You'll use these for clipping threads, trimming seams, cutting and clipping small appliqués, and while doing handwork.

embroidery scissors

Craft scissors. Use these for cutting templates from template plastic, card stock, or heavy paper.

Rotary cutter. Rotary cutting makes speedy work of cutting geometric shapes, border strips, and binding for any type of quilt. You may even prefer to use a rotary cutter for cutting templates from plastic. If so, reserve a cutter for this purpose and mark it to indicate the blade is not for fabric.

rotary cutter

rotary cutter with ergonomic handle

Q I've never heard of a rotary cutter. Where do I find one and what do I look for?

A Available in a wide array of sizes, colors, and types, the rotary cutter is one tool you will want to select carefully. Ergonomic styles are your best bet for comfort and long use. The basic cutter has a very sharp circular blade attached to a straight or shaped handle. For safety, make sure the cutter you choose has a retractable blade as well as a way to lock the blade within its safety guard when not in use.

Cutters are available in diameters of 8mm to 60mm. A cutter with a 45mm-diameter blade will serve perfectly well for most cutting jobs. Cutters with smaller blades are good for intricate cuts, curves, and small pieces. Keep one handy at the sewing machine, along with a small rotary mat, for quick trimming while you are piecing blocks.

CAUTION!
Rotary cutters are razor sharp!

Always engage the cutter's safety guard as soon as you put it down.

Always keep it out of the reach of children and pets.

Q Can I use a rotary cutter on any surface?

A For now, let's just review the basic tools you'll need. To protect both your work surface and the cutting blade, you will need a cutting mat designed for use with rotary cutters. Sometimes called "self-sealing," rotary mats are not gouged by the blade when you cut.

Choose a mat size that will fit on your worktable, preferably one that is at least 18" × 24" and marked with 1" gridlines and ⅛" and ¼" increments. It's also handy to have angled lines for 30-, 45-, and 60-degree cuts. Look for one with a matte surface (not slick or pebbly), which will help prevent fabric slippage while cutting. A smaller one to take to quilt class is also a good idea.

You will also need a transparent rotary-cutting ruler. Rotary rulers are ⅛" thick, which gives you a ledge along which to guide the rotary cutter for clean and accurate cuts. It also affords some protection from cutting yourself. *For safety's sake, do not substitute a thin, flat ruler for rotary-cutting jobs.*

You can accomplish most rotary-cutting tasks with a 6" × 24" ruler marked in ⅛" increments along its width and length. It should also have markings for 30-, 45-, and 60-degree angles to make cutting diamonds and triangles a breeze. A 12" or 15" square is helpful for squaring up blocks before joining them to make the quilt top. A 6"-square ruler with a bias line is also very useful for cutting smaller shapes and for quick trimming jobs. With these three rulers, you should be able to accomplish most cutting tasks.

Q How should I care for my rotary cutter for optimum use and accurate cuts?

A Using a dull blade can lead you to apply too much pressure when cutting. This can result not only in inaccurate cuts, it can irreparably damage your cutting mat. At the first sign of poor cutting action — if cuts require more pressure than usual or it the blade skips and misses periodically — don't assume the blade is worn. First try cleaning the blade by carefully disassembling the cutting mechanism. Line up the pieces on your work surface in the order removed. Wipe away bits of lint and add a drop of sewing-machine oil to the blade under the front sheath. Reassemble the pieces and tighten (but do not overtighten) the nut.

- -

Q What's the best way to store and care for a rotary-cutting mat?

A Since mats can be expensive, it's wise to take care of them. Here are some straightforward ways to do just that:

▶ Clean your mat periodically with a damp cloth and mild, nonabrasive detergent.

▶ Never use your cutting mats as pressing surfaces — they're heat sensitive.

▶ Develop a habit of rotating the mat periodically to avoid wearing out one spot.

▶ Store flat; do not roll or fold. Don't store your mats by leaning them against a wall. They will buckle over time and may never lie flat again.

▶ For transporting to class, lay the mat flat in the trunk of your car, out of direct sunlight, which can cause irreparable damage.

▶ Avoid cold temperatures, which can cause brittleness and breakage.

▶ Use the mat only with rotary cutters. Other cutting tools may gouge the surface or make holes in the mat. Use discarded mats for crafts projects

▶ When using the mat, place it on a hard, flat surface that is at least the same size or larger. For accurate cuts, the mat must be flat and smooth.

- -

Q My self-healing mat doesn't seem to heal itself anymore and it's full of lint. Can it be repaired or must I purchase a new mat?

A First, try using a mat smoother. Rub it over the surface to smooth out any nicks and cuts that haven't healed and to remove the lint. After several uses, you may find that the lines on the mat begin to wear off, but you should still be able to make accurate cuts using your rotary rulers. Eventually your mat will wear out, requiring a replacement. You can discard it or set it aside to use for a craft surface. Old mats make a good surface protector for projects that involve gluing, painting, or stenciling.

- -

Q How can I safely dispose of dull rotary-cutter blades?

A Dull blades are still sharp, just not sharp enough to cut multiple fabric layers. To make sure no one gets cut accidentally, put used blades back into the plastic container in which the replacement blade came (if that's how they were packaged), and add a piece of masking tape to keep it closed. Otherwise, wrap used blades in lightweight cardboard and tape the edges closed. Then throw them in a trash receptacle to which kids and pets don't have easy access.

Marking and Sewing Tools

Transferring patchwork templates and appliqué pieces from your pattern to your fabric requires accurate marking methods and tools. Pinning is essential to the piecing and appliqué processes, and you will need a few hand-sewing tools, even if you make your quilt completely by machine.

Q You've mentioned template plastic — what is that?

A Many beginners cut their templates from a heavyweight paper. Although this might work well enough for small projects, paper templates are too difficult to trace around accurately, and cardboard edges wear down from repetitive tracing, so accuracy is short-lived. Template plastic, a translucent material readily available in quilting stores and online, gives you a permanent edge so that tracing onto fabric is easier and more accurate. Many different kinds and brands are available, but they all work about the same.

You can use this plastic for appliqués as well as for piecing templates when you cannot or do not wish to use rotary-cutting methods. Heat-resistant template plastic is nice to have for preparing appliqués (*see page 174*). If you need template plastic when the stores are closed, thoroughly wash a plastic milk container and cut it apart.

You can also purchase a wide variety of precut plastic templates for popular quilt-block designs. They are a good investment if the shapes and sizes are ones you use often in your quiltmaking.

- -

Q What is the best way to draw my template shapes?

A Use a mechanical pencil with thin lead (0.5 B or HB hardness) to draw on template plastic and to trace around templates on fabrics. For temporary marks, a silver or yellow artist's pencil works well on both light and dark fabrics and washes out easily. For dark fabrics, you can use a sharpened white chalk pencil. Check at your local quilt shop for other special marking pencils for difficult-to-mark fabrics. If you use a standard #2 pencil, you will need to sharpen it often to keep the point sharp for drawing fine lines to follow when cutting.

Q Can I use a water-soluble ink pen for marking my pieces?

A Better to be safe than sorry and use only the pencils suggested above. The chemicals in fine-point water-soluble fabric markers may not come out due to fabric and dye interactions, which could ruin a quilt over time. Pressing over the marked lines may also make them permanent.

The way you remove the marks also affects long-term results. If you dab off the marks with water and a cloth, you may be sending the marks into the batting, only to have them reappear on the quilt surface later. To remove them completely, the quilt requires a good soak (or a machine washing, if you want a quilt with the softly used look you'll get from the machine's agitation). If you are making a utilitarian quilt — one that will be used and laundered regularly — the marks will come out in the inevitable wash, so whether or not you remove them ahead of time is your call. Testing first is always a good idea.

Never use these pens for tracing around templates for hand or machine piecing, as the lines they create are often thicker than a fine pencil line and contribute to cutting inaccuracies.

- -

Q What about the disappearing ink pens?

A If you plan to use an air-soluble marker, use it only when you are going to be doing the quilting or appliqué work immediately, as the ink will probably be gone the next day. In humid climates, the inks seem to dissipate in minutes!

Q Do I need any other tools?

A Here are a few must-have items that you will always want in your sewing kit:

Quilter's straight pins. Choose long, fine, steel pins with plastic or glass heads. You won't need to pin every seam, but pins are essential for holding pieces together when matching points or intersecting seams. I really like Clotilde's *(see Resources)* flower pins — the heads are flat, colorful, and easy to spot.

Safety pins. These are essential if you prefer to pin the quilt layers (top, batting, and backing) together for machine quilting. Use brass or nickel-plated safety pins and buy a box of them. You'll need lots of them to baste a bed-size quilt. These pins won't rust while they are in the quilt layers. My favorites are quilter's curved safety pins: they are easier to insert into the layers, and while they do cost a bit more, it's an expense I'm more than willing to bear.

Seam ripper. Yes, you will make stitching mistakes and you will need to do some "reverse stitching" with the aid of a seam ripper. Make sure the blade on yours is sharp.

Thimble. If you hand-piece, hand-quilt, or hand-appliqué, your finger will thank you for learning to use a thimble. Make sure your thimble fits the middle finger of your sewing hand — snug but not too tight. A metal thimble should have small dimples in the flat end to catch, hold, and guide the needle through the fabric while protecting your finger. Make sure the indentations are deep enough to hold the needle firmly in place as you guide it through the fabric layers.

Check out the variety of thimble types and styles available at your quilt shop. Metal thimbles provide the most protection, but your finger may sweat inside it during prolonged stitching sessions. Open-ended thimbles accommodate long fingernails and provide air circulation. Leather thimbles are soft and comfortable and "grab" the needle better. Newer styles from synthetic materials are also available. You may want to try several types before settling on one that suits your needs. Gold and silver thimbles are available, as well as special styles designed by clever quilters to make hand quilting easier.

CHAPTER 5

Rotary Cutting and Strip Piecing

Rotary-cutting tools have revolutionized quilting. With a rotary cutter, an acrylic ruler marked with cutting measurements, and a self-healing cutting mat, you can cut the geometric pieces for many different patchwork blocks. Rotary cutting speeds the job and improves cutting and piecing accuracy. Many pieced units can be made by combining rotary cutting and strip piecing, a quick way to sew and cut multipiece patchwork units.

First Cuts First

Accurate cutting is the first step toward ensuring that all the pieces of your quilt will fit together perfectly. Make sure you have a fresh blade in your rotary cutter, plus a rotary ruler and cutting mat to protect your cutting surface. Take your time to ensure accuracy — cutting errors only multiply due to the number of pieces in a block. Errors make fitting the pieces together difficult as well as affect the overall finished size of your project.

- -

Q How do I prepare my fabric for rotary cutting?

A First, preshrink the fabric and iron it to remove wrinkles (*see page 113*). If the fabric loses a lot of body in the preshrinking process, give it a light application of spray starch or sizing to make it easier to handle during cutting and sewing.

Do a clean-up cut (*instructions below*) before you begin cutting the shapes for your quilt. For best results, you'll need a 6" × 24" acrylic ruler marked in ⅛" and 1" increments. This is a standard ruler size you will use for strip cutting. It's also good to have an array of smaller rectangular and square rulers for cutting pieces from strips (*see page 92*). *Note:* If you are left-handed, reverse the directions that follow. Refer to the illustration on page 90 for the steps that follow.

1. Place the rotary mat on your work surface with the longest edges parallel to the table edge. Fold the fabric in half

lengthwise with selvage edges aligned and use your hands to smooth out any wrinkles so the folded edge is smooth and flat, and free of any ripples, even if that means the cut or torn edges at each end of the piece don't match (they probably won't).

2. Position the folded fabric along the length of the mat with the folded edge toward you and lying along one of the horizontal gridlines, and with the cut or torn ends to your right. Loosely fold any excess fabric that doesn't fit on the mat to the left on the work surface; to avoid cutting distortion it should never hang over the edge.

3. When you are sure the fabric is folded correctly and is wrinkle-free, use your hands to smooth and lightly crease the fold. Fold in half again lengthwise, aligning the first fold with the selvages. Smooth out any ripples or wrinkles and make sure there are none trapped in the new folded edge, using your hands to check for smoothness and to flatten the fabric along the fold (do not press). The resulting piece will be about 11" wide, an easy width to cut across without over-reaching.

4. Align the 1" horizontal line on the rotary ruler with the folded edge of the fabric that is closest to you on the cutting mat, making sure it is not skewed. Tuck a square rotary ruler against the right-hand edge of the ruler to make sure.

5. Release the safety guard on the rotary cutter. Carefully place your left hand on the ruler, spreading your fingers to secure the width of the ruler, but keeping fingers away

from the right-hand edge of the ruler. Place pressure on the ruler to keep it in place and run the cutter blade firmly along the right-hand edge of the ruler. Begin with the cutter on the mat and roll it onto the folded edge across to the opposite edge. Exert enough firm and even pressure to cleanly cut through all four fabric layers.

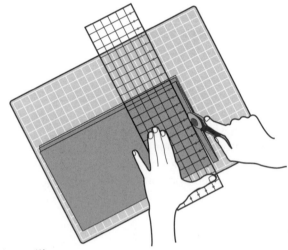

rotary cutting

6. Carefully rotate the cutting mat 180 degrees so the clean-cut edge is to your left (to the right for lefties). You are ready to cut the pieces for your quilt. After the strips are cut, you cut away the selvages on the strips.

CUTTING NORTH BY NORTHWEST

It may be easier to rotary-cut with the correct amount of pressure by positioning the mat at an angle on your work surface so the ruler points NNW rather than due north, directly in front of your body. If you cannot move the mat into this position, place the fabric on the mat at an angle (you won't be able to use the mat guidelines in this position). This trick is particularly helpful if you have limited shoulder rotation.

Cutting Strips and Patches

After you've done a clean-up cut, you're ready to cut the pieces for the blocks.

- -

Q **After I've straightened the end, how do I cut the pieces for my quilt?**

A Most rotary-cutting directions begin with cutting strips across the fabric width. Your quilt pattern will specify the correct width, the number of strips to cut from each fabric, and the size and number of shapes to cut from the strips. For patterns that utilize strip piecing and unit cutting (*see page 102*), you will make strip units and then cut shapes from them. If you design your own quilt, you will need to calculate the number of strips you will need for each shape.

Q How do I cut rectangles or squares from strips?

A First, determine the strip size, if not indicated in your pattern. The strip should be ½" wider than the finished-unit width to allow for standard ¼"-wide patchwork seams. For example, for 2" finished squares, cut 2½"-wide strips.

strips are 2½" wide

1. With the clean-cut end of the fabric to your left (reverse for lefties), position the rotary ruler on the fabric with the cut edges carefully aligned with the desired measurement on the ruler (in this case 2½"). Make sure the edge is aligned with the same line from ruler end to ruler end.

2. Hold the ruler in place and cut along the right-hand ruler edge. To keep the ruler from slipping out of place, "walk" your fingers away from you as you cut along the ruler edge. Cut one strip and open it to make sure it is straight from end to end with no curves or "bends." If there are, set the strip aside and check the fabric folding to make sure there are no wrinkles. Make a new clean-up cut and then cut a new strip. As you continue to cut, check for accuracy.

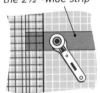

cutting squares from the 2½"-wide strip

to cut squares: finished size + ½"

CUTTING TRIANGLES

Once you've cut some squares, you are only a step away from cutting triangles. To make a half-square triangle, literally cut the square in half, from corner to corner. For quarter-square triangles, cut in half again.

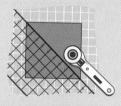

to cut half-square triangles

to cut quarter-square triangles

Q How do I make sure rotary-cut pieces are accurate?

A The more carefully you cut, the more accurate the piecing and the finished quilt will be. The following tips will improve cutting accuracy:

▶ Give limp fabric a light coat of spray starch or sizing after preshrinking, and iron it before folding and cutting. It's easier to cut crisp fabrics.

▶ Open the folded strips and check for accuracy.

▶ Trim away the selvage edges before cutting patches.

▶ Cut no more than four layers into smaller shapes for the most accuracy. The fewer the layers, the more accurate the cut patches will be.

▶ Check to make sure the strip end is square and perpendicular to the long edges of the strip after every two or three cuts from a strip. Make a clean-up cut if necessary before cutting additional shapes.

▶ Keep the cutter clean and lint-free. Lint build-up prevents smooth cutting action and causes skips in the cut.

▶ Keep the cutting mat clean; use a velvet-napped lint-removal brush to remove lint before storing the mat. If your mat develops a rough surface from extensive use, or it seals around lint and thread bits, try using a mat smoother periodically.

▶ Replace a well-used and badly scarred mat with a new one. Reserve the old one for crafts projects.

▶ Change the blade in the rotary cutter as soon as it becomes dull.

▶ Use the same ruler(s) to cut all the pieces for your quilts. Accuracy can vary from ruler to ruler and brand to brand, despite good quality control.

▶ Stand when cutting so that your head is directly above the blade for a clear view of the cutting action.

▶ Cut all of the pieces for your quilt on the same day — tension and other distractions can affect your cutting accuracy from day to day.

SEE ALSO: *Cutting Tools, pages 77–82.*

---

11 TIPS FOR ROTARY-CUTTING SAFETY

1. Keep rotary cutters safely out of the reach of children and pets.

2. Pay attention and take your time when doing any rotary cutting. Don't rotary-cut when distracted or upset.

3. Stand up when cutting so that you have enough leverage on the ruler to keep it from slipping while you cut.

4. Roll the cutter away from your body, never toward it, even though it may seem that it would be the easiest direction.

5. Never cross the hand holding the ruler in place to cut along the opposite edge of the ruler. It's too dangerous — and inaccurate.

6. Engage the safety guard every time you put the cutter down, even if you are not finished cutting. If you are prone to dropping things, wear shoes and socks while cutting.

7. Use rotary cutters only with rotary mats and rulers. The mat protects the cutting surface and the cutting blade. Rotary rulers are thicker than standard rulers to give you an edge against which to guide the blade.

8. Don't use a dull blade. Making accurate cuts with a dull blade requires more pressure, which is bad for your arm, wrist, and shoulder, and bad for the cutting mat, too.

9. Follow the manufacturer's directions for changing the blades. Keep new blades in their packaging until you need a replacement.

10. Dispose of used blades carefully; they are still sharp. Place the old blades in the packaging from the new blade or in cardboard with all edges securely taped. Throw in a trash receptacle that is inaccessible to kids and pets.

11. Keep fingers away from the edges of the ruler while you cut. If you are right-handed, steady the ruler with your left hand while rolling the cutter along the right edge of the ruler (vice versa for lefties).

Quick-Cutting Geometric Shapes

Sometimes quilt patterns include rotary-cutting and template-cutting directions for common geometric shapes other than squares, rectangles, and half-square triangles. Special rulers and ready-made templates are available for cutting many of the common geometric shapes, but if you don't have them, you can still make quick work of rotary-cutting them from strips. Some require making a paper cutting guide.

- -

Q How do I quick-cut diamond shapes?

A The most commonly used diamond is the 45-degree diamond (45 degrees at the narrow points). Other commonly used diamonds have 30-degree or 60-degree points. You can quick-cut these from strips. The height of the diamond is the straight-grain measurement from straight edge to straight edge (not from the angled edges.) Cut strips of the required height (including seam allowances) and use the appropriate angle line on your ruler to cut the diamonds. If your ruler doesn't have the appropriate angle, use a paper template with your ruler.

1. Trace the printed template along the outer solid line (cutting line) onto parchment or typing paper using a fine-point pen. Mark the pattern name and any cutting

directions on the template. Use the rotary cutter and ruler to cut out the template and check it for accuracy on the printed template.

2. Place a small masking-tape loop on the right side of the paper template and attach the template to the underside of your rotary ruler.

3. Make a clean-up (*see page 88*) along one edge of the fabric and then position the ruler on the fabric strip and use the template as your guide for cutting strips the width of the template.

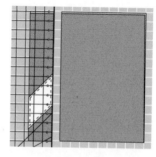

4. Reposition the ruler along the strip to cut the diamonds. The fabric strip may remain folded so you can cut two diamonds at once.

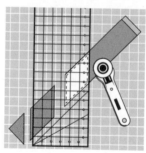

Q I've seen a pattern that calls for equilateral triangles. What are they, and how do I cut them?

A In an equilateral triangle, the length of all three sides is the same and all three points are 60-degree angles. Special rulers are available for cutting them. However, if you don't have a ruler, you can use a template to mark the triangles, or you can use a ruler with a 60-degree angle cutting line.

1. On template plastic, trace the template, including seam allowances, and cut out with rotary-cutting tools.
2. Trace around the triangle template on one piece of fabric. Remove the template and use the rotary cutter to cut the triangle. If you need several, stack up to four fabric layers with the tracing on top and cut multiples.

- -

Q Can I cut equilateral triangles from strips?

A If you need many triangles, cut strips of the required triangle height (triangle finished height plus ¾"). With the strip folded in half, trace around the template, reversing it in alternating fashion. Use the rotary cutter and ruler to cut the shapes without a template.

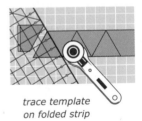

trace template on folded strip

Q Is there a shortcut for cutting half-rectangles?

A Some quilt blocks require pieced units made of two true half-rectangles (also called scalene or long triangles). These can be strip-pieced and quick-cut when you need a lot of them, using a special cutting ruler. However, this tool works only when the "parent" rectangle is twice as long as it is wide. Without the ruler, you can rotary-cut the half-rectangle shapes from full rectangles cut from strips. It's important to determine if you need mirror-image half-rectangles before you begin cutting the rectangles because the units are different and not interchangeable — the angle goes in a different direction in each one.

1. Draw the parent rectangle on graph paper and add ¼" seams all around. Draw diagonal line, corner to corner.

2. Add a ¼" seam allowance to one angled edge and cut out the resulting triangle, cutting away the sharp point. Measure the short edge of the completed template and cut strips this width.

3. Measure the long edge of the template and cut rectangles of this size from the strips.

4. If you don't need sets of mirror-image half-rectangles, cut individual rectangles in half diagonally. For mirror-image sets, leave the strip folded with wrong sides facing.

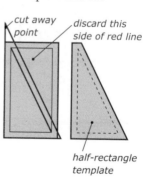

cut away point

discard this side of red line

half-rectangle template

Q I want to make a quilt using the Snowball block. Is there a quick way to cut the central shape?

A Here's one way to do it:

1. Trace the Snowball template onto paper and attach it to the underside of the rotary ruler with one of the short, angled edges aligned with the edge.

2. Cut squares from rotary-cut strips of the correct width.

3. Position the ruler on the square (stack up to 4 squares with raw edges even) and trim the corner. Rotate the squares to continue cutting off the triangles around the square.

If you prefer, you can quick-piece Snowball blocks with the folded-corner method shown on page 144. No triangles are required to complete the Snowball block with this method.

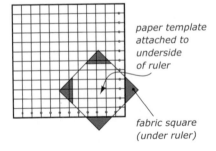

paper template attached to underside of ruler

fabric square (under ruler)

Snowball block

Solving Problems

Q Even though I made a clean-up cut, when I opened the strips some of them had a slight "bow." What happened and how do I prevent it?

A Bowed or crooked strips happen when the cuts you make are not truly perpendicular to the fold, or the fabric is incorrectly folded. With each strip you cut from a piece of fabric, strip-width accuracy can decrease. If you must cut numerous strips from a fabric — or numerous pieces from a strip — it's best to stop after every two or three cuts to check the strip accuracy. Open the last cut strip and if there's even the slightest bow, set it aside and do a clean-up cut on the fabric edge before continuing to cut more strips.

Bowed strips can also happen if you try to make very long cuts through fabric that has been folded only once (two layers) instead of folding the fabric twice to cut through four layers. Keeping cuts to 12" or shorter helps ensure cutting accuracy.

- -

Q I often find small unfinished cuts along the edge of my strips. What causes this?

A Unfinished cuts can be caused by exerting uneven pressure on the rotary cutter. Your skill will improve with practice. Also, don't try to cut through too many layers at a time — stick to a maximum of four layers. Lastly, check the blade. If it's loose, tighten the screw that holds it in place. Replace dull or nicked cutting blades.

Q No matter how careful I am, my ruler slips out of line while I'm cutting. Any tips for preventing this?

A Some rotary rulers have a frosted underside that helps the ruler grab the fabric and stay put while you hold the ruler in place. Below are several other options you can try:

▶ Attach clear ruler grips that won't obscure the ruler lines to the bottom of the ruler.

▶ Apply small drops of hot glue to the ruler corners.

▶ Smooth a clear film (available in quilt shops) onto the bottom of the ruler. It will help the ruler grip the fabric.

▶ Apply self-adhesive sandpaper dots (available from your quilt shop) to the ruler underside.

Strip-Piecing Basics

Many quilt designs require repetitive multiple units for blocks and borders. You can hasten the process for making patchwork blocks using strip piecing in conjunction with rotary cutting.

Q What is strip piecing?

A Strip piecing is a method for increasing speed and accuracy by eliminating the necessity of sewing lots of small patches together. First, rotary-cut strips are arranged in a specific sequence and sewn together to create a strip unit.

After pressing the seam allowances, you rotary cut strip-pieced segments from the strip units and then join the units to other patches or units to complete the blocks.

Strip piecing won't work for every patchwork block design. It is commonly used for simple designs such as Fourpatch and Ninepatch units or blocks, as well as with Rail Fence and two-color squares and rectangles (*see page 21*).

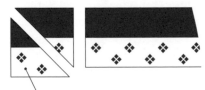

half-square triangles cut from a strip-pieced unit

Q What must I do to ensure accurate strip piecing?

A The most essential concern is cutting strips across the fabric width (from selvage to selvage), and making sure the strips are straight and true (*see page 92*).

1. Cut strips the desired finished width of the patch plus ½" for the seam allowances.
2. Since you will be cutting across the joining seam, it is essential to adjust the machine for a shorter-than-normal stitch length, such as 15 to 18 stitches per inch (or *spi*). This helps prevent the stitching from unraveling after you've cut across the seams to create strip-pieced units and before you join them to create blocks.

3. Place a stitching guide (several layers of masking tape or a strip of moleskin) on the machine throat plate to create a ledge for the strips. It's easier to stitch long strips accurately with a ledge against which to guide them. (*See page 126.*)

4. Align the raw edges of the two strips you are joining a few inches at a time and feed them under the presser foot without stretching or tugging on them. (If the strip is curved as you stitch, it will be difficult at best to cut accurate segments.) Stop often to adjust the strip edges so they are perfectly aligned. Pins are usually not necessary as quilter's cottons tend to "grab" each other.

5. Press along the seamline to set the stitches. Use the tip or side of the iron to open the seam and press the seam allowance in the direction indicated. When pressing long strip units, take care to keep the strip unit straight and true so it doesn't develop a curve. Lay the long units across the width of the ironing board, rather than along the length. If your strip units are made of multiple strips, try pressing with no steam. Too much steam during pressing can contribute to strip distortion.

6. After pressing, turn the pressed unit over to make sure the seam allowances are correctly pressed.

7. Before cutting the required segments from the pressed strip unit, trim away the selvages, making sure the cut ends are perpendicular to the long edges of the strip. (Use your rotary-cutting ruler for this job; don't just eyeball it.)

8. Follow the guidelines for rotary cutting in this chapter to cut the required segments from the strip unit.

SEE ALSO: *Press It Right, pages 113–18.*

Q How do I strip-piece Fourpatch and Ninepatch blocks?

A Cut strips of the required width and sew them together as shown. For Ninepatch blocks, you will need two different strip units to create the traditional checkerboard pattern. However, Ninepatch blocks don't always follow this pattern.

For Fourpatch blocks (*see page 128*), you will strip-piece units composed of two different strips. Press the seam allowances toward the darker strip(s) in each unit. Cut the required units at the same width as the cut strip width (to create even squares for the pattern). Arrange the units into rows and sew the rows together, making sure that seam intersections match (*see page 129*).

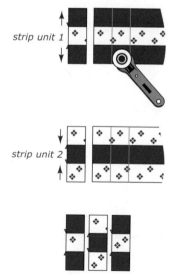

strip unit 1

strip unit 2

alternate units 1 and 2

Q Can strip piecing be used for shapes other than squares and rectangles?

A Yes, bicolor and multicolored diamond and triangle units can be cut from strip-pieced units; you can use the diagonal guidelines on standard rotary rulers or specialty rulers designed for common units. For example, half-square triangle units can be cut from bias-cut strips joined into strip units by using a ruler with a 45-degree-angle line. (They can also be made using the sandwich-piecing method shown on pages 137–8.) Two-color diamond shapes can be cut from a strip unit using the appropriate angle (30, 45, or 60 degrees) on your rotary-cutting ruler. A 45-degree-angle, two-color diamond unit is often used in an eight-pointed-star block. Strip piecing helps maintain piecing accuracy in this block design.

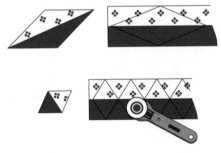

strip-pieced diamonds

CHAPTER 6

Templates, Pressing, and Piecing

Traditionalists prefer to make patchwork blocks using hand piecing, but machine piecing is a perfectly acceptable option. Hand piecing requires marking the pieces and scissor-cutting them from the fabric. For machine piecing, many patches patterns can be cut with speed and accuracy using rotary-cutting tools. The addition of strip-piecing methods speeds up cutting and sewing many geometric patchwork units and blocks. Whichever method you prefer, accurate cutting, stitching, and pressing are the skills to master.

Making Patchwork Templates

Cutting accurate patches for patchwork blocks is the first essential step. For hand piecing, you need accurate templates *without* seam allowances. For machine piecing, you have several cutting options:

▶ Use templates with seam allowances included to mark and cut the patches by hand with scissors or with rotary-cutting tools.

▶ Rotary-cut strips of the correct width and then crosscut other shapes from the strips (*see pages 92 and 96–99*).

▶ Strip-piece and rotary-cut repetitive units (*see page 102*).

▶ Use a combination of the above, depending on the block design.

You can purchase acrylic templates in a variety of sizes and shapes for patchwork blocks to eliminate the necessity of making your own templates. Follow the cutting directions that come with the templates.

Q How do I make my own templates?

A As with every other step in quiltmaking, accuracy is essential when making templates. If you start with inaccurate templates, inaccuracies are compounded throughout the piecing process, making it especially difficult to match seams when sewing blocks together.

Templates printed in books and patterns usually have the seamlines and cutting lines marked. First decide whether you will hand-piece your quilt or machine-piece it. You will need a fine-point permanent marking pen, template plastic, craft scissors or rotary cutter, and a ruler.

1. Trace each patch onto the template plastic. **For hand piecing,** trace the seamlines — usually indicated by short dashed lines — not the outer solid cutting lines. **For machine piecing,** trace the cutting lines, not the seamlines.

2. Transfer any grainline arrows and construction/matching marks to the template — dots at seam intersections, for example.

3. Cut out carefully along the lines — not to the inside or the outside of the lines.

4. Test the accuracy of the template by placing it on top of the original pattern. Make a new, accurate template if necessary.

5. Use the permanent-marking pen to write the block name and finished size on each template so that you can use it again for other blocks requiring the same size and shape.

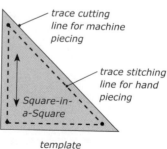

trace cutting line for machine piecing

trace stitching line for hand piecing

Square-in-a-Square

template

Q How do I use the templates to mark and cut the patches for my quilt?

A Use a sharp pencil in a color that will show on the wrong side of the fabric. After marking the templates on the fabric, take great care to cut through the marked line, not outside or inside the line, to maintain accuracy.

For Hand Piecing

Place the template wrong side up on the wrong side of the fabric, with the grainline arrow following the straight of grain (lengthwise or crosswise). Trace around the template, reversing the template if you need mirror images of asymmetrical shapes. Remember, you are marking the stitching lines. (When hand piecing, you match the drawn lines, not the cut edges, and keep the stitches on the line.) Leave at least ½" of space between shapes for seam allowances. Use sharp scissors to cut out each piece a scant ¼" beyond the marked lines — don't obsess about the accuracy of the seam width. Transfer any matching points.

Note: If you prefer to cut the patches with cutting lines marked, use a rotary ruler and sharp pencil to add the seam allowances beyond the drawn lines. Cut out on the outer lines.

For Machine Piecing

Trace around the template on the fabric wrong side, reversing the template for mirror-images of asymmetrical shapes if needed. Cut out on the marked lines. Use rotary-cutting tools when cutting geometric shapes and scissors for curved shapes. Transfer any marking points to the patches.

Q I've designed my own patchwork block. How do I make templates for the patches?

A You'll need paper, a sharp pencil, and a rotary ruler marked with ⅛" increments, a sharp straight pin, and a permanent marker with a fine tip. A large, sharp hand-sewing needle or a ⅛"-diameter hole punch are also helpful.

1. Draw the block to its full finished size on graph or plain paper (no seam allowances). Add a grainline arrow and identifying letters or numbers (if any) to each patch, making sure the arrows on all outer edges align with the straight of grain. (*See illustration on next page for all steps.*)

2. Place template plastic over the block and trace one of the patches in your block; add grainline arrows. Add ¼"-wide seam allowances to each edge of the patch. Repeat with the remaining shapes. If shapes are mirror images, you need only one. Simply mark, "Cut 1 and 1r" (reversed).

3. Extend the seamlines to the cutting lines to find and mark seam intersections for the match points on each. This is recommended where any angled lines intersect.

4. Cut out each template, using rotary-cutting tools. Check template accuracy by overlaying adjacent templates to make sure the seam intersections match perfectly. Insert a straight pin at each intersection to make a small hole at the exact intersection. Enlarge the holes with the point of a large sharp needle or a ⅛"-diameter hole punch so you can mark the match points on the fabric with the point of a sharp pencil. *Note:* For hand-piecing templates, complete steps 1 and 2, but do not add seam allowances.

5. After cutting the templates, check their accuracy on the block drawing.

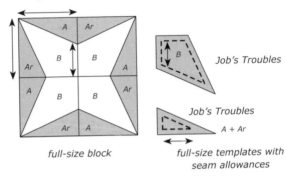

full-size block

Job's Troubles

Job's Troubles

A + Ar

full-size templates with seam allowances

- -

Q My templates slip on the fabric. How can I keep them securely in place?

A Tracing around plastic templates on fabric can be tricky. For a simple fix, add a loop of cellophane tape to the back of the template and then finger-press the template in place on the fabric.

- -

Q When I try to draw on fabric around my templates, the fabric snags on the pencil point. How can I prevent this?

A To keep the marking tool from dragging on the fabric, make a sandpaper board by attaching a piece of fine-grain sandpaper, grit side up, to the sticky side of an 8" × 10" or 16" × 20" needlework mounting board, available at crafts and needlework shops. The sandpaper grit will grab your fabric, making it much easier to trace around the template edges accurately with the appropriate marking tool. To make an impromptu sandpaper board, place a piece of sandpaper on a clipboard that you keep next to your machine.

Press It Right

Careful pressing is essential to making accurate patchwork blocks that fit together perfectly. If you're too heavy-handed with the iron, you can distort blocks — even shrink them. It's important to press — not iron. Most patterns direct you to press seam allowances to one side, to facilitate accurate seam matching.

- -

Q What's the difference between pressing and ironing?

A Ironing involves moving the iron continuously back and forth with downward pressure over fabric to remove wrinkles and creases and restore its original shape. You will do this when pressing your quilt fabrics after preshrinking them.

Pressing is a more delicate maneuver, designed to persuade a seam allowance to lie in a specific direction. It is an up-and-down motion using the tip or the side of the iron to coax the seams and edges into submission without distorting them.

Q Why do most quilt blocks have the seams pressed to one side rather than open?

A It's generally agreed that pressing seams to one side makes for a stronger quilt top. It also makes it easier to match seam intersections, as well as hide the stitches along the seamline. Usually, patchwork seams are pressed toward the darker of the two fabrics in a unit to prevent the darker color from shadowing through the lighter one. Sometimes, because of the construction requirements of a particular quilt block, you may have to press the seams toward the lighter fabric in the seam allowance. If that is the case, trim the darker seam allowance so that it is a bit narrower than the light one.

Pressing seams open is sometimes recommended when three or more seams come together at an intersection to help distribute the bulk. Some quiltmakers prefer to press all seams open.

Note: When a seam is pressed to one side in a block, you create a natural "high" (or "peak") and "low" (or "valley" or "ditch") side of the seam. Pressing seams in opposing directions on pieces that will be joined allows you to nest the high and low sides snuggly into each other for a perfect match with the seam bulk evenly distributed on each side of the joining seam. This also makes it easy to quilt in the ditch (*see page 313*).

nested seamlines

Q What's the correct procedure for pressing patchwork blocks?

A For best results with machine piecing, press as you go. Any seam that will be crossed with another must be pressed first.

1. Set the iron for cotton or for the most heat-sensitive fabric in the block you are pressing.

2. Place the pieced unit on the ironing board with the piece that will lie on top of the seam allowances on top. (Look for pressing arrows on the pattern for the block or quilt.)

3. Set the stitches by placing the iron on the stitches for a few seconds to help them sink into the fabric. This also helps smooth out any small puckers that may have occurred during stitching. Allow to cool briefly.

4. Use your fingertips and the point of the iron to direct and press the patch or strip on top so that it lies smooth and flat on top of the seam allowance. For long seams, be sure to use a lift-and-lower pressing motion rather than sliding (ironing) the weight of the iron along the seam.

5. Examine the pressed seam to make sure that the seamline is crisp and flat with no tucks. Flip the pressed unit over and press lightly from the wrong side if needed.

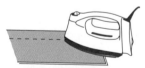

setting the stitches

pressing toward the seam allowance

Q Should I use steam when pressing patchwork blocks?

A Some quilters never use steam, claiming that steam is often the cause of block distortion. It's easy to stretch damp fabric out of shape. Others always use a bit of steam to help coax seams and edges into place. Try both methods and decide which works best for you. Keep a spray bottle handy to mist stubborn pieces as needed for a flat, crisp press.

Q If my quilt pattern doesn't include pressing directions, how do I determine the best way to press the seams in my blocks?

A Study the block(s) and draw pressing arrows that distribute the bulk of the seams in opposite directions where they will intersect in the completed block. There may be more than one way to achieve this goal as shown in the Ninepatch block on the facing page. You must also consider how the seams will connect when sewing similar blocks together side by side, so that those intersecting seams will nest, too. Mark your pressing plan on each block diagram with a pencil.

Here are some things to keep in mind:

▶ Although pressing toward the darker color is usually the recommended method to avoid color shadow-through, pressing to create flat seam intersections almost always takes precedence.

▶ Whenever possible, seams should be pressed in opposing directions where they will meet.

▶ Often patchwork blocks will "tell" you which way they should be pressed. For example, if you are joining a heavily pieced block to one with fewer seams or no seams, it's always easier to press the seam allowances away from the heavily pieced block so you don't have to deal with the bulk of the seam allowances.

▶ Block-row joining seams are usually pressed in one direction — toward the bottom of the quilt top.

▶ Borders are usually pressed away from the quilt-top center. Press the seam allowances of pieced borders toward unpieced borders on either side of it.

▶ If there is a narrow border (½" or ¾" wide) between two wider borders, it's usually best to press both seam allowances toward the narrow border strip. The seam allowances help to fill in the narrow strip, so it doesn't sink.

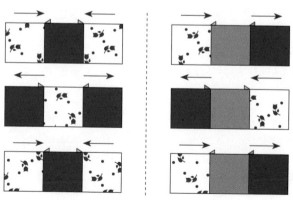

two ways to press for nested seams

FIVE "RULES" FOR PATCHWORK PRESSING

In a nutshell, these are the basic rules that help ensure accuracy and a flat quilt top with square corners. Press the blocks accurately and they will go together more easily.

1. Always set the stitches before pressing seams open or to one side. (*See page 115.*)
2. Don't drag the iron across pieces or blocks; lift and press, lift and press, not back and forth.
3. Press for opposing seams whenever possible to make seam-matching easier.
4. Press toward the darker color whenever possible to avoid dark colors showing through lighter patches.
5. Never cross another seam with stitching until it has been pressed in the correct direction.

Hand Piecing

Machine piecing is faster than hand piecing, but hand piecing offers more accuracy and project portability. It is also a good choice for seams with inset corners and blocks that have many seams intersecting in the center. Hand piecing leaves the seam allowances floating (with no stitches holding them down). This allows you to move them to one side or the other when pressing.

Q How do I hand-piece the patches together?

A Following the block diagram, arrange the pieces for the block on a piece of thin cotton batting. Join the pieces of the blocks in rows first and then join the rows with handstitching.

1. Position the two adjacent pieces right sides together with marked seamlines, (not raw edges) aligned. Place a pin at each end of the seam where the seamlines intersect, with the pins perpendicular to the seam-

pin patches together

line. Use pins along the seamlines, checking that they are perfectly aligned — it is essential that the stitching lines match on both pieces to be joined; the cut edges may not match.

2. Thread a needle with an 18"-long piece of all-purpose or cotton hand-sewing thread and insert it precisely at the point of a seam intersection, not at the raw edge. Take one small stitch forward. Check the underside to make sure the needle is in the marked line before bringing it to the surface. Take a backstitch by placing the needle back in the original hole. When hand piecing, you always begin and end at the seam intersections, not at the cut edge.

3. Fill the needle with 5 or 6 small stitches, making sure they are along the marked sewing line on both patches. Remove the pins as you reach them. The piecing stitches should be ⅛" long. With piecing practice, you'll be able to

make your stitches quite consistent. When you reach the last intersection, end with a backstitch or two.

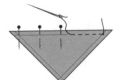

begin and end stitching at the seam intersection

4. Finger-press the seam toward the darker color in the seam and trim any triangle "ears" that extend past the edges of the pieced unit. You will do a final press of all seams later using an iron.

GET ORGANIZED

To keep hand-cut pieces organized as you cut, tuck them into individual zip-top plastic bags and label with the block's name and finished size. Once all pieces are cut, remove them from the plastic bags and arrange them into blocks. Working one row at a time, temporarily sew the pieces in the row together by stacking them and piercing the stack with a threaded needle. Slide the set along the thread to the knot, then make two knots and add the next set. After all are threaded, remove the needle and knot the thread. Tuck into a zip-top plastic bag with a copy of the block layout. Cut off sets between the double knots as you need them.

Q How do I hand-sew seamed patches together?

A The technique is the same as for joining patches to create two-patch units, but the intersecting seams must be carefully matched and left to float free of the stitching that joins the units (*as shown in the illustration below*) so you can press them as desired later. Sew pieces together in short rows and then sew the rows together to complete the block.

1. Pin the patches together, using pins at the intersecting seams to ensure that they match precisely. Use the piecing stitch described above to join the block units.

2. When you reach a seam intersection, remove the matching pin, make a stitch through the pinhole, and take a backstitch to reinforce. Then slip the needle through to the other side of the seam allowance and continue to the next seam intersection to leave the seam allowances floating free. Press the seams as directed in your quilt pattern after the block assembly is complete.

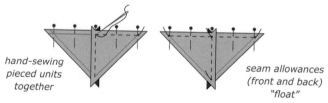

hand-sewing pieced units together

seam allowances (front and back) "float"

3. After completing and pressing all blocks, arrange them in rows and sew them together using the same piecing method. Press the long joining seams in one direction before cutting and sewing borders to the quilt top.

Machine Piecing

Accurate machine piecing goes hand in hand with accurate cutting to ensure finished blocks of the desired size. As with hand piecing, patchwork blocks and quilt-top-assembly seams in most quilts are stitched with scant ¼"-wide seams.

- -

Q Besides the obvious, how does machine piecing differ from hand piecing?

A For machine piecing, you can use templates or rotary-cut the pieces individually or from strips. You may use a combination of cutting and piecing methods within a block. Template cutting is necessary for fussy-cut patches (*see next question*). In any case, patches are cut with ¼"-wide seam allowances all around. Marking the stitching lines is not necessary (as it is for hand piecing). The patches can be arranged in rows and sewn together piece by piece and then row by row, but for many block designs, the pieces can be created with strip piecing (*see chapter 5*).

Another major difference is that *all seams begin and end at the cut edges of the patches, not at the seamlines.* Machine stitching crosses the intersecting seams — meaning seam allowances get "caught" in the stitching — so you must press seams as you go. With machine piecing, you may be able to speed up the sewing and pressing with chain piecing. (*See page 132.*)

- -

Q What is fussy cutting?

A When you want to showcase a particular motif or an area of fabric within a block or border, you must carefully plan the positioning of the ruler or template when you cut the piece. If your fabric has small motifs that you want to center within the boundaries of a patch, you would cut the squares individually (fussy cutting) rather than cutting strips and then cutting squares with only partial motifs in each square.

Cutting borders from sections of border prints is another example of fussy cutting. And you can fussy-cut appliqués from specific areas of a print to simulate a leaf, for example. If you plan to fussy-cut, purchase extra fabric. For more about fussy cutting appliqués, see page 172.

- -

Q If I fussy-cut the motif I want for my quilt squares, must I cut them on the straight of grain?

A You can fussy-cut patches with edges that are not on the true straight grain if necessary, but do take care to avoid stretching the edges. To stabilize these patches, apply a light coat of spray starch or sizing. Another way to stabilize the edges is with staystitching ⅛" from each edge. Press off-grain patches with a dry iron. It's too easy to distort patches when dampened with steam.

SEE ALSO: *All About Appliqué, pages 169–206.*

The Perfect Patchwork Seam

Consistent seam width is essential for all patchwork pieces and blocks to fit together accurately. Patches and all other quilt pieces (sashing, borders, backings) are cut with ¼"-wide seam allowances to keep the bulk to a minimum. Quilting through seam allowances is difficult; pressing the two seam allowances to one side puts two narrow layers of fabric to one side of every seam. Keeping excess bulk to a minimum makes quilting easier.

Q How do I set up the sewing machine for machine piecing?

A First, make sure your machine is in good working order. Then follow these steps.

1. Insert a size 80/12 Sharp needle for the straightest stitches. (Use a Universal needle if a Sharp is not available.)

2. Thread the bobbin and needle with a matching or neutral-color thread that will blend with your fabric colors.

3. Adjust the stitch length to 12 to 15 stitches per inch — between 2 and 3mm on the stitch-length dial (15 to 18 stitches per inch for strip piecing).

4. Make sure the tension is balanced so that the top and bobbin stitches interlock in the layers, not on either side of the seam.

5. Test the seam-allowance width to make sure it is accurate (*see next two questions*). Mark or add a stitching guide on the machine if necessary. Attach the ¼" foot if available.

6. Optional: If possible, replace the zigzag throat plate with a straight-stitch throat plate (*see page 322*) to prevent fabric from flagging — being pushed down into the wider hole in the zigzag plate. Make sure the needle is in the center-needle position. Remember that you cannot zigzag stitch with this plate or you'll break the needle.

Q **How do I sew accurate seam allowances? There is no ¼" stitching guideline on my sewing machine.**

A Even if your machine *does* have a ¼" sewing guideline etched on the throat plate, it's important to check the accuracy. As an alternative, you can purchase a ¼" patchwork foot for most sewing machines. However, to sew an accurate seam when using a patchwork foot, you must make sure that the edge of the presser foot is precisely positioned along the edge of the pieces you are joining.

Check stitching accuracy by cutting two 3" squares of quilter's cotton fabric and sewing them together. Press the seam allowance to one side and measure the resulting unit; it should measure precisely 3" × 5½". If it doesn't, cut and stitch a second pair of patches, being careful to stitch accurately. If the second patch is inaccurate, add a stitching guide to the throat plate of your machine. (*See next question.*)

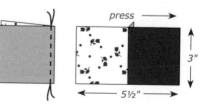

press →

3"

← 5½" →

Q How do I add a stitching guide?

A You'll need a piece of graph paper with 4 squares per inch and masking tape or moleskin (a sticky-back fabric found in the foot-care department at the drugstore).

1. Place a 1" × 3" strip of graph paper under the sewing-machine needle with the needle above the first line on the right-hand edge of the strip. Begin to lower the needle, but before it pierces the line, shift the paper slightly so the needle pierces it just to the right of the line. Lower the presser foot to hold the paper in place, making sure the paper is straight and perpendicular to the front edge of the sewing machine. This gives a scant ¼" seam allowance.

2. To mark the stitching guide on the machine, cut and apply a ¼" × 2" strip of moleskin or a piece of masking tape along the right-hand edge of the paper; secure it to the throat plate to mark the scant ¼" seam allowance. If using masking tape, add one or more layers to the first to create a slight "ledge" against which to guide the fabric. Or, you can use a short stack of sticky notes to create an easily removed "ledge" at the ¼" mark.

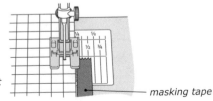

needle pierces paper just to right of the ¼" line — *masking tape*

You can leave a masking-tape ledge in place if it won't interfere with other stitching, but you will need to remove a moleskin ledge and place it somewhere on your machine for easy access later. You can remove and replace the strip several times before it's necessary to cut a new one. Use rubbing alcohol or a product like Goo Gone to remove any sticky residue that remains when removing masking-tape layers. *Note:* Some quilters use a permanent marker to draw a stitching line on the throat plates of their machines.

- -

Q Why not pierce the ¼" line precisely?

A If you stitch a seam that measures a perfect ¼", you can still lose some block size when you press the seams to one side. This is particularly true when making blocks composed of many patches requiring many seams. The procedure described above gives you a *scant* ¼" seam, which allows for the small loss of fabric at the "turn of cloth" where seam allowances are pressed to one side. Many ¼" patchwork feet are actually calibrated for this scant seam allowance, but you won't know if yours is unless you stitch a test sample and measure it as directed in the previous question.

- -

Q How do I machine-piece a patchwork block?

A First arrange the required patches in rows for a single block. Working with the pieces in one row of the block at a time, pick up adjacent patches, place the edges to be joined right sides together, and use a pin or two to hold them together. Place the pins perpendicular to the cut edge with the pin heads to the right so you can remove them easily.

Machine-stitch the patches together using the edge of the ¼" presser foot or the moleskin or tape guideline on the machine throat plate (*see page 126*). It is not necessary to backstitch at the beginning and end of the seams since they will be crossed by other seams.

Press the seam allowances in one direction, following the pressing arrows if provided in the quilt directions. After joining all pieces in each row, pin the rows together, making sure that intersecting seams match precisely, and stitch. Press the seams in one direction or as directed in the quilt pattern.

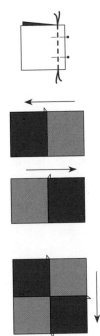

Fourpatch

Q Is pinning always necessary when sewing patches and block units together?

A Because quilter's cottons are not slippery, pins are not essential. Beginners may feel more confident pinning patches with one or two pins until they gain more experience handling the fabric pieces. However, even experienced quilters use pins in the following situations:

▶ To match intersecting seams or points

▶ At matching points on curved blocks so the pieces fit together correctly

▶ On seams that are longer than 4"; use at least one pin at the center point and each end; borders require pins spaced along the seam to prevent them from shifting

▶ On seams that require a bit of easing to make them match, because cutting and/or sewing was inaccurate

- -

Q How do I make sure the intersecting seams match when sewing pieces or rows together?

A When joining patchwork units, there are two basic pinning techniques that ensure accuracy.

Without Points

For seamed units that have no points or angled seams:

1. Nest the opposing seams and pin together by inserting pins through the seam allowances. Place the pins perpendicular to the seamline or angle the pin and catch both seam allowances in it.

2. Stitch one or two stitches past the intersecting seamline before removing the pin so the layers have no chance of shifting. *Whenever possible,* stitch with the seam that is pressed toward you on the bottom so the feed dogs won't push it out of position. You can control the top seam allowance with the point of your

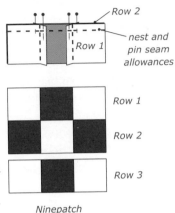

Row 2

nest and pin seam allowances

Row 1

Row 1

Row 2

Row 3

Ninepatch

seam ripper, a straight pin, or needle, or a bamboo skewer to keep the presser foot from moving it out of position.

With Points

When joining any unit with a seam to another with points to match (angled seams):

1. Press so the seam allowances oppose each other. In some cases, this may mean changing the direction that a seam was pressed originally — and that may create a twist in the seam on the wrong side of the unit.

2. To align the points, place the pieces right sides together and insert a pin at the seamline on the wrong side of the top unit. Shift the lower unit so you can see the point and insert the pinpoint at the tip and through the unit so that the pinhead is against the top layer.

3. Insert a pin on each side of the matched point to securely hold the pieces in place for stitching.

4. Remove the first pin. Stitch, removing each pin as you reach it. As you stitch across the intersection, take care to aim for the X formed by the stitching and err in favor of the point by stitching a thread or two away from it, in the seam allowance, so you don't nip off the point in the stitching.

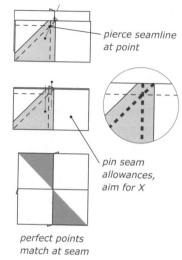

pierce seamline at point

pin seam allowances, aim for X

perfect points match at seam

Q If one row of patches in the block is slightly longer than the others, do I need to restitch the seams?

A Unless the difference is substantial, restitching the seams isn't necessary. Instead, pin the rows together, placing pins at intersecting seams and at the ends of the row. Use additional pins along the seam to ease the longer row to fit the shorter one. Stitch the seam with the shorter row on top so the feed dogs can ease the excess fabric to fit. If the difference in length is excessive, check the sizes of the pieces. It's possible that inaccurate cutting has caused the error. If so, you may

131

need to discard the row and cut new pieces or adjust the seams so they are the correct size and the intersecting seams match.

- -

Q **I have hundreds of patches to sew together. Is there a way to save time and thread?**

A Chain piecing to the rescue! Use this assembly-line sewing method whenever you are doing repetitive piecing for quilt blocks as well as when sewing units together to complete blocks. It makes quick work of piecing and saves stitching and pressing time.

When you are making a quilt with many duplicate blocks, you will join many patchwork units that are the same. Rather than stopping to clip the thread and remove a unit from the machine before sewing the next pair of patches, you can feed the next ones into the stitching and keep going until you have joined all sets of similar patches into a "clothesline." Here's how you stitch them together:

1. Prepare the units for stitching by aligning the raw edges of the two patches with right sides facing. Use at least one pin to hold them together. The pin will help you make sure you are sewing the correct edges together.

2. Stack the prepared pairs to the left of the sewing machine. Turn the stack so the edges to be sewn together are parallel to the presser-foot edge. This is an essential habit to develop for chain piecing so that you sew all pieces together correctly. It won't make a difference if both patches are plain squares but when the patches are made

of pieced units, it is essential to avoid piecing errors that require a seam ripper.

3. Stitch the first pair of patches together. When you reach the raw edges at the end of the seam, continue stitching without fabric for two or three stitches to create a thread chain. Position the next set of patches and feed them under the presser foot. It's not necessary to raise the presser foot — just feed the next set under the toe of the foot. Continue sewing and feeding prepared patches under the presser foot in this manner until you have sewn the seam in all units.

4. Take your "clothesline" of patches to the ironing board. Snip them apart and press the seams as directed in your quilt pattern.

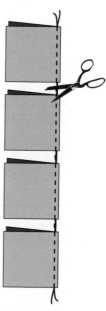

chain piecing

ASSEMBLY-LINE PIECING

You can use an assembly-line variation of chain piecing to make quick and accurate work of piecing some blocks or block sections. We'll use a Log Cabin block for a Log Cabin Quilt as an example.

First cut the center square from a strip of the desired color and then cut a 40"-long strip of each of the fabrics you plan to use for the block. Pay careful attention to placement as you sew the block to the strips. *Note:* The center square may or may not be the same size as the strip width for the logs. Cut strips and squares the desired finished width plus ½" for the seam allowances.

1. Make a reference sketch of the block and number to designate the piecing order. Use colored pencils to shade the logs to approximate the strip colors you will be using.

2. Beginning with a strip for the first log (log #1), place a center square face down on it, with raw edges aligned and stitch ¼" from the raw edges. Leaving a bit of space between squares, add the remaining squares in the same fashion.

Step 1

3. Press the stitching along the strip to set the stitches, and then use a rotary cutter and ruler to cut the strip even with the edges of the squares. With the wrong side of the center square facing the ironing board, press the log over the seam allowance, away from the center square.

4. Position a two-patch unit face down on a strip for log #2 with the center square at the top and log #1 closest to you. The raw edges of the seam allowance should face you so you will be stitching over the seam allowance. Stitch. Add the remaining units in the same fashion.

5. Trim, and press as for the first log. Add the three-patch units to a strip for log #3, rotating the three-patch unit so log #2 is closest to you. Stitch, trim, and press.

6. Continue adding logs around the center square in the same fashion, always positioning the pieced unit on the new strip so the log you added last is closest to you.

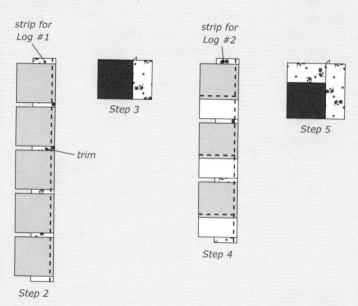

strip for Log #1

trim

Step 2

Step 3

strip for Log #2

Step 4

Step 5

Q The pieces for my block have curved edges. How do I stitch them together?

A Popular curved block designs include Drunkard's Path, Orange Peel, and Robbing Peter to Pay Paul, but curved piecing isn't as scary as it looks! In fact, curved edges have bias give, which actually helps in the piecing process. Let's use Drunkard's Path as an example of how to put together a block with curved pieces.

Drunkard's Path

1. Make templates (*see page 108*), mark, and cut the pieces to suit your sewing method of choice (hand or machine). Be sure to follow grainline placement arrows if provided. If not, make sure that the outer edges of shapes that will lie at the outer edge of the block are on the straight of grain.

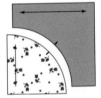

2. Match the seam intersections and place at least one more pin in the center of the seam to be stitched. The templates in your pattern may have a matching point marked at the center of each edge to be joined. If not, fold each piece in half and mark the centers before pinning the pieces together.

Step 2

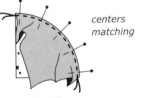

centers matching

3. Hand- or machine-piece. It's easier to work with the concave-curve on top of its convex curve partner so you can control the fullness and

Step 3

make sure that edges are always aligned. The methods are just about the same whether you hand- or machine-piece; but when hand-piecing, remember to begin and end all seams at the seamlines, not the raw edges. It may be necessary to clip the concave edge on some curved designs. Clip only if necessary — clips weaken the finished seam.

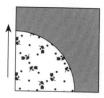

4. Press the seam toward the concave section.

*Step 4
Drunkard's Path
unit*

Speed-Piecing Methods

In addition to strip piecing (*see page 102*) and chain piecing (*see page 132*), there are several ways to speed up the piecing of common units in patchwork blocks. Sandwich piecing and the folded corner variations that follow make it easy to "mass produce" many different units for patchwork blocks.

Q What is sandwich piecing?

A This is a method for quickly piecing and cutting multiple two-color units. In some sandwich-piecing methods, a grid is drawn on the wrong side of one of two rectangles of fabric. The two fabrics are sandwiched with right sides facing and then are stitched and cut following the grid lines to yield the desired units. The most common unit made with sandwich piecing is the half-square triangle unit (also called a triangle-square unit). Accurate marking yields more accurate units than if you cut the triangles separately from each of the two fabrics and then join them in pairs. *Note:* Papers printed with stitching-grid guidelines are also available at your quilt shop.

1. Cut an 18" × 22" (or smaller) rectangle from each of the two fabrics required for the unit. Place the two rectangles right sides together with raw edges aligned. On the wrong side of the lightest color rectangle, draw a grid of squares with a sharp pencil and ruler. Leave at least ½" beyond the outer edges of the grid all the way around the rectangle sandwich. Make the squares ⅞" larger than the desired finished size of the half-square triangle unit. For a 2" finished triangle square, the grid square should be 2⅞".

2. Draw a grid with half as many squares as the total number of half-square triangles you need — you will get two units from each square.

3. Draw a diagonal line through each square in the grid, alternating the diagonal direction from square to square across each row so the final grid has rows of squares on point (*the red lines in the illustration*). There should be only one diagonal line in each of the original grid squares.

4. Attach the ¼" patchwork foot (it must sew an accurate ¼" seam; *see* Stitch Accurately *on page 140*) to your sewing machine. Beginning at the one corner of the grid (*), stitch ¼" from the grid line, pivoting each time you reach

the outer edge of the rectangle so that the stitching is
continuous, until you return to the outer edge of the grid.
Beginning at a different corner (**), stitch ¼" from the
diagonal lines on the other side in the same manner. Press
to set the stitches.

5. Using a rotary cutter for accuracy, cut along the diagonal
   grid lines between the two rows of stitching and along all
   other grid lines to make half-square triangle units.
6. Press the units open, with the seam allowance toward the
   darker color in the unit. Trim the points even with the raw
   edges of the square.

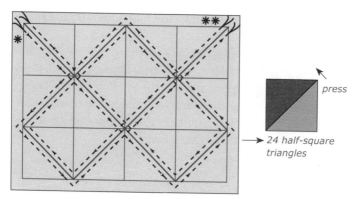

press

→ *24 half-square triangles*

sandwich-piecing grid for half-square triangles

STITCH ACCURATELY

Before you mark the grid on your fabric, test the technique with the ¼" foot and measure the resulting squares. If the resulting test squares are too small, and you can adjust the needle position on your machine, adjust it one step to the right so you will be stitching a scant ¼" from the drawn diagonal lines and test again. The other option is to actually draw the stitching lines on each side of the diagonals.

Q I don't have a ¼" patchwork foot. Can I still use this method?

A Yes. Draw accurately spaced stitching lines on each side of each diagonal line on the grid. When you stitch along the marked stitching line, stitch to the inside of the line to make sure that the resulting units are accurate. Even the width of a pencil line can make a difference in the finished size of the units cut from the grid. Do a test first.

Q What if I only need a few sandwich-pieced units?

A You can sandwich-piece half-square triangles with individual squares rather than making multiples on a rectangle grid. Here's how:

140

1. Cut two fabric squares ⅞" larger than the desired finished size of the half-square-triangle unit and place them right sides together.
2. Draw a diagonal line from corner to corner on the wrong side of the lightest square. Stitch precisely ¼" from the line on each side.
3. Press to set the stitches, and then cut the triangle units apart along the line; press the seam in each one toward the darker fabric (unless your quilt pattern specifies otherwise). Trim the seam points even with the square edges.

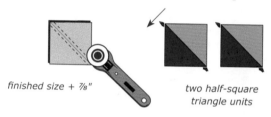

finished size + ⅞"

two half-square
triangle units

You can also sandwich-piece the units using paired strips.
1. Determine the finished size of the half-square triangle unit and add ⅞". Cut a strip of the required width from each of the two fabrics.
2. Layer the strips with raw edges even, and cut into squares. Press with a dry iron.

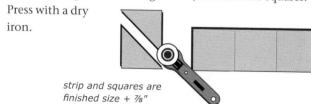

strip and squares are
finished size + ⅞"

3. Cut each pair in half diagonally. Stitch ¼"
   from the long raw edge of each triangle pair
   and press the seam toward the darker one in
   each pair. Take care not to stretch the bias
   edges while you stitch.

- -

Q Is there a way to strip-piece multiple half-square
triangles?

A Yes, the Bias Square method developed by Nancy Martin
of That Patchwork Place is a popular method for piecing
and cutting numerous half-square triangles. It involves cutting
and sewing bias strips together so that the resulting squares
have the straight-grain along the outer edges instead of the bias
grain. When squares are cut from these strip units, the resulting
squares have straight-grain edges. Cutting and handling bias
strips requires extra care, so this may not be the best method
for a beginning quilter. Directions for this method are included
with the Bias Square Ruler that you will need for the technique,
and appears in many books from That Patchwork Place.

Q What if I need lots of quarter-square triangles (Hourglass units)?

A Use the grid method shown for quick half-square triangles (*see pages 138–39*) but make squares on the grid 1¼" larger than the required finished size for the quarter-square-triangle units.

1. After cutting the grid apart and pressing the half-square triangles, place two units side by side with the colors and seamlines positioned as shown.

2. Flip the right unit face down on the left one, nest the seamlines together, and draw a diagonal line across the seamline from corner to corner. Stitch ¼" from the line on each side, cut on the line, and press. You can make two-color units or units that have as many as three different colors.

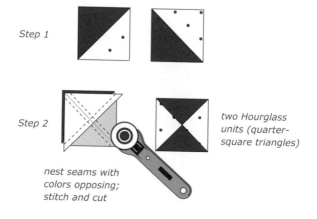

Step 1

Step 2

nest seams with
colors opposing;
stitch and cut

two Hourglass
units (quarter-
square triangles)

You can also combine a half-square triangle unit with a solid-color or print square to create mirror-image units composed of one large triangle and two quarter triangles.

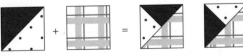

mirror-image units

- -

Q **What is the folded-corner method for piecing patchwork units?**

A It's a quick-piecing method for adding small triangles to one or more corners of square or rectangular patches or for adding a small triangle to the tip of a larger triangle without actually cutting the small triangles. It's faster and more accurate and avoids dealing with the bias edges of triangles. Although there is some waste with this method, speed and accuracy make it a popular technique.

1. Cut squares or rectangles of the required size for the unit (refer to your quilt pattern) and then cut the small corner squares that will become the triangle corners in the finished unit or block. Use a sharp pencil to draw a diagonal line from corner to corner on the wrong side of each of the corner squares.

2. Position the small square on the larger square or rectangle with adjacent raw edges aligned and the diagonal line touching the adjacent edges. Stitch on the line.

144

3. Use a rotary cutter to trim the corners ¼" from the stitching. Press.

4. Use the tip of the iron to press the triangle toward the seam allowance.

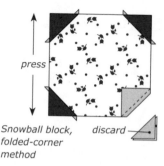

press

Snowball block, folded-corner method

discard

Note: Some quiltmakers find that it's easier to ensure accuracy by scissor-trimming only the excess triangle in the small square, leaving the background piece intact underneath to support the small triangle that remains. In this case, discard the small cutaway triangles. Also note that this method may not work when you are sewing a small light-colored square to a darker patch — the darker patch may show through the light-colored triangle.

Q Is there a way to use the cutaway triangle pairs that result with this method?

A Many quilters draw two lines on each small square — one on the diagonal and one ½" from the first. Then they stitch on both lines and cut between them. The smaller units are great for doll quilts, baby quilts, pieced borders, and other small projects.

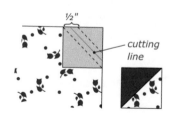

½"

cutting line

Solving Problems

Q When I start a seam, I often end up with a tangled mess of stitches on the underside. Why does this happen?

A Quilters not-so-fondly refer to these thread messes as birds' nests! They happen because the feed dogs don't have much to grab onto at the beginning of a seam. Get in the habit of holding onto the top and bobbin threads behind the presser foot whenever you begin a seam or a chain of patches if you are chain-piecing. (*See page 132.*) The resulting thread tension helps guide the fabric into the feed-dog action smoothly so the edges don't hang up or get shoved down into the hole in the sewing-machine throat plate.

If you have a zigzag sewing machine, changing the wide-hole throat plate for one with a small needle hole is a big help. (*See page 322.*) Another successful option is to begin a seam with a fabric scrap that you can use again and again. Fold a small scrap in half to make a double layer and center it under the needle. Lower the presser foot and the needle, hold onto the threads, and stitch off the edge of the scrap. Without raising the presser foot, tuck the first pair of patches under the presser foot toes and continue stitching. Cut away the scrap to use until it is full of stitches before replacing it with a new starter scrap.

Q I have difficulty joining blocks with angled seams that intersect at the points. Piecing diamonds together is particularly troublesome. How can I join them accurately?

A The pesky little diamond points must extend past the cut edges so the ¼" stitching line intersects the edges precisely. That means that the small triangle points I call "ears" must extend precisely the same distance at each end of the seam when joining triangles and diamond shapes. Many quilt-makers cut off the points — also called nubbing the points — on the pieces to make sure they match. Others use purchased templates with corners already nubbed to cut these pieces. Strip piecing (*see page 102*) and the folded-corner sandwich-piecing technique (*see page 144*) help eliminate this problem, but often you have no choice other than cutting and joining individual patches, taking care to stitch accurate seams so the seams will match perfectly.

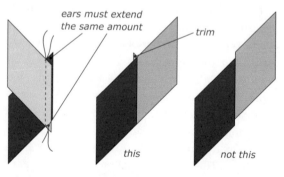

ears must extend
the same amount

trim

this

not this

joining diamonds

Q What is the best way to join triangles to squares or rectangles?

A Aligning triangle patches with squares or rectangles can be tricky. The pesky points on triangles and the bias stretch along their cut edges makes matching them to other shapes a challenge. To make it easier to align them, some patterns are printed with the triangle points cut off (nubbed) so the raw edges of the square patch and the triangle will match perfectly. You can make a nubbing template by cutting paper or template-plastic pieces for the two pieces you will be joining. Match the centers and cut off the triangle ends.

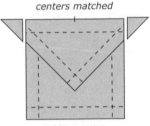

centers matched

nubbing points

- -

Q Is there a quick and easy way to rip out inaccurate machine stitches?

A On the bobbin-thread side of the seam you need to rip, use a sharp seam ripper or small, sharp scissors to lift and snip every fifth or sixth stitch along the seam. Flip the piece over and pull the thread. It should lift away easily in one piece, leaving only small thread tufts on the reverse to remove. Run a piece of masking tape over the seamline to pick them up or use a lint roller, a small foam paintbrush, or a pink pencil eraser to whisk them away. There are other ways to unstitch a seam, but I find this method the fastest, easiest, and safest.

SEAM RIPPING MADE EASIER

Just in case "unstitching" is necessary, many quilters use different thread colors in the needle and the bobbin. That way, identifying the bobbin thread is easy — and bobbin thread is usually easier to clip than the needle thread.

Q My seam ripper slipped and made a hole in the body of the block. Is there a way to salvage the block? I don't have enough fabric to replace it.

A There's nothing so disheartening as ripping the fabric when you're trying to unstitch a seam. Lightweight fusible woven or knit interfacing to the rescue! With the piece wrong side up, coax the cut edges together. Then cut a narrow strip of the interfacing and center it over the cut edges with the resin side down. Fuse in place.

If you've snipped out a small piece of fabric, leaving a hole in the block, cut a small circle of matching fabric and apply lightweight fusible web to its right side. Center the fabric under the hole, top with a Teflon pressing sheet (or parchment paper) and fuse in place. The excess fusible will adhere to the pressing sheet. Plan quilting stitches in the area to disguise your "mend."

SEE ALSO: *Special Care for Your Iron, page 76.*

Q My machine is skipping stitches. Do I need to have it serviced?

A Before you pack it off to the dealer, unthread it, clean the lint from the bobbin compartment, and check to make sure the bobbin is correctly inserted and that the thread winds off easily. Oil moving parts following the directions in your owner's manual and then carefully rethread the machine. Test-stitch on scraps. If the skipping continues, try adding a line of liquid thread conditioner, such as All-Purpose Sewer's Aid, to the spool of thread to soften and condition the thread for smoother stitching. If your test still doesn't pass muster, it's time for a machine tune-up. Once-a-year servicing, or more often if you sew a lot, is essential for the health and long life of your machine.

Foundation-Piecing Methods

Sewing patchwork blocks on a foundation is not new, but paper piecing by machine has become a new favorite for creating pieced blocks with precise points and corners.

Q What is foundation paper piecing?

A Paper piecing is an especially accurate method for constructing blocks with geometric patches, although it cannot be used for designs with inset corners (*see page 165*). This popular machine-piecing method requires a preprinted or hand-traced reverse drawing of the finished block on a paper foundation for each block in the quilt. The lines on the foundation delineate the finished patches, which are marked with the order of application. Oversized patches of fabric are cut, positioned on the unprinted side of the paper, and then stitched in place from the printed side of the foundation, through the paper.

Since you sew the pieces to the front by stitching on the lines on the back of the foundation, the printed block template is the reverse of what the finished block will look like on the front of the foundation. If the block design is not symmetrical, the paper foundation must be a mirror image of the finished design. Paper foundations add stability to the finished blocks and usually remain in the blocks until they are sewn together to create the quilt top.

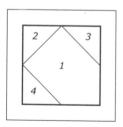

paper foundation

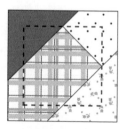

finished block with seam allowances

Q Do I need any special tools for paper piecing?

A These are the basic items you'll need:

▶ A light source for backlighting the foundation during the patch placement such as a small lamp for working at night (a well-lit window works during the day)

▶ Fine pins (called silk straight pins) to maneuver easily through the fabric and paper layers

▶ An open-toe presser foot to make it easier to see and follow the stitching lines on the foundation paper

An index card or piece of manila folder is also helpful. You will need paper on which to draw, trace, or copy the block design — one for each block. Your choices include:

▶ Foundation paper, available at your local quilt shop

▶ Copy paper

▶ Tracing paper

▶ Parchment paper

▶ Newsprint (end rolls are available at your local newspaper)

▶ Doctors' exam-table paper, available at medical-supply stores

▶ Freezer paper (found at the grocery store)

▶ Waxed paper (but you must iron it between two sheets of paper to remove the wax so you can write on it)

Q How do I make the paper foundations?

A First, make an accurate, finished-size master drawing on foundation paper for each block required for your quilt, leaving at least ½" beyond the block outline.

1. Use a sharp pencil and straight-edge ruler and trace the required number of blocks onto the paper of your choice, adding the numbers to each patch.

2. Cut out each foundation, allowing no less than ½" beyond the outer lines for the finished patches. Some patterns have only ¼" beyond the patches — an extra ¼" is better for accuracy and handling. You will trim the excess later.

3. Cut and add patches to each block foundation in numerical order.

You can also try using iron-on tear-away paper stabilizer, available at fabric, craft, or quilting stores. This product is used most often for machine embroidery, but can be adapted for foundation paper piecing. Draw the foundation on the matte side of the paper. After cutting and positioning a fabric piece, as shown in the foundation piecing method that follows, you can use a warm dry iron to press and hold the fabric in place temporarily instead of using pins. Take care not to touch the shiny side of the paper with the iron when pressing each new patch to the foundation.

- -

Q How do I cut and add the patches so they end up in the right places on the foundation?

A Set up the machine by adjusting it for a short, straight stitch (18 stitches per inch) and inserting a size 90/14 needle (to help pierce the paper for easier removal later).

1. Cut a patch of fabric for shape #1 that is at least ½" larger all around than the finished shape. (Place a ruler over the area to determine how large to cut the patch.) For half-square triangles, cut a square that is 1½" larger than one short side of the triangle and cut in half on the diagonal for two patches.

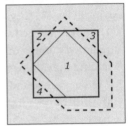

dashed lines = outline of oversized Patch #1 (wrong side against unnumbered side of foundation)

2. Holding the paper foundation up to the light with the drawn or printed lines facing you, center the fabric for patch #1 on the unprinted side of the foundation and use a few silk pins to hold it in place. There is no stitching necessary for this piece. Note that it must be positioned to extend past all lines that mark the shape of patch #1. On the printed side of the foundation paper, place an index card or piece of manila

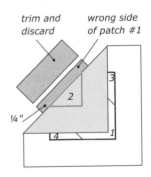

trim and discard   *wrong side of patch #1*

folder along the line of patch #2 that touches patch #1; fold the foundation firmly against the card edge to crease the stitching line and then use a ruler and rotary cutter to trim away any excess patch #1, trimming ¼" from the folded edge. Unfold the paper.

3. Cut the fabric for oversized patch #2 and place it face down over patch #1 with raw edges aligned. Pin in place.

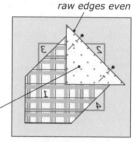

raw edges even

fabric #2

pin patch #2 in place

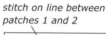

stitch on line between patches 1 and 2

4. Flip the foundation over to the printed side and stitch on the seamline, beginning and ending the stitching at the outer line for the block; backstitch or stitch in place a few stitches. Clip the threads.

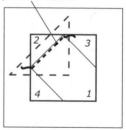

dashed lines = oversized Patch #2 on reverse side of foundation

5. Do a quick check to make sure that patch #2 completely covers the lines by flipping the patch into place on the right side of the block and holding it up to the light source

155

as you view it from the back of the foundation. If it doesn't, undo the stitching, reposition the patch, and stitch again. Clip the threads, turn the foundation over and use the tip of the iron to press the patch into place over the seam allowance. Place the foundation paper on a rotary-cutting mat with

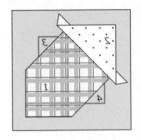

the printed side facing up and fold the paper back along the stitching to expose the seam allowances. Trim the fabric leaving a ¼"-wide seam allowance beyond the creased paper. *Note:* Undoing the stitches in foundation paper piecing is not easy. Until you are comfortable with the process, machine-baste each patch in place and check the placement, then change to the shorter stitch and stitch permanently.

6. Unfold the paper, and repeat the cutting, placement, stitching, and trimming steps to add each remaining patch in numerical order.

7. After adding all patches, trim the block precisely ¼" beyond the outermost marked lines of the completed block. Leave the paper in place to stabilize the block until you have completed all blocks and joined them to create the quilt top.

Q Do I need to pay attention to grainline when cutting the patches for foundation paper piecing?

A It's a good idea to follow grainline as much as possible. The paper foundation helps stabilize bias-cut edges, but it's still best to cut the outer-edge patches so the straight of grain lies along the outer edges of the finished block.

Q How and when do I remove the foundation paper?

A The needle perforations and the creased lines help to break down the paper, making it easy to remove in pieces. It's best to leave all the papers in place until after you have sewn all the blocks together to create the quilt top. Begin by holding each block in the quilt top at opposite diagonal corners and giving a gentle tug. The paper will pull away from the stitching lines. Use tweezers to remove stubborn bits.

Q Can I use a photocopy machine to make the foundations?

A Yes, but make sure you are always copying the original printed design. Not all machines copy accurately, resulting in a bit of size and shape distortion. Copying a photocopy creates even more distortion. However, as long as all the printed copies are the same, the blocks will fit together; the only issue is that the finished size may be slightly different.

Q Is there a quick way to make multiple foundations without a photocopier or hand tracing each one?

A Cut oversize squares of the paper you are using for the blocks and stack no more than four pieces together. Staple together in one corner of the stack. With no thread in your sewing machine and using a size 14 or larger needle and 10–12 stitches per inch, stitch carefully along each line to perforate the paper along the lines. Remove the staple and number the patches on each foundation. Follow the perforations to position and stitch patches in place.

Q My directions say to use the stitch-and-flip piecing method. What is that?

A Stitch-and-flip is another name for foundation piecing, which is similar to foundation paper piecing. Geometric shapes or strips are sewn to a layer of muslin or other similar lightweight fabric, then flipped onto the muslin and pressed before other pieces are added in the same manner. The muslin layer remains in the finished project, adding weight and stability. Typically, the stitch-and-flip method is used to make string-pieced blocks (*see next question*) to utilize your scraps. You can also string-piece oversized block patches cut from muslin and then trim them to the correct size. Some Crazy Quilt blocks can be string-pieced as well.

Q How do I make a string-pieced block with scraps?

A String piecing is a great way to use up long strips (strings) of fabric, for making patchwork fabric for garments as well as for patchwork blocks. Here's how to do it:

1. Cut the muslin foundation square 1" larger than the desired finished size of the block.

2. Cut strips of varying widths from scraps an inch or two longer than the foundation. They can be straight strips or uneven strips that are wider at one end than the other.

3. Place the first strip face up on the foundation at one edge or diagonally across the square. Place the next strip on top with raw edges aligned and stitch ¼" from the raw edges. Press along the stitching.

4. Flip the top "string" onto the foundation and press. Continue adding strips in this manner until you have covered the foundation. Trim the string-pieced block to the desired size.

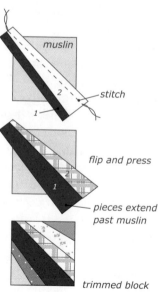

muslin

stitch

flip and press

pieces extend past muslin

trimmed block

Q What is Crazy Quilt patchwork?

A Originating during Victorian times, this random patchwork was devised as a way to use up randomly shaped scraps of elegant silk and velvet dressmaking fabrics and ribbons. Any fabric can be used for this technique, usually created on a muslin foundation. Some tips for making Crazy Quilts:

▶ The fabric pieces are arranged like a puzzle and can be sewn in place by hand, turning under the raw edges along the "seams" appliqué-fashion, or they can be machine-stitched to the muslin with zigzagging over the raw edges to hold them in place until you add embroidery.

▶ If you prefer, you can apply a layer of fusible web to the muslin foundation first, then position the fabric pieces and fuse in place.

▶ Embellish the turned or raw edges with hand or machine embroidery stitches as desired. If your fabrics are washable and you didn't fuse them in place, you can place a layer of washaway stabilizer on top of the pieces to keep them in place while you machine-embroider over the raw edges with decorative stitches. (Be sure to use an open-toe or appliqué presser foot so you can see where you're stitching.) Tear away what you can and then dissolve the remaining stabilizer with water.

▶ You can also do crazy patchwork with the stitch-and-flip method (*see pages 158–59*), but the results will not be as random since this method uses only straight seams.

Q **Is English paper piecing the same as foundation paper piecing?**

A Technically, no, but it is related. This is an essential hand-piecing method for accurately joining the edges of geometric shapes — hexagons, triangles, and diamonds — that would otherwise require multiple inset corners. Tessellated designs such as Grandmother's Flower Garden (hexagons) and Baby's Blocks (diamonds) are good candidates for English paper piecing. Some tessellated designs can be machine-stitched, but some require stitching inset corners (*see page 165*).

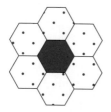

*Grandmother's
Flower Garden
(Hexagon patches)*

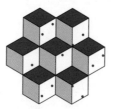

*Baby's Blocks
(diamond patches)*

- -

Q **How do you do English paper piecing?**

A Like foundation piecing, you will need a foundation for each piece in the quilt. This example is for making Grandmother's Flower Garden.

161

1. Cut a freezer-paper template for each patch (finished size) in the block — or cut from crisp typing paper or lightweight cardstock.

2. Mark each patch on the selected fabric so you can cut it out with a scant ³⁄₁₆" turn-under allowance all around.

3. Prepare as you would for an appliqué by turning and basting the allowance to the paper.

4. Align patches with right sides facing and take tiny whipstitches through just a few threads of the folded edges. Finish with a few backstitches. Do not catch the paper in the stitches. Continue adding patches in this fashion to create the desired pattern.

baste to paper

whipstitch edges together

remove basting papers

5. After the pieces are joined, remove the basting and the foundation papers.

SEE ALSO: *Turned-Edge Appliqué Methods, pages 183–84.*

Pieced and Appliquéd Blocks

Some popular patchwork designs require a combination of piecing and appliqué to complete the block. Typical designs in this category include Dresden Plate and Grandmother's Fan and variations of these traditional patterns. Appliqué is also often used to embellish pieced blocks, particularly ever-popular basket blocks. (*See the* Baltimore Album block *on page 16*.)

Q How do you piece Dresden Plate designs and prepare them for appliqué?

A Cut patches using templates for your choice of hand or machine piecing (*see pages 108–10*). Sew the "blades" together to make the "plate" with the chosen piecing method. Stitch from the *outer seamline* to the center, which will be covered by an appliquéd circle. Press seams toward the darker-color blades. Prepare the circle for the center using your favorite appliqué method (*see chapter 7*).

Machine-baste a scant ¼" from the curved outer edge of the completed plate. To make the curved outer edges easier to turn under, notch out fullness by cutting out small triangles in the turn-under allowance all around. You can use pinking shears to make quick work of this step. Turn under and press the allowance around the outer edge along the basting.

Position the plate on the block and appliqué in place, then add the prepared circle to the center.

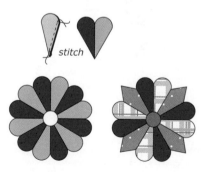

Dresden plate variations

Q Are Grandmother's Fan designs pieced and appliquéd like Dresden Plates?

A They can be prepared, positioned, and appliquéd to the corner of a background square, with the center piece appliquéd over the blades. However, many are actually created by sewing the blades together first and then sewing the fan to a curved, template-cut patch (*see the question on curved piecing on page 136*).

Depending on the number and shape of the fan blades, an appliquéd center circle may not be necessary. Individual Grandmother's Fan blocks can be arranged in interesting ways to create a number of curvilinear designs. Joining four of them with points meeting creates one variation of the traditional Dresden Plate.

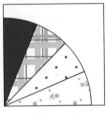
without center (pieced)

with center (pieced and appliquéd to a plain square)

Grandmother's Fan

SEE ALSO: *All About Appliqué, pages 169–206.*

Special Piecing Challenges

In some patchwork-block designs, a piece must be set into a corner. This is known as an inset seam. Stitching inset seams can be challenging. When many patchwork pieces meet at a central point, the piecing can be especially tricky.

- -

Q How do I set a patch into a corner without puckers?

A Several traditional block designs, including Baby's Blocks and the LeMoyne Star have inset corners, which are easy to hand-piece, but provide a manageable challenge when machine-pieced. For perfect, pucker-free insets, you must pin and sew the seam in two steps to ensure a perfect point or corner at the inset. This method ensures accuracy because you can see where to sew at the inset corner.

1. Adjust the machine for 15 stitches per inch. Staystitch along the seamline for 1" on each side of the patch with the inner angle. Clip to but not past the stitching with a small double-pointed scissors. Mark the seam intersection on the corner of the triangle patch to be inset.

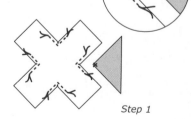

Step 1

2. With the inset patch facing down on the staystitched patch, pierce the marked seam intersection with a pin, and then pierce the inner angle at the pivot point. Secure the pin in both layers. Pin the patch to the right-hand "leg" of the inner angle.

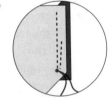

Step 2

3. Flip the pinned piece so you can see the staystitching on the inner angle. Stitch from the outer edge of the pinned patches to the pivot point. Leave the needle in the fabric, raise the presser foot,

stitch

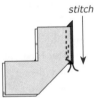

Step 3

and pivot the patches. Match the raw edges of the two patches, pin as needed, and complete the stitching.

4. Press along the stitching on both legs to set the stitches, and then press the seam allowances away from the inset patch. Add corner patches if required to complete block design.

Step 4
Crisscross block

166

Q How do I sew multiple patches together that meet at the center of a block such as the LeMoyne Star block?

A Accurate marking and stitching are essential to making a perfect match.

1. Carefully mark the upper seam intersections on the wrong side of each diamond piece. With right sides facing, sew the pieces together in pairs, beginning at the marked seam intersection, not at the cut edge.

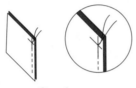

Step 1

2. For machine piecing (*see page 122*), press the seam allowances toward the darker piece in each pair. For hand piecing (*see page 118*), press later. Trim the points that extend past the patch edges.

Step 2

3. Sew the pairs together to create two half-star units. With right sides facing, match the points at the center and pin carefully. Pin the remainder of the seam and machine stitch; press the seam in one direction. For hand-pieced blocks,

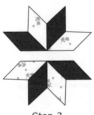

Step 3

join the block halves, then press all seam allowances in one direction, fanning out the seam allowances at the center.

4. To complete the block, add inset squares and triangles following the directions in the previous question.

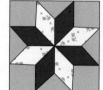

Step 4
LeMoyne Star

CHAPTER 7

All About Appliqué

Appliquéd quilts feature decorative shapes applied to the fabric surface of the quilt blocks, borders, or a whole-cloth background. With appliqué, you can create simple to extremely complex designs with detailed shapes that may have curves and sharp points in addition to straight edges. The shapes are cut from fabrics and prepared for the chosen appliqué method, then positioned and attached to the background fabric using one of several hand- or machine-appliqué methods. Choose the method that is most appropriate for your skill level, time demands, and the desired results.

Appliqué Fabrics

Choosing the fabrics for appliqué designs and backgrounds is an important first step to making a successful appliqué quilt or adding appliquéd accents to patchwork designs.

- -

Q What fabrics are best for appliqué?

A As with patchwork, most appliqué is done using quilter's cottons, but other fabrics may be used, particularly for desired color and textural effects, as long as they are compatible with the planned cleaning method for the finished project. In general, light- to medium-weight, smooth-surfaced cottons are the easiest to handle — just be sure to preshrink them first (*see page 39*).

For art quilts that won't be subject to heavy use, just about anything goes — even lamé fabrics can be appliquéd if treated to a stabilizing backing of lightweight fusible interfacing first. Nothing is off limits: you can use paper, Tyvek, or anything else you can stitch through for appliqués.

- -

Q Are there any special considerations for the background fabric in a traditional appliquéd quilt?

A Choose a fabric in a color that will act as a backdrop for the appliqué fabrics you've chosen. Solid colors, tone-on-tone prints, and subtle prints, stripes, and small checks are all possibilities. Avoid bold prints and bright colors that will make it difficult to discern the appliqué shapes against the background. To "audition" a background for your quilt, group the chosen fabrics against the background fabric choice(s). Stand back and squint at the selections to make sure the background choice doesn't overwhelm the other fabrics. If the background jumps out at it you, it is too dark, busy, or bold for the appliqué fabrics.

- -

Q Should I use solid or print fabrics for the appliqués?

A It all depends on the appliqué pattern and the desired visual effect. Folk-art appliqué is often done with solids or tone-on-tone prints (*see page 47*). Masterful appliqué often takes advantage of printed textures to add a realistic touch. For example, tone-on-tone prints and those with a hand-dyed look usually have dark and light areas in the same color family — it's easy to cut realistically shaded flower petals and leaves from them.

Cutting the appliqué shapes from different areas of a print can yield more realistic-looking leaves than those cut from a green solid. In some cases, you might be able to cut out an actual leaf motif. Wood-grain prints are perfect for buildings and tree trunks; basket-weave prints are a wonderful choice for baskets. And don't overlook colorful, large-scale prints for appliqués. When appliqué shapes are carefully positioned and fussy-cut from these fabrics, the results can be amazing.

Q What is the best way to fussy-cut appliqués?

A To test areas of a print you wish to use for appliqués, make an auditioning template by tracing the finished shape on an index card and cutting it out. Move the "window" over the fabric until you find the section you want to cut. Then mark along the cut edge, remove the template, and cut out the shape, adding the 3⁄16" turn-under allowance all around, unless you plan to do raw edge appliqué. Flip the template over for mirror-image shapes if your design requires them.

SEE ALSO: *Machine Piecing, pages 122–23.*

Q Can I use the wrong side of my fabric for the background or the appliqués?

A I think of it as the "other side" rather than the "wrong side," whether I'm making an appliquéd or patchwork quilt. Often the wrong side is a slightly different shade than the colors printed on the right side, or the print shows through to the back but is more muted. This offers more options for coordinating the appliqué pieces, instantly doubling the choices in your fabric and scrap stash.

Q In my appliqué design, the darker color shadows through. Is there any way to eliminate this?

A You can back the light-colored shapes with lightweight fusible interfacing to prevent or at least minimize shadow-through. The interfacing will change the character of the fabric and may make edge-turning more difficult. The other option is to cut away the section of dark shape that lies under the lighter one, after the appliqué is finished.

SEE ALSO: *Turned-Edge Appliqué Methods, pages 183–93.*

Q How can I test some of the fabrics in my first appliqué project before I sew?

A If you are not sure of your fabric choices or just want to confirm them before cutting and sewing them to the background squares for your quilt, make a mock-up by tracing the full-size appliqué design onto a sheet of transparent paper or clear acetate. Cut the finished appliqué shapes from the planned fabrics and attach each in position on the tracing with a small loop of removable tape or a small piece of sticky Steam-a-Seam 2 repositionable fusible web (without fusing it). Evaluate the composition and remove and replace colors that are not pleasing. When you're happy with the results, use the final mock-up as your guide while cutting the pieces and completing your blocks.

TOOLS FOR APPLIQUÉ

In addition to the basic quiltmaking tools discussed in chapter 4, you will need some additional special tools, depending on the appliqué method you are using:

▶ **Template plastic.** For some appliqué methods, you will need to make a plastic shape for each design element in the appliqué design. Heat-resistant template plastic is nice to have when preparing shapes for hand or machine appliqué because you can turn and press the edges around the template with ease. (Templar is one brand.)

▶ **Hand-sewing needles.** For hand appliqué, use the shortest, finest Sharp or Between sewing needle that you are most comfortable using. This may require a bit of experimentation. Some quilters prefer long, fine milliner's needles for needle-turn appliqué (*see page 196*).

▶ **Needle threader.** Avoid the frustration that comes with trying to thread fine needles with tiny eyes; keep a supply of good-quality needle threaders in your hand-sewing kit.

▶ **Brass sequin pins or glass-head appliqué pins.** Use to hold appliqués in place. These short pins are less likely to get caught in your thread while you hand-sew than the longer quilter's pins.

▶ **Cotton or cotton-polyester hand-sewing thread.** Use your favorite thread for hand or machine sewing (do not use quilting thread). Unless you want the stitching to show on purpose, the thread color should match the color of the appliqué — not the background fabric color. Cotton thread is very pliable and soft, and a good choice if available in the right color. Otherwise, all-purpose cotton/poly thread works well. Some quilters prefer to use silk thread in neutral colors because it is strong and the stitches are less visible.

- ▶ **Bobbin thread.** Use this thread in your machine's bobbin when satin stitching over appliqué raw edges to prevent heavy thread build-up on the underside of the work. Most bobbin thread comes in black or white, but some is available in colors. Finer and lighter-weight than all-purpose sewing thread, bobbin thread helps draw embroidery stitches, such as satin stitching, into the fabric layers or to the underside of the work so the thread doesn't show on the surface. It's best to use a bobbin thread of the same or similar fiber content as the top thread.

- ▶ **Monfilament thread.** Available in clear and smoke colors, this fine, wiry thread is available in nylon or polyester. The thread "disappears" into fabric and is essential for invisible appliqué (*see* Blindstitch *page 201*). Use it in the needle for this purpose.

- ▶ **Celtic bars.** Use to prepare narrow strips for appliquéd vines and other narrow appliqué shapes (*see page 197*).

- ▶ **Freezer paper.** You'll need this white paper (found in the grocery store) with a shiny plastic coating on one side for the freezer-paper appliqué preparation methods (*see page 190*).

- ▶ **Liquid starch.** Starch limp fabrics to make it easier to turn and stitch appliqué edges. Also use it like glue for the starch-and-press method (*see page 189*).

- ▶ **Water-soluble glue stick.** You can use this for preparing appliqués and for holding them in position on the background fabric.

- ▶ **Silver or yellow artist pencil.** Use to mark appliqué shapes on the fabric. Choose the color that shows best on the fabric and make sure it's sharp. A mechanical lead pencil may also work.

▶ **Small, sharp, double-pointed embroidery scissors**. Use to cut appliqué shapes and to clip and snip as needed for smoothly turned edges.

▶ **Duckbill appliqué scissors**. These special scissors have a paddle-shaped blade designed to protect and fan away the bottom layer of fabric, allowing for precise, con-trolled cutting close to the stitching required in some forms of machine-appliqué work.

Duckbill appliqué scissor

▶ **Open-toe presser foot**. Use for machine appliqué. The open toe makes it easy to see the appliqué edge as you stitch. The shape of the groove on its underside also rides smoothly over any decorative stitches you might use when attaching appliqués.

▶ **Nonstick pressing/appliqué sheet**. Cover fusible appliqués with this transparent sheet to prevent the fusible adhesive from transferring to your iron. Double-sided and reusable, the sheet has a coating that repels the fusible glue.

▶ **Temporary spray adhesive**. Use to hold appliqués in place for machine stitching.

▶ **Paper scissors**. Use to cut out appliqué templates from plastic, card-board, or freezer paper as directed for the selected appliqué method.

▶ **Wooden bamboo skewer or orange stick**. You may need one of these or something similar with a blunt tip to help coax edges into place as you turn and stitch the appliqué edges.

Fusible Appliqué

The traditional hand-appliqué method is called needle-turn appliqué, which is appropriate for intricate appliqué shapes. However, there are many faster and easier methods.

Fusible appliqué, is the speediest and easiest option for beginners. It requires minimal preparation and optional (but recommended) machine stitching. Fusible web — a sheet of fine intermeshed heat-sensitive fibers — makes it possible to attach appliqués to background fabric with your iron and then add machine stitching for durability as well as embellishment.

- -

Q How does fusible web work?

A Most fusible web is attached to a transfer paper to protect your iron. When heat is applied with or without steam (as the package directions dictate), the web melts, making it possible to "glue" one fabric to another. For fusible appliqué, each fabric shape has a layer of fusible web on the back. This allows you to position the shape on the background fabric and press it to fuse in place — it's that easy. To ensure permanence, the edges are usually stitched down with your choice of satin stitching, blanket stitches, zigzagging, or blindstitches (*see page 198*). All of these stitches can be done by machine. Blanket stitching by hand is also popular for those who love handwork.

Q How do I do fusible appliqué?

A Choose a fusible web of the desired type and weight (*see page 181*). Then follow the steps below.

1. Place a sheet of fusible web over the full-size appliqué pattern with the protective paper facing you. Trace the appliqué shape onto the paper side. When tracing multiple shapes, leave at least ½" of space between shapes for cutting purposes. Rough-cut each shape with at least a ¼" allowance beyond the traced lines. *Note:* Since the fusible is on the underside of the transfer paper and will be attached to the fabric's wrong side, what you trace is the reverse of what will show when the appliqué is sewn in place. Check the pattern labels: Appliqué patterns designed for fusible appliqué are usually printed in reverse. Some patterns will direct you to cut one and one reversed ("cut 1 and 1r") when mirror-image shapes are required.

2. Position the fusible web side of the cutout on the wrong side of the appropriate fabric. Following the manufacturer's directions, use the iron to attach the cutout to the fabric. Let cool. Cut out the shape on the drawn lines and carefully peel away the paper.

3. Position the appliqué on the quilt or quilt block following the placement guide and fuse in place with your iron. Stitch around the raw edges using your choice of machine stitches (*see page 198*).

fusible web shape

cut out appliqué shape on drawn line

LIGHTEN UP

Generally lightweight before they are used, fusibles get firmer and stiffer afterwards. If you are fusing large pieces, you can eliminate some of this bulk by trimming out the center of the fusible web shape — called "windowing" — before applying it to the appliqué fabric. This is an especially good idea if you plan to hand-quilt inside the appliqué piece.

fusible web

window exposes fabric in center

Q How do I make sure the appliqués are correctly positioned on the quilt blocks and borders?

A First, mark the center lines on each block (or through the border) with a removable marker of your choice. Depending on the design complexity, you may also need diagonal centering lines. Here's what you do:

1. Make a copy of the appliqué design on tracing paper cut to the same size as the background block for a master pattern. Draw centering lines on the master — some patterns may include them.
2. Position the background square right side up over the master pattern and align the centers. Lightly trace the appliqué design onto the fabric with a sharp pencil.

Position the appliqués and use a few sequin or appliqué pins to hold them in place until you are ready to attach them. For appliqués that will be stitched in place (without fusing), you can hand-baste, pin-baste, or glue-baste (with a dab of glue stick) them to the background. Temporary spray adhesive is another option for holding appliqués in place.

If you prefer not to draw the pattern on your fabric, trace the master pattern onto a sheet of acetate or clear template plastic. Place the acetate master on top of the fabric block and then carefully slip the appliqués under the acetate; adjust the placement to follow the lines, and pin in place with appliqué or sequin pins. Some quilters like to machine-baste appliqués in place after positioning them with perpendicular lines of stitching through the center of each appliqué.

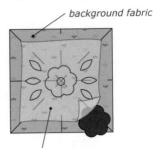

background fabric

acetate pattern overlay

Q Which fusible web is best for appliqué?

A Each has its distinct merits; testing is the only way to find out how they work and which you like best. The finer the web, the softer the results. Most webs (but not all) are attached to a release paper that protects your iron from the gummy web after it is hot.

One brand, Steam-A-Seam 2 from The Warm Company, is available in two weights and has release paper on both sides; the web is tacky on both sides (like sticky notes), allowing you to reposition an appliqué before fusing. It is essential to follow the directions carefully to take advantage of this feature, being sure to trace appliqués on the paper side that is more securely adhered to the web; the other sheet is very easy to remove.

Fusible web is available by the yard, in smaller sheets, and in rolls of narrow tape, depending on the manufacturer.

Q Will Steam-A-Seam 2 gum up my sewing machine?

A On occasion, I notice a small ball of adhesive on the sewing-machine needle when I'm sewing through fusible appliqués prepared with this product. A quick swipe with a cotton ball soaked with a little alcohol is all it takes to clean the needle and continue with the stitching, a small price to pay for the advantages this web offers.

Q How do I make sure I don't get fusible web on the iron?

A Always use a special nonstick pressing sheet (*see* Tools for Appliqué *on page 176*) between the soleplate and the fusible. Parchment paper, from the grocery store, is a good substitute. Some quilters place a sheet of it on the ironing board to keep the board free of fusible scraps and starch overspray (which can also build up on the iron and cause unwanted discoloration). A piece of lightweight muslin will work as a press cloth, too, but it can pick up stray scraps of the fusible web that might transfer to other fabrics. To prevent this, use a permanent marker to write an "R" in one corner of the cloth to designate right side. Make sure that you can read the "R" when you place the press cloth over the fusible shapes. This keeps any escaping fusible on only one side of the press cloth so you won't transfer it to your iron accidentally.

If you do get a brown buildup of fusible web on your iron soleplate, use hot-iron cleaner to remove it. Open the window for ventilation and locate the iron away from a smoke alarm. Squeeze a liberal amount of iron cleaner onto a heavy cotton cloth such as an old terry towel. While the soleplate is hot, rub the cleaner on it in a circular motion. For heavy buildup, it may take several applications to remove all the residue. To make sure the product is thoroughly removed — it's oily — rev up the steaming action, place several layers of paper towel on the ironing board, and press. Depress the steam button several times to force out any residue. Repeat until there is no residue or discoloration on the paper towel.

Q How do I store fusible web yardage to keep it from acquiring wrinkles and creases?

A Roll it around a long cardboard tube — save an empty freezer-paper tube for this purpose. Keep the empty freezer-paper box, too, and store the rolled web inside. If you have an appliqué pressing sheet, roll it into a tight roll and tuck it inside the tube to keep it wrinkle-free and readily available.

Turned-Edge Appliqué Methods

If fusible, raw-edge appliqué is not your preference, choose from several options to prepare appliqués with turned edges for hand or machine stitching.

- -

Q How do I transfer the appliqué shapes from my pattern to the appliqué fabrics?

A For most appliqué methods, you will need to make a template for each shape (to preserve the pattern or book for future use). Traditionally, appliqué patterns do not include turn-under allowances. For turned-edge appliqués, you will add turn-under allowances on all edges when you cut out the fabric shapes. A dashed or dotted line indicates an allowance that will be covered by another shape and should not be turned under.

Place template plastic over the design shapes and use a fine-point permanent marker to trace each one. Write the pattern name on the template and any number that appears on the piece, or the order of application when the overall design has overlapping shapes. If one shape repeats over and over, you need only one plastic template for that shape.

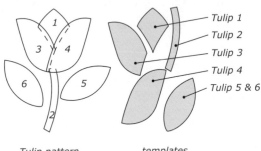

Tulip 1
Tulip 2
Tulip 3
Tulip 4
Tulip 5 & 6

Tulip pattern   *templates*

To cut the appliqué shapes for needle-turn applique by hand or turned-edge applique by hand or machine: Place the template on the *fabric right side* and use a fine-lead mechanical or colored artist pencil to trace the design onto the fabric. If tracing multiple shapes on the same fabric, leave at least ½" of space between tracings. Cut out each shape about ³⁄₁₆" from the pencil line to add the turn-under allowance to all edges.

Q Does the grainline matter when I place the appliqué templates on the fabric?

A Grainline isn't as important for appliqués as for patchwork pieces. Most can be cut following the same grain as the background square. However, bias edges are easier to turn on curves — often eliminating the need to clip curves for a smooth turn. Clipped inside corners that were cut on the bias are easier to turn without the problem of raveling (*see page 195*).

- -

Q How do I turn the edges on my appliqué shapes to prepare them for hand or machine sewing?

A Thread a needle with light-colored thread and hold the appliqué with the right side up so you can see the pencil line. Turn under the allowance along the line and hand-baste close to the folded edge. The pencil line should not be visible when the edge is turned. Do not turn under edges that will be covered by other shapes. You will remove the basting after the appliqués have been sewn in place on the background fabric. The illustration shows how to prepare piece 1 for the the tulip on page 184.

Note: You can use the freezer-paper method (*see page 190*) to prepare the shapes without the necessity of tracing templates onto the fabric.

appliqué with turn-under allowance

will be covered by shapes 3 and 4

Q How do I neatly turn under the edges at corners, curves, and points?

A To turn edges at inside corners and points, use sharp scissors to clip the fabric to the pencil line. Ease fabric fullness around curves. At points and corners, make a mitered fold after trimming some of the point away. On inside curves, you may need to do a little clipping, too.

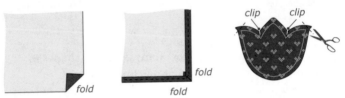

mitered corners
or points

clip inside curves and
trim sharp points

Q Some of my appliqués have very full curves and turning the edge is not easy. Any tips?

A With really full curves, there is more fabric beyond the finished shape that must fit underneath the appliqué. Keeping a smooth edge can be challenging. Hand-baste around the curved edge only, about ⅛" from the edge of the shape and draw up the basting to make the curve cup neatly to the wrong side; press and then baste.

Q How do you make faced appliqués?

A For really sharp points, where the fabric gets bulky, making faced appliqués is an excellent solution.

1. Trace the appliqué shapes onto a lightweight nonwoven interfacing (or sheer, lightweight cotton or bridal tulle). Place the interfacing, drawing side up, on the right side of the fabric and stitch on the traced lines.

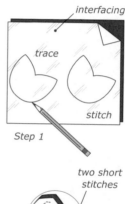

interfacing

trace

stitch

Step 1

2. At very sharp points, shorten the stitch length and take two tiny stitches across the point rather than pivoting at a sharp point. This makes a little more room for the fabric that must lie inside the point. Clip across the corners and points a scant ⅛" from the stitches to remove bulk.

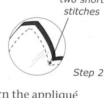

two short stitches

Step 2

3. Make a slit in the center of the facing. Turn the appliqué right side out through the slit and carefully push out the points and corners using a wooden bamboo skewer. Press so the interfacing or tulle doesn't show along the appliqué edges. You may leave the interfacing attached after pressing or you may trim out the center of it to eliminate bulk.

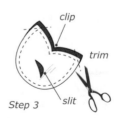

clip

trim

Step 3   *slit*

187

WASH IT AWAY

For faced appliqués, try this technique — but only if you have preshrunk your fabrics. Instead of interfacing, use water-soluble stabilizer for the facing. After sewing the stabilizer facing to the shape and slitting the stabilizer, turn the appliqué right side out and finger-press the edges or use a dry iron on the fabric side only — not on the stabilizer. After the shapes are stitched in place, wash the block in warm water to dissolve and remove the stabilizer.

Q How do I make perfect turned-edge circles for appliqué?

A Trace the finished size of the circle on heavyweight paper and cut out carefully. Trace around the circle on the fabric wrong side and cut out ³⁄₁₆" from the marked line. Hand-baste ¹⁄₈" from the outer edge of the fabric circle, leaving the thread attached when you reach the knot where you started. Center the circle template on the fabric and draw up the basting so the fabric cups around the circle. Adjust the gathers to make a smooth edge all around. Press before tying a knot in the thread tail. Carefully remove the paper circle to use again.

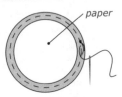

paper

Q Is there a way to prepare turned-edge appliqués without basting?

A Some quilters like the starch-and-press method; others prefer the freezer-paper method (*see page 190*), which is my favorite. Here's how to starch and press appliqués:

1. Trace and cut a pressing template for each finished-size appliqué shape from a manila folder or from a heat-resistant template plastic such as Templar. You will need to cut a pressing template for each different shape in the appliqué design. You won't need one for each of the repetitive shapes. Mark the *right side* of each asymmetrical template.

2. Place the template right side down on the appliqué fabric, trace around it, and then cut out ³⁄₁₆" from the drawn line. Dilute a small amount of liquid starch with half as much water, for example ¼ cup starch with ⅛ cup water. Protect the ironing board with an old towel covered with muslin or with a sheet of parchment paper.

3. Place each template face down on the appliqué and use a fine paintbrush to paint the turn-under allowance with the starch solution. Use the side of a dry iron or the point of a small craft iron to turn the starched edge onto the template all around and press. Allow to cool. Remove the template to use for other identical shapes and re-press the fabric shape if necessary.

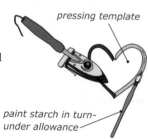

pressing template

paint starch in turn-under allowance

Q What is freezer-paper appliqué?

A This is an easy way to cut and prepare accurate, turned-edge appliqués. The freezer paper gives a slight edge against which to turn the fabric, making the shapes smoother, more accurate, and easier to handle. Purchase freezer paper at the grocery store.

1. Make plastic templates for each appliqué shape (*see page 184*). Trace around the templates on the *unwaxed* side of the freezer paper, leaving a bit of space between shapes. You will need a freezer-paper shape for each piece in the appliqué design, even the ones that repeat.

2. Place the freezer-paper template shiny side down on the fabric wrong side and press with a dry iron. This softens the waxed side so it will stick to the fabric. Cut out the appliqué shape ³⁄₁₆" from the paper edges. Clip any inner points to, but not past, the paper edge.

3. Turn the turn-under allowance over the paper, snug against the edge, and hand-baste close to the fold through the fabric and the paper. Finally, press the prepared appliqué before positioning it on the background fabric.

clip

uncoated side
of freezer-paper
template

freezer
paper

Q But won't the paper be trapped inside?

A Yes, but you can remove it in one of two ways.

▶ **For large shapes that you are hand-appliquéing,** leave a short section of the appliqué unstitched if there isn't an open edge where another appliqué shape will overlap it. Remove the basting stitches around the appliqué edge of the unstitched area and use needle-nose tweezers to reach through the opening and gently tug the paper to pull it out. Turn under the opening edge and press before completing the appliqué stitching.

▶ **For more complex shapes and for machine appliqué,** stitch all appliqués in place and remove the basting. On the reverse side, make a small slit in the background fabric under each appliqué and remove the paper through the opening. The slit will be covered by batting and backing in the finished quilt. To reduce bulk, some quiltmakers prefer to trim away the background behind each shape, leaving a 3/16" allowance inside the stitches, making it even easier to remove the paper.

- -

Q How do I detach freezer paper that has been ironed onto the back of the appliqués?

A To make it easy to lift freezer-paper templates out, make a hole in the center of each one with a ⅛"-diameter hole punch *before* adhering it to the fabric. Work the end of a toothpick under the edge and ease it around to release the paper. Take care not to stretch the fabric or poke a hole through it. If you attach the appliqués with invisible machine appliqué (*see page 201*), tug gently to detach the paper from the stitches.

Q **Can I stack layers of freezer paper and cut multiple shapes all at once? I need them for a large quilt.**

A Yes, but it's best to cut no more than four layers at once. The thicker the stack, the more inconsistent and imperfect the cuts will be. To keep the layers from slipping, trace one shape on the uncoated side of the freezer paper. Then place it on top of three more pieces of paper and staple the layers together *outside* the drawn line. Use sharp craft scissors with double points to carefully cut the shape from all four layers at once.

Q **Can I reuse freezer-paper templates when a pattern requires multiples of the same shape?**

A If you are using a freezer-paper template as a guide for needle-turn appliqué (*see page 196*), you can simply lift it from the appliquéd shape, reposition it on the next shape, press, and sew in place. Eventually, the "sticky" will wear out and you'll need a new template. If you've basted a freezer-paper template inside an appliqué and then stitched it in place by machine, you won't be able to reuse it. But, freezer paper is relatively cheap and I like to make a template for each appliqué piece so that I can prepare them all at once.

Q I really don't like to baste. Is there some other way to prepare appliqué shapes with freezer paper?

A Yes, there are two variations that eliminate the basting: the glue-stick method and the pressing method.

Glue-stick method. Trace one shape for each appliqué piece onto the uncoated side of the freezer paper, reversing the template for asymmetrical shapes. Cut out each one on the drawn line. Press each shape to the wrong side of the appliqué fabric and cut out with the turn-under allowance as shown on page 190. Apply a light coat of glue stick to the outer edges of the freezer paper and use your fingers to turn the allowance onto the paper and finger-press in place. Make sure the edges are smooth; lift and reglue if necessary. Use glue sparingly to make it easier to remove the paper shapes after the appliqués have been attached to the background fabric.

Pressing method. Cut a template for each appliqué shape and trace around each one on the *uncoated* side of the freezer paper. It is not necessary to reverse asymmetrical shapes for this method. Cut out each shape without allowances and place each one on the wrong side of the appropriate fabric with the *shiny, waxed side facing you.* Pin in the center and cut out the shape with the ³⁄₁₆" turn-under allowance. Use the point of the iron to turn and press the edges onto the freezer paper, where they will stick in place. It's best to use a small craft iron for this method and take care not to touch the waxed side of the paper with the iron.

Appliqué Stitching Options

There are a number of ways to sew prepared appliqués in place on the background blocks and borders. You can use either hand or machine methods, whichever you prefer.

- -

Q I've prepared my appliqués. How do I hand-sew them in place?

A Position and pin or baste the shapes in place on the background first (*see page 179*). To hand-sew them in place, use the traditional appliqué stitch — similar to a blind-stitch or slipstitch. For the purposes of illustration, the appliqué stitches show along the appliqué edge. In reality, they should be all but invisible.

1. Thread the needle with a single strand of all-purpose sewing thread that closely matches the appliqué color, not the background color. Make a knot in one end of the thread.

2. Bring the thread up from the wrong side of the background next to the appliqué, just catching the appliqué's folded edge. Working from right to left (reverse if left-handed), reinsert the needle in the background fabric right beside the fold where it entered the appliqué and then take a short stitch — about ¹⁄₁₆" long — in the background before catching only a few threads of

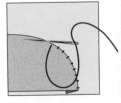

appliqué stitch

the folded edge of the appliqué with the needle. As you take each stitch, tug gently to keep the stitch snug, but without creating puckers in the fabric. Stitches should be all but invisible along the edge of the appliqué.

3. End by taking the needle and thread to the underside and finish with a few stitches in the background fabric.

- -

Q How do I prevent raveling at inside curves and points that need to be clipped in order to turn the edges?

A Minimize raveling by positioning the appliqué shape on the fabric with the inside point on the bias as shown. If you do have stray threads at the clip, take a slightly deeper stitch at the very inside point, or take several stitches very close together. You can also use a straight pin to add a drop of seam sealant such as Dritz Fray Check at these points to further strengthen them. Test first to make sure it dries clear on your fabrics. A tiny dab of glue stick on the point of the needle can help control the threads, and help tuck them under before stitching.

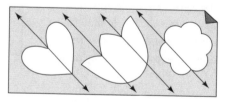

inside corners on bias fabric grain

Q So how do I do traditional needle-turn appliqué?

A For best results, develop your skill with simple appliqué shapes before trying this with more complex shapes. It takes a little practice to perfect your technique because you turn or "sweep" the allowance under with the point of the needle as you stitch, not before you position the appliqués on the background as with other turned-edge methods.

1. Prepare the appliqué shapes by tracing around the templates *on the fabric right side* and cut out each one with a ³⁄₁₆" allowance all around.

2. Position the appliqué on the background and use the tip of the needle to turn under the fabric edge just ahead of where you will take the next stitch.

traditional needle-turn

Note: If you prefer, you can use a freezer-paper template for needle-turn appliqué, eliminating the pencil line on the fabric. Cut and iron a finished-size freezer-paper shape to the right side of the appliqué fabric and then cut out the fabric shape with the ³⁄₁₆" turn-under allowance. Use the edge of the freezer paper as the turning guide.

needle-turn with template

Q My appliqué pattern has very skinny strips for vines and stems. Is there an easy way to make them?

A You need Celtic (bias) bars. These narrow bars, made of metal or heat-resistant plastic, come in widths from ⅛" to ½", and make quick and easy work of preparing vines and other narrow shapes. The results are finished strips of a consistent width. Here's how to use them:

1. Choose the bar of the desired finished width.

2. Cut bias strips twice the finished width plus ½" for seam allowances. Fold the strips in half lengthwise *with wrong sides facing* and stitch ¼" from the raw edges.

3. Insert the bar into the resulting tube and center the seam allowance on one side of the bar. Use the tip of the iron to press the seam open or to one side. Trim the seam allowance to ⅛" or slightly narrower. Press from the opposite side of the tube and then remove the bar. For long strips, just continue slipping the bar through the tube until it's all pressed, then remove it.

4. Position the tube on your block or quilt with the seam against the background fabric and baste in place through the center. Use the tip of your steam iron to apply steam as you shape the piece to follow inner curves. The steam will help shrink the piece to fit the curve. Appliqué both edges in place. When applying a stem shape in a circle, stitch along the inside curve first, then the outside. It's best to sew stems in place by hand, but you can also try invisible machine appliqué (*see page 201*).

Celtic bar

Machine-Stitching Basics

Q I would prefer to appliqué by machine. How do I do it?

A First, decide which stitch you want to use along the appliqué edge and follow the directions for that method. For all machine appliqué, attach the open-toe presser foot and apply a tear-away stabilizer to the wrong side of the background fabric pieces to prevent puckering. If tear-away stabilizer is not at hand, substitute lightweight typing or parchment paper and pin it to the wrong side of the background fabric under the appliqué area before you begin to stitch.

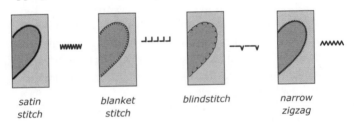

| *satin stitch* | *blanket stitch* | *blindstitch* | *narrow zigzag* |

Satin Stitch

If you want to emphasize the appliqué edges with a heavy line of stitches, choose this method. The stitch lends a satin-like sheen to the appliqué edges, hence the name. It is the most durable method for attaching raw-edge appliqués because the dense row of stitches covers the edges completely to prevent raveling. For best results, use the fusible appliqué method (*see page 178*) to prepare and attach appliqués to the quilt block or borders first. This adds durability and holds the edges firmly in place for stitching. This stitch is appropriate for simple shapes but is not recommended for complex or tiny appliqué shapes.

1. Position and fuse raw-edge appliqués in place on the right side of the background fabric that has been backed with stabilizer.

2. Thread the needle with cotton or rayon embroidery thread and use bobbin thread in the bobbin (*see page 175*). Use a densely spaced zigzag stitch (the stitch length should be not quite 0) of the desired width. The stitch should create a solid, smooth line of stitches (without visible lumps, zigs, or zags). Test on a sample appliqué first. When you look at the back of the satin stitching, the top thread color should appear as dots or a narrow row of color on each side of the bobbin-thread stitches. If you can't see a bit of the top thread color on the underside, loosen the top tension just a bit to force the tighter bobbin thread to pull the top thread to the underside.

3. Move the needle position to the right so that the inner edge of the right toe of the open-toe presser foot will ride close to the appliqué edge. As you stitch, the left swing of the needle should stitch into the appliqué and the right swing of the needle should land in the background fabric close to the appliqué edge. (*See* Tips for Super Satin Stitching *on pages 202–3.*)

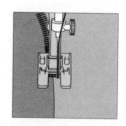

satin stitch open-toe presser-foot placement

4. Gently remove the stabilizer from the background fabric, taking care not to break the stitches. Use tweezers to lift stubborn bits of stabilizer away from the stitching.

Blanket Stitch

These stitches are more obvious individual stitches and can be done with matching or contrasting thread. The blanket stitch bites into the appliqué and then is followed by a straight stitch that lies along the appliqué edge in the background fabric. (*See illustration on page 198.*) This stitch lends a more casual, folk-art look to the finished appliqués. Blanket stitching may be done over appliqués with turned or raw edges.

1. Prepare the appliqués for raw-edge fusing (*see page 178*) or turned-edge appliqué (*see page 183–85*). Fuse or baste the appliqué in place on the background piece that has been backed with stabilizer.

2. Select the blanket stitch on your machine and adjust the length and width of the stitch for the desired visual result. Narrower stitches (1.5mm) are best for fused appliqué and for complex shapes with lots of curves, corners, or points. Use a wider stitch on large appliqués. Thread the needle with 30-weight cotton or rayon embroidery thread for more obvious stitches, or use all-purpose thread to match or contrast with the appliqué. Use thread to match the background in the bobbin.

3. Stitch appliqués in place and pull the threads to the wrong side to tie off securely. Remove stabilizer carefully.

Blindstitch

This is also called *invisible machine appliqué*. Choose this stitch if you don't want the stitches to show. (*See illustration on page 198.*) Use monofilament nylon or polyester thread so the stitches all but disappear into the appliqué edge. This stitching method can be used on raw-edge or turned-edge appliqués.

1. Prepare turned-edge or fusible raw-edge appliqués and attach to a background backed with stabilizer.

2. Thread the needle with monofilament thread. Choose clear for most colors, smoke for dark colors. Use thread to match the background color on the bobbin.

3. Set the machine for the blindstitch. Adjust the stitch width so that the zigzag part of the stitch just barely "bites" the appliqué edge and the straight stitches lie right along the appliqué edge in the background fabric. There should be no more than ⅛" between the zigzag stitches. Prepare an extra appliqué and test the stitch on a scrap to practice. If you can see the bobbin thread on the surface, loosen the top-thread tension a bit.

4. Stitch each shape in place and pull the threads to the back to tie off securely. Remove the stabilizer carefully.

5. Press the completed appliqué, using a warm iron to avoid melting the monofilament thread.

Note: In place of the blindstitch, you can use a narrow, open zigzag (1 to 1.5mm long; 1mm wide) with monofilament thread. With this method the stitch bites the appliqué on the left swing of the needle and the background on the right swing.

TIPS FOR SUPER SATIN STITCHING

Smooth satin stitching takes testing and practice in order to establish the correct stitch length and width and to learn how to maneuver around corners, points, and curves. The illustrations that follow show you how to manipulate appliqué shapes at the machine when doing the satin stitch. However, the illustrations show a more open zigzag stitch than you will be using to make it easier to see the stitches. True satin stitching has stitches that are very close to each other.

The dots in the illustrations below indicate points where you should stop with the needle down, then lift the presser foot, and adjust the work for the next stitch to maintain a smooth line of satin stitches without stitch build-up.

1. When stitching around curves, stop and pivot the needle where curves are tightest and stitches tend to be closest together.

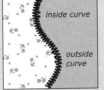

2. When satin-stitching an outside corner, stitch along the edge until you reach the corner (side 1). Stop with the needle down in the background fabric, then pivot the fabric 90 degrees, and begin stitching again. Your first several stitches (along side 2) will overlap the last few stitches of side 1.

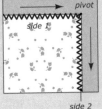

3. When satin-stitching around an inside corner, keep stitching just past the corner, bringing your needle to a stop when it is down in the appliqué fabric (side 1). When you pivot your fabric, your needle will be positioned to just catch the background fabric, and your first stitches along side 2 will overlap the last stitches of the side 1.

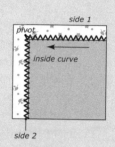

side 1

pivot

inside curve

side 2

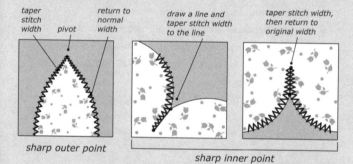

taper stitch width

pivot

return to normal width

sharp outer point

draw a line and taper stitch width to the line

taper stitch width, then return to original width

sharp inner point

These same techniques work with other machine stitches, such as the machine blindstitch and blanket stitching, but may take some practice and fine-tuning around points, corners, and curves.

TIPS FOR SUCCESSFUL MACHINE APPLIQUÉ

▶ Draw the bobbin thread to the surface before you start to stitch and take a few stitches in place — dial your machine down to 0 stitch length — then stitch over the anchoring stitches to hide them.

▶ If possible, adjust the machine to always stop with the needle down. This will make it easier and faster. Perfect stitching on machine appliqués relies on lots of stops and starts to reposition the work.

▶ Keep the appliqué stitches perpendicular to the appliqué edges. This means that you will stop often with the needle down to adjust the work so the edge of the appliqué is parallel to the presser-foot edge.

▶ Stop often to adjust the fabric when stitching curves; the tighter the curve, the more pivots are required. Pivot from the longest edge of the stitching to the tightest part of the curve.

Solving Problems

Q What if I can't find an exact thread-color match for the appliqué?

A Always select the closest color that is slightly darker than the appliqué fabric. With a multicolor print fabric, use a neutral color that blends well with the colors in the print.

Q When I hand-sew, my thread always gets tangled. How can I prevent this?

A Because of the way fibers are twisted and then wound on the spool, it is essential to knot the correct end to avoid sewing problems. When removing thread from a spool, cut off the length you need (18" or less is recommended for most handwork) and knot the end you just cut (*see page 294*.) However, if you are cutting thread from a bobbin, knot the end you pull from the bobbin.

Note: If you are cutting thread from the spool on your machine, unthread the machine before cutting the length you need. Drawing it through the threading mechanisms and tension discs puts undue stress on the thread, stretching and weakening it.

- -

Q I want to appliqué light colors on a dark background but the background shows through. How do I prevent this?

A You can back the light-colored shapes with lightweight fusible interfacing or with a second piece of the same fabric using the facing method for preparing appliqués (*see page 187*). Both add bulk to the finished appliqué but shadow-through will be minimized. Appliqués cut from fabric with fused interfacing on the back are easier to handle because the two fabrics act as one.

- -

Q My finished appliqué blocks are often smaller than intended. Why is that?

A Background blocks (and border strips) often shrink a bit due to the stitching process, particularly with machine-appliqué techniques. To fix your current problem, measure to find the smallest block and trim it to a square of the largest possible size, making sure the design is centered in the block. Then trim all remaining blocks to that size.

In the future, cut the background block or border strip so that it is oversized — at least 1" larger all around than you want it to be when it's finished. In addition to allowing for shrinkage, it also allows for inaccuracies in placement. Trim to size after all appliqués are positioned and pressed, taking care to keep the design correctly positioned in the trimmed piece.

- -

Q My bobbin thread is showing on the surface of my satin-stitched appliqués. What do I do to fix this?

A The top tension is too tight. Loosen the upper-thread tension on the machine so the bobbin tension will pull it into the fabric layers. Test your stitching first on scraps prepared the same way you will be doing the appliqué. It's okay if the top thread shows a bit on the wrong side of the satin stitching, as long as the fabric doesn't pucker. It's essential to adjust tension correctly for any stitch you use for appliqué, making sure that the bobbin thread doesn't show along the stitches on top. (*See* Adjusting Tension, *on page 311*.)

CHAPTER 8

Settings and Borders

When you've completed the blocks for your quilt, you're ready to assemble them to make the quilt top. You'll also need to choose an arrangement for your blocks — a setting — and add any additional pieces required. Adding the borders is the last step before quilting and finishing. These steps require the same care and consideration that goes into planning, cutting, and sewing the blocks. Careful sewing and pressing at this stage is essential to creating a finished quilt that is true and square with flat, ripple-free edges.

Quilt Settings

The two basic settings for quilt blocks are straight settings and diagonal settings, also called on-point settings. You can set blocks together, side by side, in either of these two settings, or you can set them apart with sashing strips (also called lattice) or with sashing strips combined with sashing squares (also called cornerstones). Sashing squares may be plain or pieced.

Sometimes patchwork or appliqué blocks are set off with alternating plain squares called setting squares. These are cut to the same size as the blocks and offer open space for interesting quilting designs to complement the busier blocks. In some quilt designs, two different patchwork blocks alternate in the layout and the result is an interesting secondary design due to the way they connect.

- -

Q How do I know which setting to use for my blocks?

A It depends on the blocks you've created and the desired finished look. Planning your own setting is lots of fun; you can copy something from a quilt-pattern book, choose from all the possibilities shown on pages 210–211, or create your own layouts.

The easiest way to choose a setting is to work on a design wall (*see page 212*) and arrange the blocks in straight and diagonal settings, with and without sashing. It's often easiest to set blocks that have multiple seams with sashing — eliminating the need to match piecing seams block to block.

Diagonal settings often create a more dynamic visual effect in the finished quilt. Some blocks, such as pieced basket blocks, look better in diagonal sets and others take on an entirely different look when set on point.

When you choose a diagonal setting, you will also need setting pieces to fill in the spaces around the points of the outer blocks — corner setting triangles and side setting triangles. These are often cut from the same background used in your quilt blocks or from a coordinating fabric that helps unify the blocks. For some layouts you will need setting squares to place between the blocks.

Playing with the blocks on your design wall will help you determine whether a straight or diagonal setting is best for your quilt. If you're not certain about your setting choice, arrange the blocks and pieces in a straight set and take a digital photo, then rearrange them in a diagonal setting and take a photo. Compare the photos to make your final selection. Computer software programs for quilt design, such as Electric Quilt, offer another way to play with and select a setting for your blocks, as well as plan the borders, fabric selection, and quilting.

- -

SET GALLERY

Shown here are the most common sets used for quilts — but there are many variations. Planning the setting for your blocks is a very personal, artistic, and aesthetic choice.

Straight set: block to block, side by side

Straight set: block to block with alternate setting squares

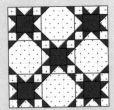

Straight set with alternating patchwork blocks

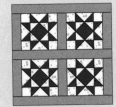

Straight set with simple sashing

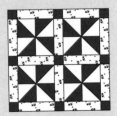

Straight set with sashing and sashing squares

Diagonal strip setting

Diagonal set, block to block

*Diagonal set with sashing
and sashing squares*

*Diagonal set with
alternate setting squares*

Straight strip set with sashing

Diagonal set with simple sashing

Medallion (on point)

Q What is a design wall?

A Essentially, it is a large expanse of wall covered with a napped fabric on which you can place the pieces for a block, finished blocks, or the blocks and pieces for an entire quilt top. The cotton blocks will "stick" to the napped surface without pins, allowing you to step back and review your work as well as move pieces around to facilitate the design process. (*For more on this fabric, see the next question.*)

It's best if you can place the design wall so that you can walk away from it. Viewing your setting from a distance makes it easier to see "problem" areas. You can also get a more realistic idea of how the finished quilt will look by viewing it through a reducing glass or a door peephole (from your local hardware store). This gives you the opportunity to evaluate the layout and make any changes before you sew the pieces together.

Once the quilt blocks are assembled, use the design wall to arrange the rows of blocks and setting pieces. If you have a digital camera, take a photo and print it out to keep as a reference. As you sew the quilt pieces together, row by row, replace them on the design wall until you are ready to sew the rows together.

If you don't have a design wall, you can plan quilt settings on graph paper. For on-point (or diagonal) settings, you will need on-point graph paper. Draw the blocks to scale and color them with colored pencils. Cut them out, move them around, and glue them down when you're happy with the arrangement. Draw in the setting pieces (if any) and the desired borders to create your own assembly diagram.

TAKE A PHOTO

While you are experimenting with the placement of your blocks, take digital photographs of the different options. Keep a copy of the setting you choose in your notebook to refer to later. You might also keep copies of the "runners up," in case one of those designs might appeal to you at a later date.

Q How large should the design wall be and how do I make one?

A Size depends on available space. A 4' × 8' design wall is large enough to hold the pieces for a twin-size quilt. Some quiltmakers give up an entire wall in their sewing room for a design wall.

There are many ways to prepare a design wall that allow you to make it as large as possible for your workspace. If possible, the napped fabric should be mounted on a firm, permanent surface. If that's not possible, try covering foam-core board with flannel for a portable version that you can store easily.

1. Choose a white napped fabric for the wall. Possibilities include a flannel top sheet (twin-size or larger); several yards of wide cotton flannel fabric; a large piece of thin cotton batting; or a large piece of sturdy, washable felt or headliner cloth — the fabric used to cover ceilings in cars, trucks, and boats. (Polyester batting is not recommended as it pills and is not as thin and smooth as cotton batting.)

Headliner cloth is more expensive, but is relatively lint-free and easy to vacuum. It is available from online sources (type "headliner fabric" into a search engine). A large flannel-backed tablecloth is another fabric option. If you keep your design wall clean (vacuum or wash as appropriate), it can also provide the perfect backdrop for photographing finished quilt projects.

2. Purchase a 4' × 8' piece of ½"-thick, porous building board at your local building supply store. It is white on one side.

3. Work on a large flat surface. Place the white side of the building board against the wrong side of the napped fabric. Wrap the fabric around the board so it is smooth and taut and use a staple gun with ⅜" staples to attach it. Miter the corners as smoothly as possible.

4. If possible, attach the covered board to a wall using drywall anchors and screws. Make sure it is level before you mark the placement for the screws — and try to anchor it to wall studs if possible.

Q I've chosen a diagonal setting for my blocks. How do I cut the setting triangles?

A If you are following a pattern, the cutting dimensions for the setting triangles will be included in the cutting directions. When planning your own quilt designs and settings, you will need to calculate the correct sizes and cut squares to cut into triangles. You will need four corner triangles (half-square triangles) and two side setting triangles (quarter-square triangles) for each row that doesn't finish with a corner triangle (the number of diagonal rows in your quilt, minus 2).

Choose the correct equation below to cut the triangles you need. The triangle size you use for corner triangles will be smaller than the triangle size for side setting triangles because you will cut only two corner triangles from a square. You will cut the larger squares for side setting triangles twice diagonally for a total of four side setting triangles. This ensures that the long edges of the triangles are on the straight grain so the outer edges of the quilt won't stretch during handling.

Corner Setting Triangles. Finished size (length/width) of the block ÷ 1.414, rounded up to the nearest ⅛" plus .875 = size of square to cut in half diagonally. You will need two squares of this size for the quilt, to yield a total of 4 corner triangles.

straight grain

cutting corner setting triangles

Side Setting Triangles. Finished size of block × 1.414, rounded up to the nearest ⅛", plus 1.25 = size of square to cut twice diagonally. Each square will yield 4 side setting triangles.

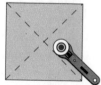

straight grain

cutting side setting triangles

SEE ALSO: *Cutting Charts, pages 404–5.*

Quilt-Top Assembly

Accuracy is just as important in this step as in all other quilt-making steps. Keeping your pieces in order so that you sew them together correctly can be challenging, especially with more complex designs and settings.

- -

Q I'm ready to assemble my quilt top. What's the next step?

A First, trim thread tails, check the pressed seams on the back of the blocks to make sure there are no twists, and give the blocks a final press. If you find twisted seams, it's not necessary to undo and redo stitching. Just make sure the twisted seams are pressed as flat as possible on the back of the quilt top. Check the blocks to make sure they are the same size and square up any uneven edges.

- -

Q How do I square up my blocks?

A Squaring up blocks can be as simple as pressing them, but sometimes finished blocks need a bit of trimming. It's a good idea to check all of the finished blocks for your quilt top to make sure they are the same size and to trim any discrepancies along the outer edges if possible. A square ruler that is larger than the block is handy for this process.

1. Place the ruler over each block and align the inner adjacent corners with the grid lines for the unfinished size of the block (½" larger than the pattern-specified finished block size). If the block is too large, any excess will extend beyond the ruler edges. If there is excess, determine whether you can trim it from one side or whether you must center the block under the ruler and then trim.

2. Trim only if necessary to remove any bits of excess beyond the ruler edges. If your blocks have patches with points along the outer edges, trimming may not be possible — there must be a ¼"-wide seam allowance beyond the points so you don't "lop" them off when you sew patches together. If there isn't a ¼" allowance beyond the points, you may need to make a new block if you have enough fabric, or try to correct the sewing on the block.

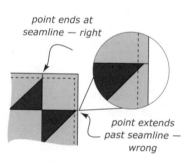

point ends at seamline — right

point extends past seamline — wrong

Note: If all of your blocks are the same size but are a bit smaller than what your pattern calls for, you can still use them for your quilt. Adjust the cutting dimensions for any setting pieces (squares, sashing strips, and sashing squares) to fit the new block size.

Q What if I don't have a full ¼"-wide seam allowance?

A If what you have for the seam allowance is less than ⅛", discard the block and make a new one if possible, taking care to cut and sew accurately. If you have at least ⅛" beyond the points, you can probably still use the block. To make sure you don't stitch into the patches, turn the block over and center a square ruler on top with the seam allowances extending at two adjacent edges. Use a sharp pencil to mark the seamlines. It's possible you will have full ¼" seam allowances on some edges of the block with skimpy seam allowances on the other(s). In addition, the seam allowance may be ¼" wide at each end, narrowing to ⅛" in some places.

- -

Q How do I sew the blocks together when one seam is skimpy and the other is ¼" wide?

A When joining blocks with seam allowances that vary in available width, mark the full seam allowance on the wrong side of both blocks. Then pin the blocks together, making sure that the marked seamlines on both blocks match. Place straight pins along the marks with the pinheads close to you and the points toward the sewing-machine needle on the block with the skimpy seam. Stitch, removing pins as you go. You may want to machine-baste these blocks first to make sure the stitching is accurate.

Q Some of my blocks are slightly smaller than others. What do I do?

A Because even minor cutting and stitching inaccuracies can affect the size of your blocks, it's not unusual to have a set of blocks with a few that are ⅛" or so different in size. Making new blocks is one option if you have enough fabric leftovers and you don't have to replace too many of them. However, you should be able to make them fit together with a little finessing while you pin and stitch. With only ⅛" to ¼" extra, the fullness should all but disappear in the piecing and pressing. After you add quilting stitches, differences will be even less obvious. For differences of more than ¼", see the question on page 226.

1. Arrange the blocks in the desired setting with the smaller blocks in the uppermost row or rows if possible.
2. As you sew the blocks together, row by row, place the smaller block on top of the longer one with pins at each end of the seam and at any intersecting points that must match. As you stitch, the feed dogs will help ease the bit of excess in the larger block into the seam.
3. When you press to set the stitching (*see page 115*), steam press from the larger side along the stitches to help further ease in the excess.
4. When you join rows, pin at the intersecting seams and ease in the excess in the same manner. In some cases you may need to gently stretch a section of a block to fit.

Q Some of my blocks measure the same on all four sides but don't look square. Can I rescue them?

A Try "blocking" your blocks with the steam iron to return them to a true and square shape.

1. Use a fine-point permanent ink pen to draw a full-size block with all seamlines marked on a piece of paper or on heat-resistant template plastic. *Note:* If the block is not symmetrical, turn the traced block over, tape it to a window, and trace over the lines to make your squaring template. Mark this side "face up" for the blocking.

2. Place the squaring template face up on the ironing board and then place the block right side down with seamlines aligned. With straight pins, secure the corners and centers of each edge to the ironing board. Stretch or ease the block to fit the pattern.

3. With the iron set on steam at the cotton setting, steam the block thoroughly, using your hands to help reshape the block to match the drawing as it begins to cool down. Press, don't iron. Allow to dry thoroughly before removing it from the blocking template.

Note: If you have several blocks to block, make a tracing for each one so you can block them all and allow them to cool. Don't use photocopies — the ink may bleed and transfer to your blocks.

Q I've squared up the blocks and given them a final press. What's next?

A Refer to the quilt photo and/or the quilt assembly diagram to arrange the blocks into rows. If you are designing your own quilt, refer to your setting plan (*see page 208*) or choose a setting from those shown on pages 210–211.

Arrange the pieces on your design wall, a large flat work surface, or on the floor in the desired finished arrangement. When you are happy with the setting, sew the pieces together in each row, press the seams in opposing directions from row to row, and then sew the rows together. Press the row-joining seams toward the bottom edge of the quilt top. For on-point settings, arrange the blocks in diagonal rows with the required setting pieces and sew together in diagonal rows as shown in the illustration. If setting pieces or sashing strips are required, press all seams toward the setting pieces before joining the rows and adding the corner squares last.

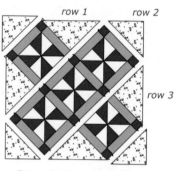

diagonal setting assembly

Q How do I keep the quilt pieces in order, so they end up in the right places and right direction?

A Number the rows and attach a label to each block with its row number and position from left to right (1A, 1B, 1C, etc.) Use scrap paper or sticky notes pinned in place. Attach the label close to the upper edge of each piece, but out of the way of the seam allowance.

▶ Working with one row at a time, stack the blocks (and setting pieces if any) in order, beginning at the right-hand edge of the layout, ending with number 1 on top of the stack for each row.

▶ Take the stack to the machine to sew them together in numerical order. After pressing the seams, return the completed row to the quilt layout.

▶ Complete the remaining rows in the same manner and then join the rows to complete the quilt-top center.

More ways to keep the pieces in order while you stitch:

▶ Lay a piece of masking tape across the center of each row of pieces so that you can take the entire row to your sewing machine. Remove from the tape, one by one, pin, and stitch the pieces together in order.

▶ Use your digital camera to take a photo of the quilt layout; make an 8½" × 11" printout to keep at your sewing machine for a sewing guide.

Q How do I use continuous sashing strips (without cornerstones) to join rows of blocks?

A First, arrange the blocks with space for the sashing strips between the blocks and between the rows.

1. Cut vertical sashing strips of the desired finished width plus ½", and the length of the blocks from top to bottom edge. Cut all vertical sashing strips the same length.

2. Sew the blocks together with the short sashing strips. Press the seams toward the sashing.

3. To cut the long sashing strips, measure the length of one completed row through the center of the blocks, ending at the raw edges; cut strips to match this length. For large quilts, you may need to join two or more sashing strips with bias seams (*see page 352*).

4. Sew the block rows to the sashing, lining up the vertical sashing strips to keep the quilt top square. Use an air- or water-soluble marking pen to draw lines on the sashing for matching purposes. Pin carefully, matching the seamlines to the marks. Stitch.

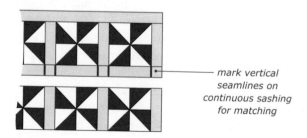

mark vertical seamlines on continuous sashing for matching

Q I am planning a diagonal setting for my 12" blocks. How do I know how large the quilt-top will be?

A Determine the width across the block from point to point by multiplying the finished block size by 1.414 and rounding up to the nearest ⅛". For example, 12" × 1.414 = 16.968 (17"). A quilt top with 3 blocks across and 4 blocks down would measure (3 × 17") × (4 × 17") or 51" × 68" before adding borders.

- -

Q I cut side setting triangles for my quilt, but the finished quilt wasn't square. What happened?

A By their nature, side setting triangles have two bias edges. Stretching them even a little while joining the diagonal rows can cause inaccuracies; the triangles may draw inward, resulting in edges that are not straight and true. Even the corner triangles can cause problems.

Many experienced quiltmakers cut the outer-edge corner and side setting triangles oversize, allowing room to trim the excess at the outer edges to square up the quilt top. Determine the correct size for the squares (*see the chart on page 409 or use the equations on page 215*) and then cut them 1" to 2" larger before cutting on the diagonal. (You may need additional yardage.)

Note: Sometimes, on-point blocks are allowed to float on the background. This means that an extra margin of background fabric is left beyond the block points when trimming away the excess on the oversize setting pieces. This makes it easier to attach borders without the worry of "clipping" the block points by catching them in the seam allowance.

- -

Q I participated in a block exchange. How do I make very different blocks work together in a quilt?

A Digital camera and computer to the rescue! Adding sashing strips and borders that pull the blocks together is a great way to do this, but taking all the blocks to your fabric store to choose the perfect sashing fabric for a large quilt could be challenging. If you have or can borrow a digital camera, you can take a photo and make a quilt-top mockup to take to the quilt shop for auditioning sashing fabrics.

1. Place your blocks on a design wall (or large flat work surface) in the desired arrangement with even spaces between the blocks where you will place the sashing strips. Take a digital photo of the final arrangement.

2. Transfer the photo to your computer and adjust the size of the images in a photo software program so that the "quilt" will fit on an 8½" × 11" sheet of acetate (from your office supply store). Be sure to select "transparency" for the paper type in your printer software, and then print the photo on the acetate. (As an alternative, you can print the photo on white paper, cut the blocks apart and glue them to a sheet of acetate, leaving space for the sashing.)

3. Take the quilt mock-up to the shop and lay it on top of fabric choices to find the perfect sashing.

- -

Q The blocks I received for a birthday quilt are not all the same size. Some are ½" smaller than the others. How can I make this work?

A You have several choices, depending on the block style of your quilt:

▶ If the blocks are appliquéd, trim all of the blocks to the same size — the size of the smallest square in the batch. Be sure to keep the appliqués centered in the blocks. You may be able to trim patchwork blocks to the same size, but not if the edges have intersecting seams where trimming would chop off the points of the patches.

▶ Add a frame of strips around all of the blocks to bring them up to size. Choose from those shown below. *Cut the strips for the frame wider than you will actually want the blocks to be when finished* so that you can custom-trim each framed block to a standard size. Some of the frames will be slightly narrower than others after trimming but they will all fit together in a straight or diagonal setting.

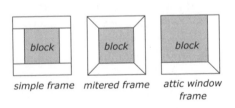

simple frame   mitered frame   attic window frame

▶ Frame the blocks with oversized triangles or half-square triangles and trim them all to the same size.

triangle frame

226

Q How do I add triangles to squares? What size should they be?

A Cut squares of the appropriate size for the triangles. (*Refer to* Cutting Triangles from Squares *on page 406.*) You will need two squares for each square you want to enlarge with corner triangles. Cut the squares and cut each in half diagonally. Sew the triangles to opposite sides of the square and press the seams toward the triangles. Add the remaining triangles to the remaining opposite edges and press toward the triangles.

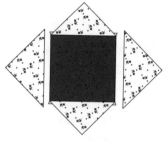

adding triangles to a square block

Adding the Borders

Borders add a "frame" to most quilt tops to draw the eye to the quilt center. They may be plain strips enhanced with quilting. Pieced borders and appliquéd borders are other options to consider. Although not always necessary, most quilts have at least one border. Quilts with uneven outer edges don't have borders unless the quilt-top edges are appliquéd to an outer border strip. In general, borders are used to:

▶ Enlarge a quilt top to the desired finished size

▶ Add a decorative frame of a single or several colors —
much like matting a piece of art

▶ Add visual interest

▶ Complement, emphasize, or repeat quilt colors and shapes

Q **I've sewn together the blocks for my quilt. How do I cut and add borders?**

A Decide on the number of borders you want to add and how wide each one will be. Before measuring and cutting the borders, you must choose which of the two basic methods for adding borders you want to use: *mitered* or *straight-cut* (sometimes called butted or blunt corners). Straight-cut corners are best for beginners; mitered corners are a bit more challenging but something to try after you have a little more experience. Marking the seamlines in the mitered seam is the challenging part. Borders with corner squares — plain or pieced — are another easier option for beginners.

When more than one border is added to a quilt, mitered corners are often chosen for the look of one continuous border around the quilt. Borders composed of patchwork blocks or pieces (pieced borders) are the most challenging border style; precise measuring and piecing are required for a perfect fit of border to quilt top. Appliquéd borders are more time-consuming but add a lovely frame to patchwork or appliquéd quilts.

straight-cut border

mitered border

Q What are the design factors I should consider when planning a border for my quilt?

A Planning the border design is one of personal preference if you are not following a specific pattern. Study quilts in books for ideas, and consider the following:

▶ Borders are often cut from one of the fabrics used in the quilt blocks for a unified finish.

▶ Pieced borders often repeat a block or a shape found in the quilt blocks. For a quilt composed of Fourpatch blocks, consider using similar blocks in the pieced border. For visual interest, set them on point in the border strip.

▶ If you are adding a pieced border, you may want to use a solid or tone-on-tone print in a contrasting color for a narrow inner border to set the pieced strips off from the complexity of the pieced blocks. You may want a third border beyond the pieced border.

▶ Appliquéd borders can be a nice contrast to geometric pieced blocks, particularly if appliqué is used elsewhere within the quilt design.

▶ A single, wide border provides a nice space for an interesting quilting design to surround the quilt top.

▶ Narrow contrasting borders are often used to set the quilt off from additional wider borders.

▶ Pieced borders can be planned as part of the quilt top when using diagonal settings, as advocated by quilting expert Sally Schneider in her books.

▶ When using multiple borders, keep them in proportion to each other. For example, a ¾"-wide inner border requires an outer border that finishes to at least 1½" (2 × ¾") or 2¼" (3 × ¾") or 3" (4 × ¾") wide. Or a 1½"-wide inner border with a 3"-wide outer border (2 × 1½") would work well.

▶ Don't forget to add ½" seam allowances (¼" on each side) to your border widths before cutting. So, for a 3" border, you would cut a border strip that is 3½" wide.

▶ Don't forget that you will lose some finished border width if you choose a contrasting binding. If you bind the quilt with the fabric used for the outer border fabric, this is not a consideration because the color will be continuous.

▶ Drawing the quilt top to scale on graph paper and playing with different border widths, colors, and combinations is a good way to determine the best proportions. Computer software for quilt design is also available for quilt top and border planning.

- -

Q How do I measure my quilt for straight-cut border strips and attach them?

A It is essential to keep the quilt square when you add the borders, no matter which border style you choose. Do not make the mistake of measuring each edge of the quilt and cutting border strips to match each one; unless you are a perfectionist, the opposite sides of your quilt will probably not be exactly the same size due to slight cutting and piecing inaccuracies or because the outer edges have been stretched unevenly during handling. You must measure, cut, and sew borders in a manner that makes the opposite edges the same length, to create a "square" quilt rather than one that ripples along one or more edges and will never hang straight. Measuring through the quilt-top center is always more accurate.

1. Press the completed quilt top, taking care not to stretch it out of shape. Arrange it on a flat surface — use the floor if your cutting surface is too small. Make sure that it is lying flat and smooth.

2. Use a long ruler (or a long tape measure) to measure the length of the quilt through the center. Use this measurement to cut the side border strips at the width you've chosen for that border (remembering, of course, to add in seam allowances).

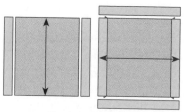

*measure through quilt centers to cut
accurate border lengths*

3. Fold the quilt in half crosswise and mark the center point at the edge; repeat with each side border strip. For large quilts, fold the pieces and mark the quarter points too.

4. With right sides facing and centers matching (and quarter points), pin the border to the quilt-top edge at the markings and at the ends; place pins perpendicular to the quilt-top edge. Pin the remainder of the border strip to the quilt

edge, gently easing any excess fullness in the quilt top between matching points to fit the border. Stitch ¼" from the raw edges and press the seam toward the border strip.

5. To add the top and bottom borders, measure the quilt-top (with appropriate side borders added) width through the center and cut the border strips to this measurement. Mark the matching points, pin to match, stitch, and press as you did for the side borders.

6. Add successive borders, if any, in the same manner — sides first, then top and bottom — always measuring through the quilt-top center to determine the cut length for the strips.

- -

Q My quilt-top edges are longer than the border fabric I plan to use. How do I make strips to fit?

A Cut enough strips of the correct width to piece into one long border strip that is longer than the distance around the quilt (perimeter), plus one more strip than is necessary to make it around the perimeter. For example, if the quilt is 25"× 45", you will need a 140"-long strip (50" + 90"), plus extra for seaming. Since quilt yardage calculations are usually based on 40" of usable width, you will need at least 4 strips; cutting 5 strips is even safer. After cutting the strips, sew them together with bias seams (*see pages 352–56*) and press the seams open. Then measure for the borders as described above and cut the border strips from the continuous piece. For smaller quilts, it may not be necessary to sew all of the border strips together.

Usually, straight-cut borders are added to the lengthwise edges of the quilt first (as the quilt will lie on a bed or hang on a wall), and then to the top and bottom borders, but occasionally you will see exceptions to this rule due to the quilter's preference.

- -

Q Why should I use bias seams when joining binding or border strips for my quilt?

A End-to-end seaming requires less fabric, but the results are better and stronger when you use bias seams. Strips that are joined end to end are far more noticeable to the naked eye than bias seams and detract from the beauty of the finished project.

When piecing binding strips together, the same thing applies. In addition, bias seams distribute the seam bulk in double-layer binding (*see pages 352 and 356*) on an angle. End-to-end seams in bindings result in a lump where the seam stacks up on itself in the turned layers.

- -

Q How do I sew an accurate bias seam when my border strips have straight ends?

A You'll need your rotary mat, cutter, a sharp pencil, and a small square ruler for this.

1. Place one strip facing up on the mat and cross it with the second strip at a perfect right angle. (Use the grid on the cutting mat to assist in accurate strip placement to make the right angle.)

233

2. Place a small ruler with the edge on a 45-degree angle from corner to corner and draw a diagonal cutting line. Remove the ruler and pin the strips together across the line. Stitch on the line.

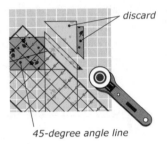

discard

45-degree angle line

3. Trim ¼" from the stitching and discard the cutaways. Press the seam open.

Q **Do I need to be concerned about where border-piecing seams fall along the quilt edge?**

A When trimming borders to the correct length from a long strip made of two or more shorter strips, take care to "walk" the strip along the edge (check the positioning) to which it will be joined. Make sure that no seamlines fall close to the quilt-top corners or close to the center of an edge. You may need to "waste" some of the border length in order to cut the strip to best advantage, keeping seams away from corners and centers. On large quilts, you may need to add another strip or portion of another strip to make the border long enough to keep the seams as inconspicuously positioned as possible.

Q Should quilt borders be cut across the grain or along the lengthwise grain?

A Cutting borders across the grain (fabric width) saves fabric, but because woven fabric has more give in the crosswise direction, border strips cut in this manner will have a certain amount of give or stretch; that can be helpful when fitting the borders to the quilt-top edges. Cutting borders with the length along the lengthwise grain adds stability to the borders because the lengthwise threads in woven fabrics are stronger than those used in the crosswise direction. For this reason, the outermost border is best cut along the lengthwise grain. This is especially true for wall quilts so that they lie flat and true against the wall.

For larger bed quilts, it is not necessary to cut the borders along the lengthwise grain; follow the directions on pages 230–232 for measuring your quilt and cutting the border strips to fit it. This method saves yardage and many quilt patterns are written in this manner. If you prefer borders cut along the lengthwise grain, it will be necessary to recalculate the border yardage required. As a general rule of thumb, the yardage for lengthwise-cut outer borders should be several inches longer than the longest dimension of the finished quilt to allow for shrinkage. Also note that unless the border strips are wide (up to 13" cut width), there will be extra fabric when you cut borders along the lengthwise grain.

- -

Q I want my quilt to have border squares. How do I measure and cut the borders and squares?

A The width of the border determines the size of the border square — or vice versa. Measure the quilt length through the center and repeat for the quilt width. Use these measurements to cut the top and bottom borders of the desired width. Cut corner squares to match the border width. Sew the long borders to the quilt top and press the seams toward the borders. Sew a corner square to one end of each of the shorter borders and press the seams toward the border strips. Sew the border/corner square strips to the quilt top and press.

- -

Q How long do I cut the border strips for a border with mitered corners?

A Measure the quilt top through the center as described for straight-cut borders to determine the length and the width measurements. (*See pages 230–32.*) On very large quilts, it's a good idea to take three measurements in each dimension and average them if they are different. Once you have an accurate measurement for your quilt top, add it to twice the border width plus 4" for seam allowances and "wiggle room." For example, for a 3"-wide finished border on a quilt that measures 45" × 54":

Quilt length/width + (2× border width) + 4" = cut length for mitered-corner border

45"+ (2 × 3") + 4" = 55" top and bottom border cut length

54"+ (2 × 3") + 4" = 64" side border cut length

Q How do I attach borders with mitered corners?

A Accurate measuring and marking is the key to perfectly mitered borders.

1. Fold each border strip in half and mark the center point. Divide the determined quilt-top length in half and carefully measure and mark that distance from the center in each direction on the side border strips. Measure and mark the top and bottom border strips in the same manner.

2. Mark the center of each edge of the quilt top.

3. With right sides facing and centers matching, pin one border strip to the quilt-top edge. Work from the quilt-top side. The raw edges at each end of the quilt top should match the pins on the border strip. With the wrong side of the quilt top facing you so you can control the seam allowances in pieced blocks, stitch the border to the quilt top. *Begin and end the seam precisely at the ¼" seam intersection at each corner — not at the quilt-top's raw edges.* Backstitch for security and take care not to stitch into the seam allowances at either end of the seam. It's better to stop stitching a thread or two from the seamline rather than even a thread past the seamline. Add the remaining borders in the same manner. Press to set the stitches (*see page 115*) on each border seam but don't do any directional pressing yet.

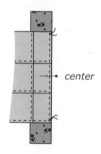

center

begin and end seam
at seamlines with
backstitches (not at
quilt-top edges)

237

4. To sew the mitered seam at each corner, fold the quilt diagonally at the corner and pin, making sure the outer border edges are perfectly aligned. Draw a 45-degree-angle stitching line from the end of the border stitching to the outer cut edges. Place straight pins along the stitching line (not across it) and carefully open the quilt. Use a square ruler with a true-bias line to check the accuracy of the seamline; adjust if necessary and then stitch on the line. Trim the excess border strips ¼" from the stitching and press the seam allowances open. Then press all border seam allowances toward the border strips.

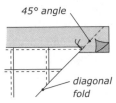

45° angle

diagonal fold

- -

Q How do I attach multiple borders with mitered corners?

A First determine the total *finished width* (not cut width) of the combined borders. For example, if your quilt has a ½"-wide finished inner border, a 2"-wide finished middle border, and a 3½"-wide finished outer border, the combined finished border width is 6". Use this width in the formula on page 236 when determining the cut lengths. Cut all borders the determined measurement(s) and sew them together in the desired order to create a single pieced border for each side of the quilt top. Apply the border strips as described above, carefully matching the seams at the mitered corners. Pin and then machine-baste the mitered seams first, to check the match. Make corrections as necessary and then permanently stitch, trim, and press.

- -

Q **How wide should a border be? Are there any guidelines?**

A If you're following a quilt pattern, follow the designer's directions for the border width(s) — unless you prefer a wider or narrower border than is shown. When creating your own quilt settings, determining the border width(s) should be based on your personal preferences and how the quilt will be used. Adding borders is one way to enlarge a quilt top to fit a specific bed, for example.

Multiple borders are more interesting when they are varying widths. The narrowest border is usually a contrasting color and is commonly placed next to the blocks to give the quilt top an obvious frame. Usually each successive border is a bit wider than the previous one. Border widths should be in proportion so the quilt top remains the central focal point and the borders act as a frame to draw the eye into the center.

As you can make more and more quilts and develop your own design eye, you'll know instinctively what border widths will best frame your finished quilt top.

Solving Problems

Q My quilt calls for border strips 42" long but my fabric is only 40" wide after preshrinking. Now what?

A The best approach is to cut five strips across the fabric width. Use bias seams (*see page 233*) when sewing them together to make a continuous border strip from which you can cut the four required lengths. After seaming the strips and pressing them open, measure the quilt top and cut the strips to the required length, taking care when cutting to make sure that the bias seams don't lie at the end of a strip. If you don't have enough fabric for this strategy, you can add corner squares of another fabric (*see page 236*).

- -

Q Despite careful cutting, stitching, and pressing, my narrow borders (less than 1" wide) are often "wobbly" — the width is inconsistent. How do I avoid this problem?

A Narrow borders are often a contrasting color, so cutting and stitching discrepancies are more noticeable than in wider borders. First, take great care when cutting narrow border strips to avoid uneven cut widths along the length of the strip. Always stitch long seams with a ledge of moleskin or layers of masking tape at your ¼" seam guide (*see page 126*). Consider my (almost) foolproof strategy to ensure even-width narrow borders when they will finish to 1" or narrower.

1. Cut narrow border strips ¼" wider than required. For example, for a 1" finished border, cut the strips 1¾" wide (1 + ½" for seam allowances + extra ¼" = 1¾").

2. If you must piece strips to make them long enough, sew them together on the diagonal (*see pages 233–34*).

3. Pin the quilt top to the border strip with the pins on the quilt-top side so you can control any seams at the outer edge. If there are intersecting seams, make sure that the point where the stitching crosses is ¼" from the border's raw edge so you won't stitch over the points of the patches.

4. Stitch with the quilt top facing you so that you can aim for the X (*see page 131*) at each intersecting seam (so you don't stitch into the block).

5. Examine the finished seam on the border side to find any obvious stitching inaccuracies (or "wobbles") that can be corrected. Before fixing them, put a different color thread in the needle and stitch from the border side. The new color identifies your corrections. Clip the stitches in the offending wobbles and remove them.

6. Press the seam toward the border (never toward edges with patchwork seams).

7. After adding the side and the top and bottom borders, place the quilt top on your cutting mat and trim the borders to the desired finished width plus ¼". Line up the ruler with the stitched and pressed seamline, and trim the excess. Don't be surprised if the amount you trim varies in places along the length of the strip.

8. Take great care when pinning and stitching the next border to the narrow border so the seams are accurate. Press both seam allowances toward the center of narrow borders that finish to ½" or wider. For ¼"- or ⅜"-wide borders, press the seams away from the quilt top.

FAKE IT

Flat piping (*see page 391*) is a good alternative to a really narrow border and is easier to control. Since it lies on the quilt top, it covers the seam intersections at the quilt top edge, eliminating the worry about accidentally stitching off the points of patchwork points and corners.

Q I'm making a quilt with pieced borders, and the borders ended up too long for the quilt edges. Now what?

A This is not an unusual predicament. The more piecing seams in the quilt and the border, the more likely it is that this will happen. To make the border fit, first determine how much too long it is. Then take slightly deeper seams in enough areas of the pieced border to make it fit the quilt top. It's not necessary to undo any of the seams; just stitch them again with a slightly wider seam allowance and press. There will be two rows of stitching in the seams that you adjust. It may only require taking a few deeper seams, evenly distributed along the border strip. The differences will be unnoticeable in the finished quilt, particularly after it is quilted.

CHAPTER 9

Quilting Choices

For some quilters, making the blocks and assembling the quilt top is the most enjoyable part of the process. For others, it's the quilting — they love to see the quilt come alive with the depth and texture that quilting stitches add. Once done only by hand, today machine quilting is not only acceptable but has also become an art form all its own. The rhythmic motion of hand quilting can be soothing and meditative, but it will take longer to finish your quilt. Machine quilting may be faster, but it also requires careful planning and care when manipulating the quilt sandwich under the needle. Both methods take practice and patience.

Planning Considerations

Before you can make the quilt sandwich with the quilt top, batting, and backing (*see chapter 10*), you must plan the quilting design. This is a very personal part of the process, based on how you want the finished quilt to look, and on your stitching skills. Machine quilting requires practice and patience, so starting simple and working up to more complex designs is a good idea.

Quilt the same quilt or block three different ways and each one will look different, depending on the design and stitching method used. That's difficult to illustrate on the pages of a book, but you can get an idea by examining the "quilted" blocks on pages 246–49. Lee Cleland's book, *Quilting Makes the Quilt,* clearly demonstrates this concept. (*See* Resources.)

- -

Q Why is quilting necessary?

A Whether you quilt by hand or machine, the quilting stitches serve a utilitarian function: holding the batting in place between the top and backing so the batting fibers won't shift. In addition to this functional aspect, the quilting stitches create an overall visual and textural effect. For quilts that will be used often, quilting is essential. For wall and art quilts, designs and quilting methods are chosen for their decorative attributes; heavy quilting is not necessary since fiber shifting during laundering these is usually not an issue.

Q Are there instances when hand quilting is a better choice than machine quilting?

A Choose hand quilting if you prefer traditional methods and have the time to do extensive handwork. Intricate designs, especially those with many tight curves, may be easier to quilt by hand since you have more flexibility in positioning the quilt while you work. If you plan to use your quilt and launder it regularly, machine quilting may be the best choice. Many quilters believe a hand-pieced quilt deserves hand quilting, but you can choose to machine-quilt it or do a little of both.

Q How do I choose a quilting design for a finished quilt? I don't know where to start.

A Study the basic quilting styles in this chapter, check out quilting pattern books, and visit quilting stencil companies online. Here are some things to consider when making your choices:

▶ Straight lines are the easiest for beginners and there are many quilting patterns that are easy to mark on the quilt top using your rotary ruler and an appropriate marker.

▶ Simple open shapes such as a star or heart motif are easier to stitch than designs with lots of tight curves. You can add other quilting patterns inside these for more interest.

▶ If you choose designs with long straight lines, crooked and uneven stitches may be more obvious; short curved lines camouflage these flaws.

Quilting Styles

Every quilting pattern changes the character of the blocks and overall visual appearance of the finished quilt. Many quilters design their own quilting patterns; others choose decorative quilting stencils that are widely available at quilt shops and from online sources. There are also many ways to quilt that don't require stencils as well as methods for quilting that don't require marking the actual quilt top.

- -

Q What are the basic quilting styles to consider when planning the quilting?

A Examine the illustrations and accompanying descriptions below to learn about your quilting style options and see how they affect the look of the finished quilt.

Utility Quilting

Simple straight-line stitching patterns designed to hold the quilt layers together come in many styles including:

▶ **Quilting-in-the-ditch.** Requires no marking because it follows the seamlines in the patchwork. It is often used to set the quilt layers together along the major seamlines before adding more intricate patterns or motifs in the blocks and borders.

Quilting in the ditch

▶ **Outline quilting.** Stitching ¼" from the seamline, inside the patch, is a no-mark method that highlights patchwork shapes. Use the edge of a presser foot or masking tape as a stitching guide. You can also outline appliqués.

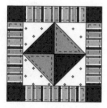

Outline quilting patchwork

Outline quilting appliqué

▶ **Allover designs.** Cover the surface of the quilt, often with no attention to the actual seamlines in blocks and borders. These may be used in plain setting blocks, in the background of appliquéd blocks, in sections of pieced blocks, and in borders and sashing. Marking these designs is covered in this chapter.

allover crosshatching

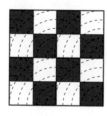

allover fan design

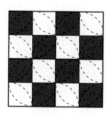

allover Orange Peel design

247

▶ **Echo quilting.** Looks like ripples in the water. This no-mark method is often used to outline and enhance appliqué shapes with concentric rows or rings of evenly spaced stitching, usually ¼" apart. Some experienced quilters do echo quilting with free-motion machine quilting (*see page 320*), but beginners are usually more comfortable using machine-guided stitching with the edge of a narrow presser foot as the guide for line spacing. Low-loft batting is the best choice when doing extensive echo quilting.

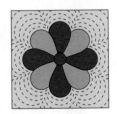

Echo quilting

▶ **Motif and selective quilting.** Stitching that follows specific shapes (motif) that have been marked on the quilt top like the one in the center of the illustration below. Following a motif in a printed fabric is an example of selective quilting.

Continuous-Line Quilting

Lines and curves that are joined to create continuous lines you can follow without stopping, clipping threads, and repositioning the quilt. This eliminates the work of tying off the top and bobbin threads and burying them in the quilt layers (*see page 314*).

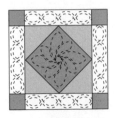

center: motif quilting
sashing: continuous-line quilting

248

Stippling and Meandering

Randomly stitched curves and swirls, a bit like puzzle shapes, done with free-motion stitching. Low-loft batting is the best choice for quilts that will have stipple quilting.

quilt-in-the-ditch in the appliqué

stipple quilting around appliqué

▶ **Stippling stitches** are closely spaced and free-form. They are used to fill background areas with dense stitching that compacts the quilt layers and often puts other areas in raised relief. Stippling (and meandering) stitches typically do not cross each other and no marking is required. Some high-end computerized sewing machines offer a built-in stippling stitch that you can customize somewhat by adjusting stitch width and length settings.

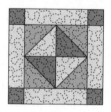

meander quilting

▶ **Meandering stitches** are done like stippling, but are more widely spaced to cover larger areas or the entire quilt top in an allover pattern to make fast work of quilting.

Note: If you own a computerized sewing machine with an embroidery unit, you may enjoy using it to stitch digitized motifs on your quilt. Check at your sewing-machine dealer or with online sources for the array of available quilting designs.

- -

Q Are there any guidelines for choosing a quilting pattern?

A First you need to decide what you want the quilting to do and then create a quilting plan that achieves that goal. Your timeline for completing the quilt is also a factor to consider. Here are the most common quilting options:

▶ **Hold the layers together with simple stitching.** You can't go wrong with quilting in the ditch, and it's an easy way for beginners to get started. Stitch in all the vertical and horizontal seams that join the blocks and in the seams of the patchwork seams within the block. Add an interesting border design motif and the quilting is finished. Other options include allover designs such as meandering over the quilt or using a planned allover design such as clamshells or fans.

▶ **Enhance appliqué shapes and fill the space around them.** Outline and echo quilting are excellent choices. They can be stitched using the edge of the presser foot as the spacing guide, but can also be free-motion quilted (*see page 320*) if you have developed that skill.

▶ **Fill the quilt surface with quilting stitches and interesting texture** — without requiring intricate stitching. Consider allover patterns, including simple meandering, channel, or grid quilting. Marking the design on the quilt top is required for all but meandering.

▶ **Emphasize the piecing lines in patchwork blocks.** Outline quilting inside the block patches achieves this. On the machine, stitch with the edge of a ¼" patchwork foot along the seamlines to keep the stitching an even width from the seamline. For hand piecing, use ¼" masking tape along the seamlines as a stitching guide. Allover patterns can also be done within the outer edges of individual blocks.

▶ **Add texture.** Stippling, echo quilting, and closely spaced grids are all possibilities.

▶ **Fill empty spaces and blank setting squares.** Stippling or meandering; crosshatched grids; repetitive rows of straight-line or decorative stitching; motif quilting within blocks, borders, and sashing can all make blank spaces more interesting.

▶ **Enhance unpieced setting blocks and fill borders and sashing.** Motifs such as simple shapes, medallions, wreaths, feathers, and continuous-line patterns, as well as grids confined inside the squares are all options.

▶ **Accent pieced blocks.** Using motifs or curvilinear designs in a geometric patchwork block and add interesting movement to the surface of the finished quilt.

▶ **Tie the quilt.** Instead of stitching, use simple hand stitches secured with square knots, spaced across the quilt to hold the layers together. This is a particularly appropriate approach for utility quilts made with thick polyester batting that is difficult to hand-quilt and difficult to maneuver under the sewing-machine needle.

SEE ALSO: *Tying a Quilt, pages 340–41.*

Q How do I know if the quilting motif I've chosen is the right size and proportion for my quilt top?

A The motif should fill the area (block or border) without making it look too crowded; if it's too small, the design will look skimpy and the background area beyond the motif may look puckered after quilting. It's best to allow for at least ½" of breathing space beyond the motif outline. The same holds true for border designs. *Note:* You can draw your own quilting motifs, trace them from a variety of books with quilting designs, or purchase or make quilting-design stencils.

- -

Q What is a quilting stencil and how do I use it?

A Many wonderful quilting designs are available on thin plastic squares and strips, with the stitching lines cut out for marking purposes. Small bits of plastic, called bridges, are spaced along the cutout lines to give the stencil stability and keep it intact. You'll find a wide array of motifs for blocks, plus border designs, some of which have coordinating designs for the border corners. They came in assorted sizes to fit different block and border sizes. The size is usually punched or marked on the stencil, along with a design number.

After selecting the stencil(s) you want to use for your quilt, position one in the desired location on the quilt top and use the marker of your choice (*see page 259*) to trace along the openings onto the quilt top. When you remove the stencil, there will be skips in the lines where the bridges were. There's no need to connect the lines over the skips unless you want to.

- -

Q How do I create a corner design that coordinates well with the border design I've chosen?

A With some designs, it's easy to make them meet naturally at a 90-degree angle in the corners, particularly if the design is geometric or composed of straight lines. For curvilinear designs that flow through the corners, try placing a mirror at a 45-degree angle on the border pattern and slide it along until you see a design that you like. Mark the mirror location on the pattern with a diagonal line and then trace the corner design and a mirror image of it onto paper to create the corner pattern. Next determine how many border repeats you'll need for each of the borders and draw them on a strip of butcher paper. You may need to adjust the finished border designs (*see page 255*) to make them fit the two border dimensions (top and bottom and sides) perfectly.

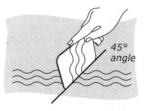

Q When I choose a stencil for the motif, sometimes it's too small or too large. How do I adjust it to fit?

A First make a tracing of the design by drawing inside the cutout areas of the stencil with a black pen on a square or strip of paper — the matte side of freezer paper is a good choice. Take the tracing to your local copy center and reduce it or enlarge it to the desired size on their copier. While there, you might want to make several reductions and enlargements of the design to have various sizes on hand for future projects. This process is also appropriate for adjusting designs to fit borders and sashings. Transfer the adjusted design onto the quilt surface on a lightbox or make a marking or stitching template (*see pages 260 and 263*).

- -

Q What is a continuous-line quilting design?

A As the name implies, you can quilt one of these designs in a continuous motion, starting and stopping only once. These designs are available in motifs and border designs. Quilting is easier and faster when you limit the number of starts and stops. Use a wooden bamboo stick or orange stick to follow the design lines in order to determine if the design is continuous.

continuous-line motif — begins and ends at the same point

If you must stop anywhere and start again before reaching the starting point, it's not a continuous design. In some designs, you may be able to double back in some areas to eliminate stops and starts. For borders, it may be worthwhile to modify a design to make it continuous by connecting motifs with added lines or curlicues or eliminating parts of the design.

double back to stitch continuously

Solving Problems

Q When I join the repeats in a continuous-line quilting motif, the design doesn't fit the borders. How do I fix this?

A Here's a good solution to this problem:

1. Prepare border designs on long strips of tissue paper cut to match the border width. Draw them with the required number of full design repeats using a fine-tip permanent marking pen.

2. Determine how much too long or too short the strips are to perfectly fit the borders of the quilt and how many ⅛" increments of change are necessary along the length of the border design. For example, if the border-strip pattern

is 1" too long, remove 1" in eight ⅛" increments spaced equally along the length of the strip to make it the correct length. Cut the strip apart in eight places, overlap the edges by ¹⁄₁₆" for a total of ⅛" at each cut, and tape in place. This usually distorts the quilting design somewhat so reshape the quilting lines as needed.

3. To lengthen a strip, follow the same procedure, but "slash and spread" the pattern where you need extra length: add tissue where openings occur and correct the stitching lines. The slight difference created in the pattern won't be obvious when you are careful to spread the change along the length of border.

tissue paper   extra tissue paper under spreads

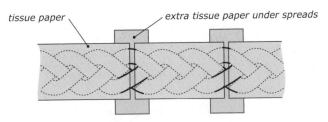

slash and spread to lengthen (or overlap to shorten)

4. Once the borders are finalized, make tracings of each one on new pieces of tissue paper so there is a strip for all four borders. Then, apply the strips to the borders, one at a time, using a light coat of temporary spray adhesive to hold them in place.

5. Stitch along the drawn lines, through the tissue paper and the border. The paper is easy to stitch over and the adhesive helps to control the fabric and eliminate puckers in the top fabric layer.

6. After stitching, simply tear away the tissue paper. The adhesive dissipates over time, but you can also wash your project after quilting to give it the "popcorn" texture that is characteristic of heirloom quilts.

- -

Q How do I know if the quilting design I've planned will enhance my quilt?

A An easy way to do this is to tack the completed quilt top to your design wall (*see page 212*) or to a plain wall in your home. Then take a straight-on digital photo of it and print it on your computer, making the print as large as possible (or take a nondigital photo and have it printed on an 8½" × 11" sheet). Next, place a sheet of tracing paper over the print and use a fine-tip colored pen to draw the quilting plan on the quilt with short dashed lines to represent the stitching. If you're not happy with the plan, rethink it, and do a new drawing on a clean sheet of paper. For a more close-up view of your quilting plan for a symmetrically designed quilt top, crop the photo so it shows only a quadrant and then draw in the quilting designs. For a full view, photocopy the quadrants three times and tape them together.

Marking the Quilting Design

Often the quilt top is marked with the quilting pattern before layering it with batting and backing. Depending on how you plan to quilt your quilt, choose from an assortment of design-transfer methods, including some nonmarking techniques (*see page 263*) that save time. The method and the marker you choose may depend on the type of design you are transferring and the color of your quilt top.

- -

Q **My quilt top is finished and I've planned the quilting. How do I prepare the top for marking?**

A Before making the quilt sandwich, take the time to clean up the quilt top, front and back.

1. Trim all stray piecing threads on the back of the quilt top so they won't shadow through lighter colors. Check all seam allowances to make sure they are correctly pressed. Watch for twisted seams, puckers, and tucks in the seams and correct if needed so the quilt top is smooth and flat on both sides. *Note:* Sometimes twisted seams are necessary for easy seam matching from block to block. If there are twisted seams, make sure they are pressed as flat as possible.

2. Check the front of the quilt top for stray threads and snip as needed.

3. Press the quilt top, taking care not to "iron"; pushing the iron across the seamlines on the surface can distort the

top, creating a finished quilt that may not be true and
square.

4. If you plan to stitch in the ditch, free-motion quilt without following any set pattern, or use one of the no-mark
methods described on pages 263–66, your quilt top is
ready to layer and quilt. For other quilting strategies
requiring marking, spread the quilt top on a large flat
surface and smooth out any wrinkles. Secure the edges to
the surface with 3"-long pieces of masking tape centered
lengthwise over the fabric edge.

- -

Q **What do I use to transfer a quilt design to the quilt
top?**

A Since the marks must be easy to see, choose a marker
color that will show on the quilt fabrics and test the
chosen marker to make sure you can remove the marks easily
after the quilting is completed; be sure to follow the manufacturer's directions. Keep the package directions for markers
in your quilting notebook (*see page 26*) for future reference. If
marking directly on the quilt top is undesirable, use a stitching
template as discussed in No-Mark Transfer Methods, on page
263. Following are the traditional options for marking on the
quilt top:

▶ Washable graphite pencils and thin-lead mechanical
pencils

▶ Fine-point water-soluble markers; you can also use air-
soluble ones, but only if you plan to quilt right away

▶ Silver or yellow artist pencils

▶ Chalk wheel and powdered chalk or a sharp dressmaker's chalk pencil

▶ Powdered chalk with a pounce pad for pierce-and-pounce marking

▶ Masking tape (for straight-line designs)

– –

Q I've chosen a marker. How do I use it to transfer the quilting design?

A Choose from the following marking methods. Also see No-Mark Transfer Methods, beginning on page 263. Select a marking tool appropriate for your quilt top (*see previous question*).

▶ **Direct tracing.** For light-colored quilts, trace over the designs on a paper template with a permanent pen to make them easy to see. Then place the quilt top over the tracing on a light box and use a removable marker or chalk to trace the design onto the quilt top.

▶ **Pierce-and-pounce.** For dark-colored quilts, draw the design on lightweight paper with a permanent marking pen and machine stitch with an unthreaded, larger-than-normal sewing-machine needle to pierce the design. Position the pierced paper template on top of the quilt top and use a pounce pad to gently push and deposit powdered chalk through the holes. Carefully lift the paper and connect the dots using a marking pen or pencil of your choice.

Most of the powdered material will rub away during quilting. Brush away any remaining powder after quilting.

▶ **Bridal-tulle stencil.** Trace the design onto a piece of bridal tulle with a fine-point permanent marker. Place the tracing on the quilt top and pin in place. Trace over the design with a chalk marker or with a water-soluble marking pencil (if you plan to wash your quilt).

▶ **Stencils.** Trace along the cut lines of ready-made templates.

▶ **Masking tape.** Position masking tape on the quilt top to create straight-line and grid patterns. Use ¼"-wide tape for single-line grids. If you want two parallel lines of stitching, stitch along each edge of the tape. Remove tape after stitching. It's best to tape small areas because leaving tape in place for long periods may leave a sticky residue. For more closely spaced parallel lines of quilting, use a twin needle (two needles attached to a single shank) in the machine and two spools of thread — but only if you don't mind a zigzag stitch on the back of the quilt. The bobbin thread zigzags between the two needle threads on the underside of your work.

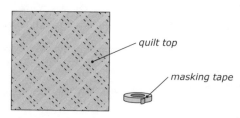

quilt top

masking tape

Q How do I remove the pounced powder marks?

A They will probably wear off as you work; that's why it's important to follow the pounced dots with a marker before you begin to quilt. If they don't disappear during the quilting, use a dry washcloth to rub them out or try a nylon stocking to brush them away.

Q I don't have a light box. Is there another way to trace the design?

A If you have a glass-top dining or coffee table, simply put a lamp underneath it. Place the quilt top on the table, turn on the light, and trace the design. Otherwise, purchase a large piece of clear acrylic (custom framers or glass companies may stock it) and place it on a stack of books (of even heights) at each end so you can slide a flat under-cabinet light beneath it.

If the edges of the piece are sharp, wrap them in wide masking tape to protect your fingers, or have a professional cutter finish the edges so you don't cut yourself. Or, if your dining table has leaves, open the table and place the acrylic on top with a table lamp underneath. Store the acrylic sheet under a bed or in the back of a closet when not in use.

No-Mark Design Transfer

Many quilt tops can be quilted without marking at all, saving time and the necessity of removing marks later. Stitch-in-the-ditch quilting is one example. No-mark methods leave no marks on the quilt, but you will need to make stitching templates. This requires transferring the design to paper of some type so you can attach it to the quilt and stitch around or through it. You can use freezer paper or Con-Tact paper for repositionable quilting templates that can be used several times.

- -

Q How do you prepare and use paper stitching templates?

A You will need a fine-point permanent marker and tear-away stabilizer paper that you can see through — a lightweight vellum-type or architect's yellow drawing paper (available in rolls of varying widths from Golden Threads) works well. (Waxed paper will work as a substitute.) Use permanent ink so there's no chance of the needle dragging color through the paper and onto your quilt.

1. Place the paper over the design and trace carefully. Pin the tracing in place on your quilt where you want the design.
2. Thread the machine and prepare it for free-motion stitching (*see pages 321–22*).
3. Free-motion stitch along the marked lines and tear away the paper. The needle punches holes as you stitch, making it easy to lift the paper away — but do take care that

you don't stretch or break the quilting stitches by stressing them too much. Work from the center of the quilt out, working on one block or quilt section at a time for easier handling.

Note: If you're uncomfortable with free-motion stitching, apply the paper to the quilt with a light coat of temporary spray adhesive, attach an open-toe presser foot and stitch with the feed dogs engaged for machine-guided quilting (*see page 309*).

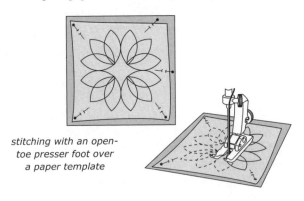

stitching with an open-toe presser foot over a paper template

---

Q I'm quilting each block in my quilt with the same design. Is there a speedy way to make the paper-stitching guides?

A Cut oversize squares of the paper and trace the design on only one of them. Stack them with the tracing on top — up to 15 layers works fine for this speed-marking method. Pin the layers together. Drop the feed dogs on your machine, attach a darning or free-motion presser foot, and insert a large unthreaded needle in the machine (size 100/16). Free-motion–stitch (*see page 321*) along the design lines through all layers to mark the design with fine holes to follow when quilting. Use the same method to prepare stitching templates for borders, setting squares and triangles, and sashing strips.

If you have trouble seeing the perforations in the paper, darken them with a permanent marker or try one of the following alternate methods for paper templates.

Freezer-Paper Quilting Templates.
For simple quilting motifs — a shape like a heart, for example — trace the design onto the uncoated side of the freezer paper. Cut out the shape, position it on the quilt top, and use a warm iron to press it in place. Quilt around the template by hand or machine (free-motion quilting is easiest) and carefully remove the paper template to use again. Discard the template when it becomes difficult to make it stick to the quilt top.

stitch around freezer-paper template

Con-Tact-Paper Quilting Templates. You can prepare templates for simple shapes using clear Con-Tact paper in the same fashion as for freezer paper, removing the backing paper before adhering the shapes to the quilt for stitching. If the shape you wish to quilt is asymmetrical, trace the reverse image onto the paper backing. Cut the shape from Con-Tact paper, remove the backing paper, and position on the quilt. Then simply stitch around the outer edge and remove the template to use again until the "sticky" wears out. You can add other quilting in the center of large simple shapes if you wish — stippling, cross-hatching, echo quilting, or other simple motifs, for example.

Glad Press'n Seal Templates. This new "plastic" product from the grocery store has a "sticky" side that will adhere to the quilt top. (The freezer-weight version is easier to handle but either weight will work.) Use a fine-tip permanent marker to draw the quilting design (motif or border designs) on the nonsticky side of the plastic. If you are making a template for a block, draw the finished block size on the plastic to help with positioning. Use your hands to smooth and press it into place; do not press with an iron. Stitch through the Press'n Seal along the marked lines and then gently tear it away along the stitched lines.

For multiples of the same design, layer sheets of the Press'n Seal with scrap fabric in between, and stack and stitch with an unthreaded machine needle to perforate the design (*as outlined for the* Pierce-and-Pounce *on page 260.*) The fabric is necessary to keep the Press'n Seal layers from sticking to each other.

Use this method for borders too, by cutting strips the length and width of the finished border before tracing the design onto them. You can also piece shorter lengths by overlapping pieces by ½". If you prefer to chalk-mark your quilting design using a perforated Press'n Seal template, you will need a pounce pad and loose chalk (*see page 260*).

CHAPTER 10

Making the Quilt Sandwich

The quilt top is finished, and you've planned the quilting, and marked it on the quilt top as directed in chapter 9. You're almost ready to start stitching. But first, you'll need to create the quilt sandwich. When the sandwich is ready to quilt, go on to chapter 11, Quilting the Quilt.

Preparing the Quilt Backing

The backing for your quilt can be as simple as a single piece of fabric — perhaps a print in a coordinating color or one of the fabrics you used in the quilt top. For added fun and interest, as well as out of necessity, quilt backings can be pieced using panels of several different fabrics.

- -

Q How do I determine the size of my quilt backing?

A Measure your quilt top and add a 2" to 4" margin beyond each edge to allow for the natural shrinkage that occurs during the quilting. For small quilts, the 2" allowance is adequate. For example, if the finished quilt top is 36" × 40", add 4" (2" + 2" to include both sides) to the quilt dimensions and cut a piece that measures 40" × 44". For a quilt top that measures 72" × 90", add 8" (4" + 4" for both sides) and cut a 80" × 98" piece. Since most backing fabric ends up being about 40" wide after preshrinking, you'll need to sew two or more pieces of fabric together to get the correct size. (*See next question.*)

- -

Q How do I cut and sew the pieces together for a large backing?

A Look at Pieced Backing Options on pages 270–71 and choose the option that best suits your quilt. Preshrink the backing fabric and trim the selvages. Determine the cut size for the backing as described in the previous question and then choose one of the following piecing methods.

Method 1. Note that seams in quilt backings may cross the width or the length of the quilt.

1. Divide the width or length of the backing cut size by 40" (the width after preshrinking). Round up to the nearest full number. This is how many panels you need to cut.
2. Sew the panels together with ¼"-wide seams, and press the seams open for easier quilting. For machine quilting, you may press seams toward the outer edges.

Method 2. For a two-panel vertical layout, the seam will run down the center of the quilt, or split one panel and sew each half to the long edges of the full panel. If the backing slips off center during the quilting process, it won't be obvious because there is no center seam. Here's how to do it:

center
crease

1. Split the total yardage for the backing into two equal lengths and place them right sides facing with selvages even.
2. Stitch ½" from each selvage and trim the seams to ¼" to remove the selvages.
3. Fold the tube in half with seamlines aligned; press one folded edge. Cut along the fold. Press the seams open or away from the center.
4. Cut along the fold and press the seams open or away from the center panel.

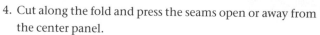

PIECED BACKING OPTIONS

Standard Pieced Backings. These are the most common ways to piece a backing:

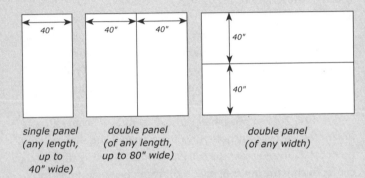

single panel
(any length,
up to
40" wide)

double panel
(of any length,
up to 80" wide)

double panel
(of any width)

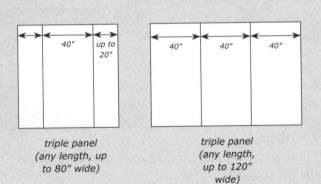

triple panel
(any length, up
to 80" wide)

triple panel
(any length,
up to 120"
wide)

Creative Pieced Backings. The backing of your quilt can be made using several different fabrics for a pieced look. Check out the options below:

▶ **Offset Seam.** Not enough of one fabric? Make up the difference with a different fabric — perhaps backing leftovers from another quilt.

▶ **Patchwork.** Use various size pieces of different colors and prints — perhaps cut from leftovers from the other quilt components for the quilt top — to make an interesting pieced backing. The pieces you use shouldn't be too small; avoid making backings with lots of pieces as the multiple seams will make quilting, particularly hand quilting, more difficult.

▶ **Inset Strip.** Insert a narrow strip of color in one or both directions. Offsetting the strips makes for a more interesting "design" on the quilt back. This is a great solution for a quilt that is a bit wider than the 40" you may have to work with after preshrinking the backing fabric.

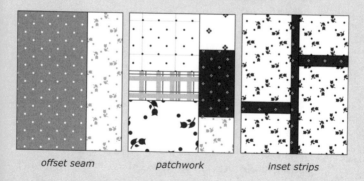

offset seam   *patchwork*   *inset strips*

Q How do I guesstimate the required backing yardage my quilt will need?

A A quick rule of thumb for backing yardage: If the quilt top is more than 36" wide but no wider than 72", add 4" for small quilts or 8" for large quilts to the quilt top length, and then double that measurement for the actual fabric length required in inches. To allow for shrinkage, multiply this result by 1.05, and then divide by 36 to determine the required yardage for the backing. This will give you enough fabric to cut and sew two lengths together for the backing (*see page 269*). There may be some waste with this method, but at least you will be sure to have enough yardage for the backing.

For example, if the quilt top is 45" × 78", your math would look like this:

> **Quilt top length = 78"**
> **78" + 8" = 86"**
> **86" × 2 = 172"**
> **172" × 1.05 = 180.60"**
> **180.60" ÷ 36" = 5.10 yards**
> **5.10 yards = 5⅛ yards**

- -

Q The backing for my quilt is not quite wide or long enough. Can I add strips of fabric to enlarge it?

A Adding fabric is the only way to enlarge it, but I wouldn't add narrow strips to the edges if you only need a few inches to make the backing wide enough. The seam could end up too close to the binding seam since backings are cut several inches larger than the quilt top and trimmed to match the quilt edges after quilting. It's better to make a vertical and horizontal cut through the center of the backing and add more fabric there as shown on page 271 for inset strips. This keeps the seams for the additions out of the area that could otherwise end up in the binding seam. The resulting backing develops character and looks like a deliberately planned artistic backing.

Preparing the Batting

Select the batting for your quilt based on the recommendations on pages 56–58, and then cut it to the correct size for the quilt sandwich — the same size or just slightly smaller than the backing.

- -

Q Do I need to do anything to prepare the batting before I make the quilt sandwich?

A It depends on the type of batting you've chosen and your plans for the quilt's use and care. Some possibilities and suggestions follow:

▶ Polyester battings don't require preshrinking but you should remove the batting from the bag, unfold it, and allow it to relax overnight before using it.

▶ If you are making a thin quilt with cotton flannel for the batting, launder the flannel as you would normally wash and dry it, and then press to remove wrinkles. Trim away the selvage edges, or use ½"-wide joining seams if you must piece it to fit your quilt, and then trim the seam allowances to ¼" wide after stitching.

▶ If you are using cotton batting or a blend that is primarily cotton and you plan to launder your quilt once or regularly, it's best to pretreat the batting with a modified wash — but only if the manufacturer's directions so specify. In addition to controlling shrinkage, which can be as much as 5 percent in cotton batting, prewashing removes cottonseed oil, which could stain your finished quilt.

▶ If you prefer the highly textured look of an old quilt that has been laundered repeatedly, you may decide not to presoak cotton batting. If you *don't want* that "popcorn-like" surface, then be sure to presoak cotton batting following the manufacturer's directions.

- -

Q **If I need to wash the batting, how do I go about it? Won't it just fall apart?**

A Manufacturing methods used for batting are designed to hold the fibers together, but you do need to take care in the washing process. To wash the batting, first remove it from the package, open it out, and shake it lightly to remove wrinkles and folds. Then use one of the two following methods to wash it.

Method 1. If the package specifies presoaking in the washing machine with minimal agitation:

1. Fill the washing machine with warm water and immerse the batting; allow it to rest in the water at least 10 or as long as 30 minutes. Drain the water.
2. Allow it to spin for 10 to 15 seconds only and turn off the machine.
3. Dry on regular heat in the dryer. When you launder the quilt the first time, the batting will shrink more to produce the heirloom look you want. Laundering a test block with batting and backing is a good idea.

Method 2. If the package recommends presoaking without any agitation (which could compromise the characteristics of some cotton and cotton-blend and wool battings):
1. Place the batting in a large plastic laundry basket in the bathtub.
2. Add enough lukewarm water to the tub to cover the batting. Allow to soak for 10 minutes.
3. Empty the tub. With the batting still in the basket, use your hands to push out as much excess water as possible.
4. Lift the basket from the tub and remove the batting carefully to avoid stretching. Lay it flat to dry on a sheet (outside in the shade and covered with a second sheet). Dry for one hour and then flip the batting and dry for another hour or until completely dry.

Q How large should I cut the batting for my quilt?

A Cut the batting the same size as the backing — at least 2" to 4" extra inches beyond the quilt top on each edge. I prefer to cut the batting slightly smaller than the backing so that I can see and manage all three layers of the quilt sandwich.

Q Does batting have a grainline?

A No, but it may stretch more in one direction than the other. Test your batting to determine which direction has the least amount of stretch and use that as the "lengthwise grain" (the least amount of stretch along the length of the quilt). This is especially important for quilts that will hang on the wall and for bed quilts that will get a lot of use.

Q I removed my polyester batting from the bag and spread it out, but it's full of wrinkles. How do I remove them?

A Allow it to relax for several hours after spreading it out in a single layer on a flat surface. If large, deep wrinkles don't relax and you cannot smooth them out with your hands, toss the batting in the dryer with a damp towel and tumble on the low setting for 10 to 20 minutes to help further relax the wrinkles. Don't use an iron, which will flatten the batting.

Assembling the Quilt Layers

With the batting and backing prepared, you're ready to baste the quilt top, batting, and backing together to create the quilt sandwich so you can start quilting.

- -

Q **How do I hold the quilt layers together so they don't shift while I quilt?**

A The key to successful quilting without getting puckers in any of the layers is in the basting. For machine quilting, you may pin-baste, hand-baste, tack-baste, or use a spray-on temporary adhesive to hold the layers together. (*For spray-basting how-tos, see the question on page 283*). The directions that follow are for preparing for machine quilting. See page 286 for hand-basting a quilt sandwich (best for preparing for hand quilting on a frame or in a hoop).

Begin with the backing securely attached to the surface on which you are working. (*See page 278.*) Two large banquet tables pushed together are often large enough to accommodate a large quilt. (You might be able to schedule time at your church or school or community center to borrow their tables when you're ready to baste your large quilt. It also helps to enlist a quilting buddy to assist you.) If you don't have a table surface large enough, use the floor or the carpet — but vacuum first.

1. Press the finished quilt top and check for any stray threads on the back and on the front. Mark quilting patterns as desired (*see page 258*).

2. Make sure the backing corners are true and square (perfect 90-degree angles). Press the backing to remove any wrinkles.

3. Spread the wrinkle-free quilt backing face down on a large flat surface, preferably one that is at counter height (*see* Table It, *facing page*). Beginning on one end, use short lengths (2" to 3" long) of masking tape to secure the backing to the work surface. Do the same at the opposite end, pulling it taut and smooth but not so tight that you are stretching the fabric.

4. Using a long ruler and a large square ruler to keep the piece square and true, tape the remaining sides in place.

5. Smooth the batting in place on top of the backing, making sure there are no wrinkles. Use the edge of a yardstick to "sweep" across the batting from the center out when working on a large quilt to smooth out stubborn wrinkles. If the quilt is large, you may want to tape the batting edges down before adding the quilt top.

6. Center the quilt top on the batting and smooth out from the center. Use a long ruler and a large square ruler to make sure that the quilt is true and square along all sides and the corners as well as along the block and row seams. (Run your hand along the edges of the ruler you plan to use to make sure it is smooth and snag-free first.)

7. Pin-baste (*see next question*) or hand-baste (*see page 286*) the layers together for quilting.

TABLE IT!

Depending on the size of the quilt layers and the width of your tabletop, you may be able to clamp the quilt layers to a table using jumbo binder clips from an office-supply store instead of using masking tape to hold it in place.

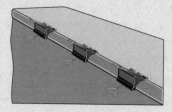

Q How do I pin-baste the quilt-sandwich layers together?

A Work from the center out and use safety pins — curved basting pins are easiest to use (*see page 85*) to pin through all three layers. You will need about 100 pins for small bed quilts and as many as 350 for a queen-size quilt. Place pins no less than a hand's width apart — about 4" — in a grid-like arrangement to ensure the layers are adequately secured. Keep pins away from the long horizontal and vertical seamlines if you plan to quilt in the ditch (*see page 313*) and out of any areas that you plan to echo-quilt (*see page 248*).

Do not close the pins until you have positioned all of them — then check the back of the quilt to make sure there are no undesirable pleats, tucks, or wrinkles. Adjust the pins in any area where you spot problems and then close all pins. If you have lots of pins to close on a large quilt, use the serrated end of a grapefruit spoon (or a Kwik Klip tool) to lift the pointed bar from the quilt surface and push it into the clasp to make it easier on your fingers. You will remove pins as you reach them during the quilting process. To protect the outer raw edges of the quilt, wrap and baste the outer edges of the backing to the front (*see illustration on page 286.*)

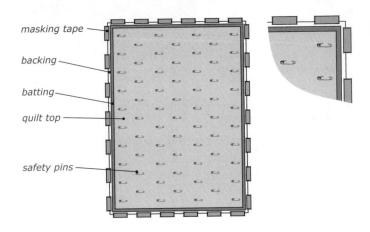

masking tape

backing

batting

quilt top

safety pins

OPENED — NOT CLOSED

As you remove safety pins during the quilting process, leave them open and store in a box — on a high shelf away from children and pets. Closing them when you put them away just prolongs the pin basting and the wear and tear on your fingers.

Q **Is there a way to hold quilt layers together besides safety pins?**

A You can hand-baste the layers (*see page 286*) but for small quilts and quilted projects, I prefer to use temporary spray adhesive (*see page 283*) to hold quilt layers together for machine quilting. The adhesive dissipates over time. If you are a purist or are creating a masterpiece quilt, you may not want to use the spray.

Another tool, a quilt-basting gun, shoots plastic tacks (like those that hold price tags on clothing) through the quilt layers after you have prepared them as described for pin basting. The tacks have a T-bar at each end. However, the plastic tacks and the gun needle that carries them through the quilt layers do make holes

quilt-basting gun

that are larger than a large needle. A shot of steam may be all that is required to remove the "holes" after you remove the tacks. Laundering the finished quilt also does the trick — if you prepared your quilt fabrics with washing in mind.

You can buy a special plastic grate to position under the quilt to keep the tacks from shooting into the carpet if you work on the floor or on a padded work surface. (Lighting grates are larger and work for this purpose too; look for them in the lighting department at your local homebuilding supply store. If the gun needle is longer than the grate holes are deep, place a piece of foam under the grate first to protect the work surface).

The plastic tacks are easy to quilt around and usually stay in the quilt unless they are in the way of the quilting pattern. To remove them, clip the tacks with a sharp craft scissors from the back of the quilt and discard the pieces. Quilters like the speed and ease of the quilting-gun tacking method. There's no chance of the presser foot getting caught in a safety pin and the tacks are very flexible and easy to move out of the way while quilting.

One precaution: Don't try to use the tacks in appliqués that have been fused in place. The fusible stabilizes the fabric, making it difficult for the gun needle and the tacks to penetrate without leaving a large hole that may not seal later.

For added control of the quilt layers to prevent the layers from shifting while you quilt, try inserting the gun needle down through the layers and back up through the backing, batting, and quilt top so both T-bars of the tacks are on the quilt surface. If the gun misfires and the tack doesn't penetrate the quilt layers, it's probably time to replace the gun needle.

- -

Q How do I use spray adhesive for basting my quilt layers together?

A Some quilters love basting spray; others won't touch it. It's my favorite way to baste quilt layers together for wall quilts and other small quilted projects because it's fast and easy. I'm not sure I would like it for large quilts because of the space it requires to avoid adhesive overspray on furniture, walls, or the like.

Temporary spray adhesive — specifically designed for quilting, machine embroidery, and other crafts — allows repositioning if necessary. It dissipates over time, but if you're concerned about any long- or short-term negative effects on your quilt, launder the project after it is finished to remove the adhesive immediately; of course this means you must have prewashed the quilt fabrics so that you can launder the quilt. Because of the temporary nature of the spray, it's wise to use it just before you are ready to quilt; it may not be the best way to baste large quilts for that reason.

Basting spray is available from several different manufacturers (OESD 505, Sullivan's, June Tailor, and Sulky). Each one has individual features, including scent and sticking power. Try them all and decide which you like best — or ask a quilting buddy for recommendations.

Note: If you are chemically sensitive, this may not be a product you want to use — check the contents. If you do use it, you may want to wear a face mask while you apply it.

1. Read the directions on the can before you begin. Work in a clean well-ventilated area and protect surfaces from

overspray — use large sheets that you can launder to mask off areas where you don't want overspray.

2. Prepare and press the quilt top and the quilt backing and prepare the batting (*see page 273*). Spread the quilt backing out on a large fat surface and smooth out any wrinkles. Use small pieces of masking tape to secure it to the surface to keep it smooth and taut, or use binder clips (*see page 279*) to hold it in place on a large table.

3. Apply a light mist of the adhesive to one long half of the backing wrong side. Don't overdo it; it doesn't require nearly as much spray as you might think.

4. Fold the batting in half lengthwise, position on the quilt back with the adhesive and then flip the other half onto the backing so you can you use your hands to smooth the batting in place in the adhesive. (Some quilters spray the batting, not the backing; try both to decide which works best for you.) Flip the remaining half of the batting back onto the first half and apply spray to the remaining backing. Flip the batting over and smooth in place.

5. Apply a light coat of spray to half of the batting and repeat the positioning process with the quilt top. Smooth out wrinkles and make sure the horizontal and vertical seamlines, outer corners, and edges are true and square.

Q Is it true that the adhesive from the spray gums up the sewing-machine needle?

A It can be true if you use too much or if you are doing lots of closely spaced quilting, such as stippling. If you get a sticky buildup and skipped stitches, clean the needle shaft with rubbing alcohol on a cottonball. Use less spray on your next quilt.

- -

Q If the adhesive is temporary, won't it come undone during the quilting process?

A If you didn't use enough spray it could, but in my experience, even a light mist holds the layers well during the machine-quilting process. If you know you won't quilt right away, you can still use spray adhesive to hold the layers together and then pin-baste or tack-baste with a quilting gun for permanency.

- -

Q Is there a way to remove the adhesive without washing the quilt?

A On small projects, using a steam iron to press the quilt front and back after quilting often dissipates the adhesive. It's important to use a light touch so you don't distort the texture of the finished quilting. Laundering a large quilt is easier than pressing to remove the adhesive.

Q **When is hand-basting the quilt sandwich preferred and how do I do it?**

A You will need to use this method if you plan to hand quilt in a hoop or on a frame. Some machine quilters also prefer this method to pinning, but it means taking care not to catch the toes of a presser foot in the basting stitches.

Follow the directions beginning on page 277 for layering the batting, backing, and quilt top. Then pin the outer edges of all three layers together at 6" intervals. Using a long doll-making needle or a curved upholstery needle and white cotton thread, hand-baste through all the layers in a grid of stitches that are no less than 3" apart. Make the stitches about 2" long. The closer the rows of stitches are spaced, the more control you have of the layers. For large quilts, add diagonal basting lines from the quilt center to the outer corners.

To protect the outer raw edges of the quilt while you quilt, fold the excess batting and backing onto the quilt top and use safety pins or hand basting to hold it in place.

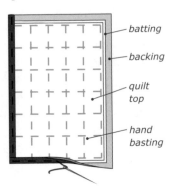

batting

backing

quilt top

hand basting

Solving Problems

Q There appears to be a layer of netting in my batting. What is it?

A This open-work fabric is called scrim and is added to batting to help support the fibers. It adds stability to the finished batting to control stretch. If the scrim is closer to one side of the batting rather than in the center of the fibers, put the scrim side closest to the backing when layering the quilt.

SEE ALSO: *All About Batting, pages 56–62.*

Q I always find small pleats of fabric caught in the quilting on the quilt back. How can I prevent this?

A First make sure that the backing is held smooth and taut on your basting surface. If it's not, you will pin or baste wrinkles into it. If your backing fabric is overly soft, it's easier for pleats to form. Starching the backing to make it firmer before you layer and baste the quilt sandwich can discourage unwanted pleats from forming. I've also discovered that using temporary spray adhesive to hold the layers together helps cut down on unwanted tucks and pleats.

Q How can I layer and pin-baste a large quilt without crawling on the floor?

A Push two folding 32" × 72" banquet tables together when you're ready to layer your quilt; put them away when not in use — or keep one up for a comfortable work surface if space permits. Raise them to waist height with tubes of black ABS plastic pipe, accurately cut to the correct length so that you can slip them onto the table legs with the leg crossbar resting on the pipe edges. Determine the desired height before having the hardware-store personnel cut the pieces for you. (If you don't have banquet tables, you may be able to use tables at your church or local recreation or senior center.) Another temporary alternative is to place a hollow-core door on two adjustable sawhorses to provide a large surface for basting quilt layers together. The door and sawhorses can be stored out of sight in the garage, shop, or closet when not in use.

CHAPTER 11

Quilting the Quilt

After you've planned the quilting and marked the quilt top as discussed in chapter 9 and made the quilt sandwich as directed in chapter 10, you're ready to quilt. Now you need to decide whether you will hand- or machine-quilt the design. Hand quilting is the choice of traditional quilters, who prefer it to machine quilting. It offers portability and flexibility not possible with machine quilting. Machine quilting is faster than hand quilting, but offers its own challenges, particularly when working on a large, bed-size quilt.

Hand Quilting

Choose hand quilting if you prefer traditional methods and have the time to do handwork. Intricate designs and those with lots of tight curves may be easier to quilt by hand as you have more flexibility in positioning and maneuvering the quilt while you work. At the machine you are confined to the space under the needle and the inflexibility of the machine needle itself.

Choose machine quilting if you want to finish your quilt quickly and especially if you plan to use your quilt and launder it regularly. You might think that a hand-pieced quilt deserves hand quilting, but that doesn't mean you can't machine-quilt it — and vice versa. The choice is yours.

Q Do I need special tools for hand quilting?

A Besides needle, thimble, and thread, the only other tool you will need is a frame or hoop to hold the layers while you stitch. Or, you can lap-quilt (*see page 300*) without a hoop at all. Large quilts are often mounted on a floor frame, which requires dedicated space in your home, with the quilt remaining attached until you have completed the quilting. Due to space limitations, many hand quilters opt for a round or oval hoop on a floor stand or an even smaller hand-held lap hoop. Some of these are mounted on stands to make holding the quilt in your lap easier. Using a smaller hoop makes your work more portable — a distinct advantage for hand quilting. A hoop isolates the area you are quilting, but it must be removed and repositioned as you fill the area with stitching. If you use a frame, rehooping is not an issue.

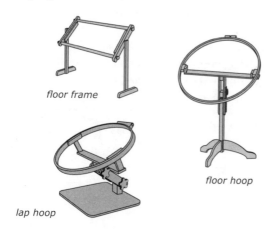

floor frame

floor hoop

lap hoop

Q How do I attach the quilt layers to a floor frame for hand quilting?

A Some hand quilters make the quilt sandwich and hand-baste layers together (*see page 286*) before attaching them to the quilting frame. Others attach the backing first, followed by the batting, and then the quilt top. How you prepare and attach the layers may depend entirely on the type of frame you have. Follow the manufacturer's directions for best results.

Q What should I look for in a wooden floor-stand or lap hoop?

A Your hoop should be made of sturdy wood and be at least 1" deep. It may be circular, oval, or a half-oval. A 10-inch-diameter hoop is handy for small projects. Choose a 14"-diamater hoop for larger quilts. Half-circle and oval hoops are a good choice for quilting borders. Inexpensive square and rectangular quilting hoops of PVC pipe are also available. Like many other quilting tools, you may find you need several hoop styles to meet your needs.

half-circle hoop
(wooden)

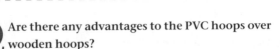

rectangular hoop
(PVC pipe)

Q Are there any advantages to the PVC hoops over wooden hoops?

A Each one has its advantages. PVC hoops are easy to assemble and lightweight. They are available in several sizes as well as on floor stands. You may like using a square one when quilting within blocks, and a rectangular style for working in border areas. They can be disassembled for convenient storage. Long, flexible clips (not shown in illustration) wrap over the quilt and the bars of these hoops to hold the quilt in place.

Q Is it essential to use a hoop or frame for hand quilting?

A Some quilters prefer to "lap quilt" without a frame and develop a beautiful hand-quilting stitch with this method. (*See page 300.*) Others find it necessary to use a floor frame for large quilts and wooden or PVC frames for smaller quilts. A hoop holds your work smooth and taut while you stitch. The smaller the hoop you choose, the more often you will need to reposition it to complete the quilting. Working with a hoop supports your work and helps to achieve more even stitches.

- -

Q What needle should I use for hand quilting?

A The traditional advice is to use a very short, thin needle (a size 12 Between) to achieve short, even, hand-quilting stitches — the shorter the needle, the shorter the stitches will be. However, it may be easier to begin with a longer Between needle, a size 7 or 8, and graduate to shorter and shorter needles as you gain experience. (Some experienced quilters actually prefer long, fine milliner's needles instead of the short Betweens.) Experiment with other needle types and sizes to find the one that works best for you. Remember that as the number-size gets larger on hand-sewing needles, the needle gets thinner and shorter. That also means the needle eye is finer and may be more difficult to thread. I keep a supply of quality needle threaders on hand to save my eyes and my sanity!

Q What's the best thread for hand quilting?

A Thread manufacturers offer special hand-quilting cotton thread, which is heavier and stronger than all-purpose or cotton sewing thread and is waxed for added sewing ease. Cut the thread no longer than 18" — about the length from your fingertips to your elbow crease — to avoid undue wear on the thread. If you don't have hand-quilting thread, run the thread through a cake of beeswax (available in a slotted plastic container at your fabric store) or through white paraffin. Place the waxed thread between two layers of paper towel and press with a warm iron to melt the wax into the thread. This strengthens it and helps prevent kinks and knots.

- -

Q I've waxed my quilting thread but knots still form in my thread. Is there anything else I can do?

A It's essential to pay attention to which cut end of the thread you insert into the needle. Hand-quilting is done with a single thread; don't double it and knot the ends together.

1. To prevent thread twisting and knotting, cut an 18" length from the spool, making the cut at an angle to make it easier to thread.

2. Insert the fresh-cut end into the needle.

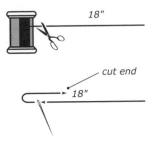

18"

cut end

18"

3. Draw the thread through the needle and make a quilter's knot at that end. (*See next question.*)

knot this end

Q How do I make a quilter's knot?

A After threading the needle and drawing it though, place the cut end that went through the eye perpendicular to the needle and extending about ½" above it. Make three thread wraps around the needle and use your fingernail to hold them firmly as you slide the wraps down the length of the needle, over the eye, and down the length of the thread, ending the "slide" within ½" of the end. The result is a small secure knot, easy enough to hide in the quilt layers.

place needle across thread end

make 3 wraps and then slide wraps down needle to end of thread

---

Q What is the basic hand-quilting stitch?

A For quilting in a hoop, it's simply a short running stitch through all three layers of the quilt. It takes practice to learn how to rock the needle through the layers to produce short stitches of consistent length on the front and back of the quilt. Although you begin and end with a quilter's knot, the knots won't show on either side of the quilt once you know how to "pop" the knot between the layers. First hoop the area of the quilt where you want to start quilting. Always begin in the center of the quilt and work outward, rehooping as needed.

1. Thread a short needle (size 7 to 12 Between) with an 18" length of hand-quilting thread and make a quilter's knot (*see previous question*). Place a thimble on the middle finger of your sewing hand to protect it and guide the needle into and through the layers as you stitch.

2. Hoop the quilt top, making sure the layers are smooth and taut. Insert the needle in the quilt top only ½" from where you actually want to start stitching and then up through the top at the starting point along the quilting pattern. Before continuing with the stitching, "pop" the

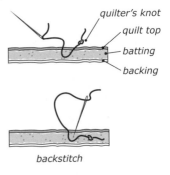

quilter's knot
quilt top
batting
backing

backstitch

knot between the layers by tugging gently on the thread so that the knot separates the fabric threads and slides in between the layers, becoming entangled in the batting.

3. If a tail of the thread lies on the quilt-top surface, clip it close to the quilt top, or use the point of the needle to open the hole in the fabric so you can use the needle tip

to work the thread tail inside the quilt
layers. Take one short backstitch and
bring the needle up at the point where
you wish to start quilting.

start quilting

4. With your sewing hand relaxed in a backward C shape and
   the needle perpendicular to the quilt top, pierce the quilt
   layers with the needle and stop pushing when you feel the
   tip of the needle with a finger on your
   other hand next to the quilt backing. Use
   a rocking motion with your needle and
   thimble to bring the tip to the quilt-top
   surface and fill the needle with several
   stitches (about ¼ of the needle's length).
   Use the thimble to push the needle
   through the quilt layers to remove the
   stitches from the needle.

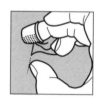

*rock needle through
quilt layers to fill
with short running
stitches*

5. Continue making short running stitches in this fashion
   as you follow the quilting design line. Work to develop a
   smooth rocking rhythm to your stitching. The stitching
   motion brings the needle parallel with the quilt top (rock
   down) and then almost perpendicular (rock up) as each
   stitch is loaded on the needle.

6. When you reach the end of the thread or the end of the
   quilting, pull the thread taut. Wrap the thread around
   the needle point two or three times, and then insert the
   needle into the quilt top and pop the knot inside. Slide the
   needle along through the layers for an inch or so before
   bringing it out on the quilt backing. Trim the thread tails.

Note: To mark patches for outline quilting (*see page 247*), place ¼"-wide masking tape next to the seamlines inside the patch. Stitch along the tape's inner edge and remove. Tape only the hooped area and don't leave masking tape on the quilt for long periods to avoid leaving residue.

Q Can I move from one area of the hooped quilt to another without ending and starting again?

A When you finish a line of stitches, if the next area is an inch or so away, slip the needle into the quilt top and batting (but not the backing), move it through the layers, and draw it out at the location where you want to start stitching.

Q Any tips for hooping the quilt to get ready for stitching?

A First, make sure the quilt layers are basted together without puckers or pleats on either side (*see page 279*). For the most control, space hand-basting stitches closer rather than farther apart. Choose a hoop size appropriate for the size of your quilt — but no larger than the length of your forearm (16" to 18"). You should be able to reach the center of the hoop. Hoops on floor stands may be slightly larger (22" diameter) since you can tilt the hoop to reach the center.

1. Place the inner ring of the hoop on a flat surface and spread the area you want to quilt on top.

2. Place the outer hoop on top, feeling for the edge of the inner hoop. Slip the hoop in place and tighten the hoop nut so that quilt is held loosely, just tight enough that it can't slip out of place.

3. Carefully turn the hooped quilt over and make sure there are no wrinkles in the backing.

4. Tighten the hoop nut so that the quilt is held taut but not so tight that it's difficult to make the running stitches. You will need to experiment to determine how taut you like it.

Note: When using PVC hoops, there is no nut to tighten. Clips secure the quilt around the "tube rails" of the hoop.

Q How is the quilting stitch made when quilting on a frame?

A Because the expanse of the quilt is held in the frame, it's difficult to rock the needle through the layers as for basic hand quilting. Instead, begin and end the stitching by popping the knot (*see page 296*) and then change to the stab stitch: Push the needle down through the quilt, catch it with your other hand, and push it straight up through the top. Continue in this fashion along the lines. Frame quilting takes longer than hoop quilting because each stitch is individually formed.

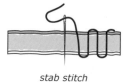

stab stitch

Q How does lap quilting differ from hoop or frame quilting?

A There is no apparatus to hold the layers taut. That means you can use your underneath hand to grasp the quilt in the area where you will be stitching to help slide the fabric onto the needle as you take the short running stitches. As you work the needle through the quilt to form the stitches, allow the needle to slant back toward the thread rather than keeping it perpendicular to the quilt top. You can use your thumb on the top of the quilt and the other four fingers underneath in the outer areas of the quilt but in the center areas you may need to place your thumb underneath, too.

Q What are the hallmarks of fine hand quilting?

A Unless you are going for a primitive, rustic look with large stitches of uneven lengths, hand quilting exhibits the following characteristics, whether you do lap quilting or quilt in a hoop or a frame:

▶ Stitches are an even and consistent length and tension.
▶ Stitches are the same length on the front and back of the quilt.
▶ There are no puckers in the fabric layers.
▶ Stitches are small — 10 to 12 per inch. (Large stitches can catch and break during use).
▶ All stitches go through all three layers.
▶ There are no visible knots on either side of the quilt.

Solving Problems

Q I can't make tiny hand stitches. Are slightly longer stitches okay?

A Yes, if you are beginner, aim for stitch-length consistency first while you learn to maneuver the needle through the layers. As you gain more hand-quilting experience, shorter stitches will come more naturally. Using a fine, short needle makes it easier to take small stitches, but it takes practice to use one. Your needle will develop a bit of a curve as you use it, and it will eventually break. It's essential to keep a good supply of quilting needles on hand.

- -

Q I have difficulty pulling the needle through the quilt layers. Any tips?

A Purchase a package of finger cots (like the tips of rubber gloves) at your drugstore or an art shop and wear them on your fingertips to add the necessary traction for pulling needles through stubborn layers. Packages of small circles called "needle grippers" are also available at quilt and fabric shops.

Note: Finger cots are typically made of latex. If you have a latex allergy, try a pair of cotton gardening gloves with rubberized fingertips.

finger cots

- -

Q How do I avoid breaking my needle?

A Whenever you encounter a thick area — for instance, at a seam intersection — use a stab stitch (*see page 299*) instead of trying to fill the needle with running stitches.

- -

Q I have trouble threading those tiny hand-quilting needles. Any suggestions?

A Invest in fine wire needle threaders. When you need to thread one needle, thread several at a time. You can slip the wire through 3 or 4 needles and pull the thread through all of them at once. Leave all but the one you need to use threaded on the spool after cutting off a length of thread. Knot the cut end of the thread on the spool to keep the threaded needles attached until you need the next one. Then snip the knot, remove the next needle with enough thread and knot the end you just snipped. Knot the thread on the spool.

- -

Q How do I keep my thimble on while hand quilting? It often slips off.

A First, make sure you are wearing the correct size — not so tight that it cuts off circulation and not so loose that it can slip off easily. Even when a metal thimble fits correctly, you can lose it occasionally. To prevent slippage, wear a finger cot (see previous page) or cut the fingertips from lightweight surgical gloves to wear underneath your thimble. You may also find it easier to maneuver the needle by wearing finger cots or glove tips on your other fingers.

- -

Q The borders aren't wide enough to fit in my hoop. What do I do?

A If you turned the backing over the batting and quilt front and basted it (*see page 286*), release the stitches to see if there is enough to hoop. If not, simply lap long strips of muslin or scrap fabric over the raw edges of the quilt and hand- or machine-baste in place. This will give you the extra fabric you need to fit into the hoop. Remove it after the quilting is completed.

- -

Q My fingers are really sore from hand quilting. Can you recommend something to soothe them?

A Some quilters swear by Preparation H as an overnight healer. Others suggest a lip balm such as Carmex to treat small cuts and pinpricks. Another way to ward off skin damage before you begin to hand-quilt is to apply several layers of New-Skin Liquid Bandage or a similar product to the fingers of the hand under your work — your "nonsewing" hand. Some quilters wear thimbles on both hands as protection — something that will take practice to get used to. Others recommend wearing a guitar thumb-pick on the guide finger that's on the underside of the quilt to protect it from constant pricking.

- -

Q I pricked myself while quilting and bled on my quilt. How do I get it out?

A If it's still wet, use a bit of your own saliva to dissolve it and dab it with a little cold water. Or, dip a cotton ball or Q-tip in hydrogen peroxide and dab it on the stain, then follow with a little cold water. If any blood is left and you plan to wash the quilt, treat it with a stain remover before you wash it.

Machine-Quilting Basics

Choose from two basic ways to maneuver the quilt at the machine. **Machine-guided quilting** requires a special presser foot (*see next page*) with the feed dogs up (engaged). **Free-motion quilting** requires disengaging the feed dogs and using a spring-loaded darning or embroidery foot. It's essential to make sure your machine is in excellent working order before you begin quilting.

It is easier to quilt more complex designs with free-motion stitching, but this method does require some practice to gain proficiency. With either method, manipulating a large quilt under the arm of the sewing machine can be challenging.

More and more quilters are purchasing new long-arm and mid-arm machines that have more space for easier maneuvering of the quilt layers. Others are choosing to have the quilting done by quilters who specialize in long-arm quilting.

Q Are there any special tools required for machine quilting?

A Insert a new Sharp sewing machine needle when you begin quilting. For large quilts or those with extensive quilting, you will need to change it often to maintain consistent stitch quality and prevent skipped stitches.

Most quilters use specialized presser feet (*pictured on page 73*) to make machine-guided quilting easier. These and other useful tools include:

▶ A ¼" patchwork foot allows you to easily space quilting lines ¼" from seamlines for outline quilting (*see page 247*) and to do echo quilting (*see page 248*).

▶ A walking foot is good for smooth quilting on thick layers.

▶ An open-toe appliqué foot helps you follow lines easily.

▶ A spring-loaded darning or machine-embroidery foot (open- or closed-toe) is good for free-motion machine quilting.

▶ An adjustable quilting guide (*see page 307*) for the presser foot is helpful for maintaining even spacing for cross-hatching (*see page 247*) without the necessity of marking the quilt top.

▶ Narrow masking tape is handy for marking straight quilting lines on a quilt top, using the edge of a carefully positioned rotary ruler as your placement guide. Stitching along both edges of narrow masking tape is one way to create closely spaced parallel rows of quilting (*see page 261*).

▶ A twin needle (two needles attached to a single shank) makes quick work of doubling stitch patterns — particularly effective with channel and grid quilting. However, the stitching on the quilt backing is a single row of bobbin stitches forming a zigzag between the two needle threads.

In addition to special presser feet, some quilters prefer to replace the zigzag throat plate with a straight-stitch throat plate (*see page 322*). This helps prevent the needle from pushing the quilt (often called flagging) into the throat plate, which causes puckering and stitch jamming. They also use this plate for patchwork piecing seams for easier stitching (*see page 124–5*).

SEE ALSO: *Needles and Presser Feet, pages 71–72 and Marking the Quilting Design, pages 258–62.*

Q What is a walking foot?

A This special sewing-machine presser foot (*see page 73*) is designed to grip and feed the top layer of fabric just as the feed dogs grip and feed the bottom layer while you stitch. A clip on the side of the foot fits over the presser bar to make the foot "walk" in concert with the feed dogs, rather than sliding over the fabric surface. It keeps the foot from pushing the top fabric layer forward, preventing uneven stitching and puckering. It's usually necessary to purchase this as an extra accessory for your machine. Some machines have a built-in even-feed mechanism, making a walking foot unnecessary. Check with your dealer. The walking foot is especially useful for machine-guided quilting in straight lines — quilting in the ditch and outline, channel, and grid quilting.

- -

Q How do I use a quilting guide?

A A quilting guide is used to make parallel lines of stitching on your quilt. Here are a few pointers on how to use one:

▶ Mark the first row of quilting on the quilt top, and layer and baste the quilt sandwich. Stitch along the marked line.

▶ On close examination, several basic and specialty presser feet have a hole in back with a screw. Loosen the screw on the back and slip the bar on the quilting guide through the hole. Adjust the guide the desired distance from the needle and tighten the screw.

▶ Tuck the sandwich under the presser foot, loosening the screw and adjusting the guide as needed to fit the quilt under the foot.

▶ Lower the "toe" on the quilting guide so it just grazes the quilt surface along the first line of stitching. Tighten the screw to hold this position.

▶ Lower the foot and stitch slowly to keep stitching lines straight. Continue in this fashion to complete all rows.

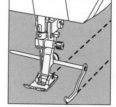

quilting guide

307

Q What type of needle should I use for machine quilting?

A Sharp needle is essential; use a size 75/11 or 80/12 for quilts with thin batting and a 90/14 for thicker, heavier batting. If you are using specialty threads such as rayon or metallic embroidery thread, choose a needle designed specifically for the thread type.

SEE ALSO: *Needles and Presser Feet, pages 71–72.*

Q What thread should I use for machine quilting?

A It depends on the desired finished appearance and your skill level. Beginners often use monofilament nylon or polyester thread in the needle and the bobbin because the stitching hardly shows. Some quilters choose it because it blends into all of the colors; use clear for most colors, smoke for dark ones. You can also use matching or contrasting thread — but the stitching will be obvious and so will any mistakes.

Many quilters prefer to use cotton machine-quilting thread in colors to match or blend with the fabrics in the quilt top. The bobbin thread usually matches the backing fabric; cotton quilting thread is the best choice, but make sure it is designated for machine quilting, not hand quilting. Hand-quilting thread has a waxed coating that can clog the tension discs and adversely affect the machine stitch quality.

SEE ALSO: *Thread Selection, pages 64–68.*

Q My machine has a stitch that simulates hand quilting. Do I need special thread for this stitch?

A Use regular quilting thread in the bobbin to match the
backing and put smoke-colored monofilament thread
in the needle. This color doesn't catch the light and is more
"invisible" than reflective clear monofilament thread.

Machine-Guided Quilting

Machine-guided quilting with feed dogs up (engaged) is best
and easiest for straight lines and gentle curves — and is probably the best choice for beginners.

Q How do I set up the sewing machine for machine-
guided quilting?

A For straight-line designs, sew with a presser foot of your
choice and the feed dogs engaged.

▶ Attach the walking foot or engage the even-feed feature on
your machine. Or, attach an open-toe presser foot so you
can easily see the seamlines. For outline stitching ¼" from
a seamline, attach the ¼" presser foot.

▶ If possible on your machine, set the needle to stop in the
needle-down position when you stop to pivot or adjust the
quilt, so it won't slip out of place. Otherwise hand-lower
the needle into the quilt before pivoting.

▶ Adjust the machine for 6 to 10 stitches per inch.

▶ Thread the machine with the desired thread in the needle and the bobbin. Many quilters prefer clear monofilament thread in the needle, with machine-quilting thread in the bobbin to match or contrast with the quilt backing.

▶ Make sure the tension is correctly adjusted for beautiful stitching on both sides of the quilt.

- -

Q **Adjust the tension — how do I do that? I'm afraid to play with the machine tension settings.**

A The easiest way is to do a test. Here's how:

1. Set up the machine as described in the previous question using the threads you plan to use.

2. Make a 6"-square sample quilt sandwich with your batting choice between two scraps of quilter's cotton. Stitch the layers together and remove them from the machine.

3. Examine the top stitching and the bobbin stitching. If the bobbin thread is pulled to the top or the top thread is pulled to backing, rethread both the needle and the bobbin to make sure they are correctly threaded.

4. Stitch another test row and check both sides (*see* Adjusting Tension *on the facing page*). Adjust as needed.

5. If you haven't had your machine serviced and tension problems persist, clean and oil the machine, and test again. If that doesn't help, it's time for a machine tune-up at your dealer.

ADJUSTING TENSION

Once you've done a tension test as described in the previous question, look for one of these results:

A Balanced stitches look smooth and even on both sides. The two threads interlock and are buried within the quilt layers, not showing on either surface. If your stitches look like this, you're all set.

B If the bobbin thread is pulled up to the quilt surface and freckles of bobbin thread show, the top tension is probably too tight. Loosen it in small increments and test-stitch to determine the correct adjustment.

C If the bobbin threads lie on the backing surface with little freckles of the top thread showing, tighten the top tension in small increments until it pulls the bobbin thread into the center of the quilt layers. Test-stitch until the stitching is perfect on both sides.

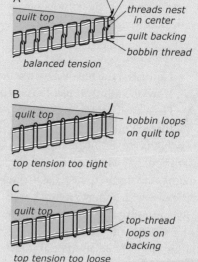

A   *needle thread*   *batting*
threads nest in center
quilt top
quilt backing
bobbin thread
balanced tension

B
quilt top
bobbin loops on quilt top
top tension too tight

C
quilt top
top-thread loops on backing
top tension too loose

Q If I see how the tension is not right, is it better to adjust the bobbin or the top tension?

A You may be able to adjust the bobbin tension on some machines, but it's always a good idea to try to adjust the top tension first. If you're not satisfied, check your machine manual for bobbin-tension adjustments. Adjusting the bobbin tension by tightening the tension screw on the bobbin case draws the top thread further down into the layers.

I have an extra bobbin case (marked with nail polish) that I use for quilting so I'm not afraid to play with the tension settings. Different batting, thread, and fabric combinations often require fine-tuning the tension. I make notes in my quilting notebook (*see page 26*).

- -

Q I adjusted the tension on my bobbin case for quilting. How do I adjust it back to a "normal" setting?

A Place a full bobbin in the case and suspend it by the thread tail over your other hand. Jiggle the thread. The bobbin case should gently drop toward your hand in small increments. If it drops fast, tighten the tension screw on the case with a small screwdriver in increments until it's correct. Finally, test the tension by stitching on two layers of quilting fabric. Make additional adjustments if necessary.

- -

Q How do I quilt in the ditch?

A If you plan to quilt in the ditch of the seams in patch-work blocks and along borders and setting pieces, take the time to determine the best stitching path to follow to minimize the number of times you must stop and start within a block. Aim for a continuous line if at all possible to avoid lots of threads to clip and hide in the quilt.

Use your finger to trace along the seamlines to determine a path to follow that will take you back to the starting point without stopping, or with only one or two stops. When you have identified the path with the fewest stops, place a piece of tracing paper over a drawing of the block and mark the stitching path with colored pencil lines and stitching-direction arrows. Then stitch in the ditch of the block seams following your predetermined pattern. (*See* The Set Up *on page 315.*)

1. Place the quilt under the needle at the place where you want to start, and lower the presser foot. Use the hand wheel to lower the needle to catch the bobbin thread. Draw the bobbin thread to the quilt-top surface.

2. Begin stitching, holding onto the top and bobbin thread tails to prevent tangles. To lock the stitches at the beginning and end of a stitching path, change to a very short stitch length and stitch for ⅛", then return to the stitch length you've chosen for quilting (usually 6 to 10 inches).

3. Stitch in the ditch (valley) of the seam, not through the pressed seam allowances, jogging slightly if necessary when the pressed direction of the seam changes at seam

313

intersections. Use your hands to spread the fabric along the seamlines to make it easier to stitch in the valley. Don't let the needle bite into the area where the seam allowances lie because the errant stitches will show and flatten the texture of the quilt where they jump the seamline. When quilting in the ditch in

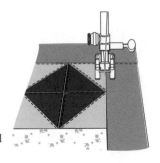

quilting in the ditch

patchwork blocks, stop with the needle in the quilt before raising the presser foot to pivot at points and corners.

Q **How do I hide thread tails where I start and stop quilting?**

A If you start and stop with tiny stitches as directed in the previous question, you can simply clip the thread tails close to the surface. However, I usually draw the thread tails to the back of the quilt, thread them with their bobbin thread tails onto a needle and work them into the quilt layers — just to be safe. If you don't start and end with tiny stitches, you must draw the tails to the back and work them into the quilt layers in this manner. I always pair up the top and bobbin threads at each location, then make an overhand knot in them as close to the backing surface as possible, and then thread them into a needle and work them into the layers, popping the knot (*see page 296*) to hide it.

THE SET-UP

Before you begin to machine-quilt inside the blocks and borders, it's a good idea to set the layers of the quilt sandwich by stitching in the ditch of all major vertical and horizontal seams. This stitching outlines the individual blocks, borders, and sashing, to anchor the layers for further quilting. Once the set-up stitching is done, you may be able to remove most if not all of the pins or basting-gun tacks you used to baste the quilt layers together.

These "setting stitches" also offer the opportunity to make sure there are no unwanted wrinkles or tucks caught in the backing before proceeding. Begin the setting stitches along the center vertical seam, working out to one side, before reversing the placement of the quilt at the machine to stitch from the center to the remaining outer edge. Repeat for the horizontal lines.

Note: If you don't want this stitching to be a permanent part of the quilted pattern and you plan to wash the quilt, use water-soluble basting thread in the needle and bobbin for this step so that you can remove it after completing all of the other more decorative quilting.

Q Can I do machine-guided stitching on motifs with straight or curved lines?

A Yes, but it is easier to do stitching motifs with a presser foot and the feed dogs engaged on small to lap-sized quilts. Use the walking foot for straight lines and switch to a

¼" foot or an open-toe foot so you can see the marked lines to follow. For large quilts, it's worth learning how to free-motion quilt to make it easier to quilt along the marks without constantly adjusting the quilt as you stitch along the markings.

Straight, geometric designs. Stop to pivot the quilt at corners and points of the design. Stop with the needle in the corner before raising the presser foot to adjust the quilt.

Curved designs. Use an open-toe presser foot and a slightly shorter stitch than you normally would for machine quilting. Stop often with the needle down so you can raise the foot and adjust the motif position under the needle and foot for smooth stitching. As you gain experience, you will discover that you can use your hands to gently manipulate curves under the foot without having to stop and raise it frequently. Practice, practice, practice.

Positioning your hands on each side of the presser foot like a hoop and using them to exert a little pressure on the quilt sandwich (*see illustration on page 323*) helps keep the layers from shifting while you stitch. Use your fingers to help coax or ease any excess fabric under the presser foot. If you are using a walking foot or even-feed setting, puckering on the top should be minimal as long as you have basted the layers together.

- -

Q How do I handle the bulk of my large quilt at the sewing machine?

A The most typical way to handle the bulk of quilts that are larger than 36" square is to roll the quilt from two

opposite edges toward the quilt center and
secure the "rolls" with bicycle or quilt clips
or large safety pins. Leave about 12" of the
quilt unrolled at the center where you will
start the stitching. The clips or pins allow
you to stitch from the center out, unrolling
the quilt gradually as you work toward the
outer edges. Unpin and re-pin as needed.

*roll sides toward
center for machine
quilting*

For a very large quilt or one with
thicker batting, try accordion-pleating the quilt sandwich
along both long edges (instead of rolling). You may not need
to secure the folds, but if you do, try spring-loaded bull-nose
binder clips or clothespins that you can release and replace easily as you work from the center toward the outer edges of the
quilt.

For extra-long quilts, place the rolled quilt in your lap and
over your shoulder to hold it as you begin to stitch.

▶ Until you are ready to quilt the borders, you can fold the
excess backing and batting over the edge of the quilt and
pin or baste it in place (*see page 286*). That will give you less
width and length to manage and it also keeps the fuzzy
edge of the batting from becoming a magnet for dust, lint,
and stray threads.

▶ Another way to handle the bulk of a large quilt is to cut
the batting to the correct size for your quilt as directed on
page 276, and then carefully cut it into three long pieces
of equal width. Center one piece on the wrong side of the
prepared backing and smooth the quilt top in place on top

317

of it. Pin or hand-baste the layers together in the center section only (*see* Assembling the Quilt Layers *on page 277*) and quilt that section only. Since there is no batting in the outer thirds of the quilt, it's easier to fold or roll and handle it at the machine. End all quilting about 2" from the long edges of the batting in the center section so you can fold the top back and splice the next strip to the center strip (*see page 63*). Baste the layers and quilt, connecting with the previous quilting lines as required. Repeat to add the remaining strip of batting on the other edge of the center panel and finish the quilting.

▶ If you are doing straight-stitch quilting in a grid of straight lines, it's easier to work in one quadrant at a time because you can keep the other three sections of the quilt to the left and behind the needle while you work on the quadrant. To quadrant-quilt, first set the layers together by stitching in the ditch along all of the long vertical and horizontal seams (*see* The Set-Up *on page 315*). Then refold or roll the quilt so you can work comfortably in one quadrant of the quilt with the rest of the quilt behind and to the left of the machine — or in your lap. *Note:* If you don't want the setting stitches to stay in the quilt, stitch with water-soluble thread in the needle and bobbin thread on the bobbin. The stitching will dissolve when you launder the quilt (allowing you to pull the bobbin threads free).

Q When I use my walking foot, it often hangs up at seam intersections and the stitches are smaller where several layers of fabric come together. Isn't a walking foot supposed to prevent this problem?

A It's not unusual for this to happen, particularly where several seam allowances intersect. If this is a consistent problem, get into the habit of stopping the machine with the needle down and lifting the presser foot so the layers will relax under the foot. When you drop the presser foot, you should be able to continue stitching with ease over the thicker area. This works with other types of presser feet, too.

- -

Q I found several tucks caught in the stitches on the back of my quilt. How can I avoid this problem?

A Tucks happen! Sometimes they happen because the backing layer wasn't smooth and taut before the batting and quilt top were added. They are more likely to happen when working on a large quilt and when doing machine-guided quilting. All the tugging and moving to manage the quilt under the machine needle can disturb even the most carefully basted quilt layers.

If the quilt will be used and loved and laundered and the tucks in the backing are not large, don't worry about them — who will see them anyway? If tucks annoy you, undo the quilting stitching for a few inches above and below the tuck. Use a hand-sewing needle to draw the thread tails (top and bottom) into the quilt layers. Use hand basting to secure the layers in the unstitched area, easing the excess fabric in with the basting. After basting, restitch from the right side, filling in the unstitched area. Overlap the existing stitches at each end of the line as you begin and end the quilting. Draw the top thread to the underside and thread the top and bobbin threads in a needle; bury the threads in the quilt layers. Remove the basting if it is visible.

Free-Motion Machine Quilting

Learning to free-motion quilt opens up a world of stitching options not possible when you use a presser foot for machine-guided quilting. With a little practice and the mind-set that practice makes perfect and you can live with your "mistakes," you can learn to do beautiful free-motion quilting.

Q What is free-motion quilting?

A In this method, the feed dogs are dropped, disengaged, or covered, and a special presser foot (spring-loaded darning, or free-motion quilting or embroidery foot) is used (*see page 73*). The foot is spring-loaded so that it moves up and down with the needle while you stitch. Since the machine is incapable of moving the quilt without the feed dogs and the usual presser foot, you must move the fabric under the needle to follow the desired quilting pattern. You control the stitching speed and direction as well as the stitch length.

You can move the fabric forward and back or from side to side to follow the direction of the quilting pattern, expanding the range of possible designs you can stitch with ease on the machine. Free-motion quilting can be used to follow a marked pattern on the quilt top, or to create freehand motifs of your own design without marking. Stipple quilting and meandering are two popular types of free-motion quilting.

- -

Q **How do I do free-motion quilting?**

A To begin, mark the quilting pattern you wish to follow on the quilt top (although for stipple and meander quilting, no pattern is needed). Make the quilt sandwich (*see page 277*) and proceed as follows.

Note: The speed you move the fabric controls the stitch length.

1. Thread the machine needle and bobbin with your choice of thread types and colors. Use a bobbin thread in the bobbin (*see page 175*). The thicker the thread, the smaller the number: 30-weight thread is thicker than 60-weight thread. Test the stitch on sample quilt layers and adjust the tensions as needed (*see page 310*).

2. Drop the feed dogs (or disengage — see your machine manual), attach a darning or free-motion presser foot, and insert a new 75/11 or 80/12 needle. If you don't have a darning or free-motion foot, use an open-toe presser foot so you can see where you're stitching.

3. Raise the needle and presser foot. Although you will control the stitch length as you move the fabric under the needle, it's best to set the stitch length to 0. If possible, change the needle plate from a zigzag plate to a straight-stitch needle plate.

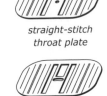

straight-stitch throat plate

zigzag-stitch throat plate

4. Adjust your sewing chair so that your arms can rest on your sewing table to avoid arm and shoulder strain. You should be looking down at your stitching, not up or level with it. Provide room to the left and behind the quilt to hold the quilt — don't let it drag over the edge of the sewing surface.

5. Place the area of the quilt you wish to stitch under the presser foot and needle. Plan ahead so that as you stitch in an area, you can work your way out of the "corner" that is closest to you so that you don't box yourself in.

6. *Drop the lever on the presser foot to engage the stitching mechanism.* Use the hand wheel to lower the needle and raise it to draw the bobbin thread to the surface. Hold the two threads away from the needle and take several stitches in place to anchor the stitches. Trim the thread tails close to the quilt surface.

7. Place your hands about 2" from each side of the presser foot to act like a hoop as you guide the quilt and settle your foot on the foot pedal. Try to maintain a consistent, medium speed — move the quilt at the same speed that the needle is stitching (controlled with the foot pedal). Jerky motions and uneven speed result in stitches of uneven length. Don't rotate the quilt, but instead use directional movements to stitch in the desired direction. To avoid lumps and knots, don't allow the needle to stitch over and over in the same place.

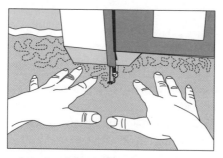

shape hands around foot to act as a hoop

Note: Some top-of-the-line sewing machines have a special foot or mechanism with an electronic eye that "reads" the speed at which you move the needle when free-motion stitching. This means that when you slow down or speed up, the machine automatically adjusts so that your stitch length remains consistent — the hallmark of perfected free-motion stitching. If you have trouble mastering free-motion stitching on your own, investing in a machine with this feature may be a good idea.

8. To end the stitching, take five or six stitches in place, pull gently on the needle thread to bring up the bobbin thread, and clip both threads close to the surface.

SAFETY CAUTION

When free-motion quilting, take care to keep your fingers out of the way of the needle. A spring-loaded darning foot has a closed toe if you prefer more finger safety than provided by an open-toe darning or quilting foot.

Q Why use a straight-stitch needle plate?

A By its nature, your machine will stitch better when going forward and backward. Because you move the fabric in many different directions when free-motion quilting, stitch tension can be problematic. Using the straight-stitch plate usually improves the stitch quality and tension and helps prevent skipped stitches because there is no extra room for the needle to push the fabric layers into the hole like there is in a zigzag plate.

Q How do you stipple quilt? And what can you do about meandering?

A Practice both types of free-motion designs (*see page 249*) to develop a smooth stitching rhythm while moving the fabric under the needle and maintaining a consistent stitching speed.

Note: First, take the time to "set" the blocks and borders by machine-basting in the ditch of the major seams to anchor the layers. Stitch in the ditch of the vertical and horizontal center seams first and then along all others. You can use wash-away thread in the needle. The bobbin thread will be released in the wash, or you may need to pull it free from the quilt after it is dry.

1. Prepare the machine for free-motion quilting (*see pages 321–22*). Thread the machine with lightweight cotton thread in the needle and on the bobbin.

2. Begin stitching in a corner and guide the fabric with your hands in smooth back-and-forth and side-to-side movements to create curved, closely spaced lines of even-length stitches. Make patterns that look like puzzle pieces. Do not cross any of the lines of stitching. Don't quilt yourself into a corner. Do not turn the quilt — move it with your hands as you stitch yourself out of the corners.

3. Try to use a medium to fast sewing speed to maintain stitch consistency while making smooth loops and swirls. Do not strive for uniformity of shape — the look should be more random. (*See* Stitching Practice *on the next page.*)

STITCHING PRACTICE

▶ Use a pencil as your "needle" and practice drawing lines that look like stippling or the larger meandering stitch to train your eyes and hands before you try it on fabric layers.

▶ Unthread the needle and practice stippling or meandering on paper. Draw your own curving lines and doodles on paper if you think you need a line to follow until you are comfortable with the free-motion technique.

▶ Thread the machine with the thread(s) you plan to use and make a 12"-square sandwich of fabric, batting, and backing to practice the stitching pattern.

▶ Do a warm-up session before you start, to retrain your hands, eyes, and feet until the stippling motion becomes second nature.

Q What is the optimal speed for free-motion quilting?

A If you move the fabric fast and stitch at a slow speed, the stitches will be too long. If you move the fabric slowly and stitch fast, the stitches will be too small. A medium-fast stitching speed with controlled fabric movement is optimal for creating smooth stitches of a consistent length. If you can control the speed of the machine motor (check your manual), try adjusting it to half or two-thirds of the normal speed and then stitch a little faster than you are normally inclined to stitch.

Q Can I free-motion stitch other patterns, instead of always using the jigsaw-puzzle shape?

A By all means. Try doodle-stitching on small quilt sandwiches or just plain sheets of paper to come up with your own designs — loop-de-loops, circles, spirals, bows, words, geometric shapes, leaves, and flowers are just a few of the possibilities. Unlike stippling and meandering, stitching lines can cross in free-motion doodling designs.

Q I can't drop the feed dogs on my machine. Can I still do free-motion quilting like stippling?

A Set the stitch length to 0 and securely tape an index card over the feed dogs. Make sure all edges of the card are taped down so they won't catch on the back of the quilt. Puncture a hole in the card by raising and lowering the needle through it several times.

Q Is there anything I can do to make it easier to move the quilt under the needle?

A Get a better grip with latex gloves or rubber fingers. Special gloves for machine quilting are available at your quilt shop. Or, try a new pair of lightweight cotton gardening gloves with rubberized fingertips. Special slippery mats (*see page 331*) are also available to attach to the bed of the sewing machine to help the layers glide more evenly.

---

14 TIPS FOR STRESS-FREE MACHINE QUILTING

1. Clean and oil your machine and have it serviced once or twice each year by a qualified technician. Regularly check the needle and needle bar as well as the bobbin area and bobbin case for lint, and remove it with a soft brush. Also remove the needle plate to check for lint you might have missed. Do not use "canned air" to blow lint out of the machine interior — it will only blow it further into the machine.

2. Sit in the seat of your chair, not on the edge, with your body centered directly in front of the needle, not to one side. Position your chair as close as possible to the machine to avoid leaning and curving into your work, which causes back, neck, and arm strain.

3. Make sure your sewing machine and chair are correctly adjusted for your height, and have adequate lighting. Sit high enough while you quilt but not so high that you have to hunch over your work.

4. Set up your machine following the guidelines for machine-guided (*see page 309*) or free-motion quilting (*see page 321*).

5. Unless you are doing zigzagging or decorative stitching, switch to a straight-stitch throat plate (*see page 322*) to improve the appearance of the quilting stitches on the back of the quilt. This offers more support as the needle pierces the quilt backing. Don't forget to switch back to the zigzag plate for other sewing projects or zigzag stitching.

6. Make a map of the quilting order or the quilting path (use directional arrows). Follow it to avoid too many stops and starts with threads to tie off. Try to work from the center out to the sides as much as possible. Quilt specific motifs or grids first, and then fill in backgrounds and smaller areas.

7. Make a stitching test sample with a scrap of the fabric or a leftover block and the actual batting and backing you are using. Check and

adjust the tension as needed before you start on the quilt. Different combinations of fabric, backing, and thread type require fine-tuning tension for the optimum results.

8. Practice stitching complex designs before you stitch them on your quilt. Trace the design onto scrap fabric with a permanent marker, remove the thread from the needle and bobbin, and then stitch along the lines, learning how to guide it for the smoothest flow. This kind of practice trains your eye and your muscle memory.

9. Take the time to carefully layer and baste the quilt sandwich (*see page 277*) so that puckers, tucks, and wrinkles on the front or back won't be a problem while stitching. After basting, check the backing to make sure there are no unwanted wrinkles.

10. Keep the largest part of the quilt to your left while you stitch and make sure there is adequate support for the quilt to your left and behind the machine.

11. Always pull the bobbin thread to the top of the quilt layers before you start stitching. Otherwise, they will get tangled and knotted in the stitching on the back, and may be difficult to undo or remove.

12. To keep your work flowing smoothly, don't watch the needle — watch where you are going instead.

13. Replace the needle often to avoid snags and pulls. Machine manufacturers recommend changing a needle after four hours of stitching — even if it doesn't seem dull or to have any burrs. Remove it and discard. (Wrap in masking tape before tossing into the wastebasket.)

14. Breathe and relax and take breaks to revive your body and relax your shoulders, hands, and arms. If you are tense, your stitching will be, too. Sing or hum while you stitch to help relieve tension.

Solving Problems

Q Why do I keep breaking needles while I machine-quilt large quilts?

A Stress on the quilt layers can strain the needle and cause breakage, so don't allow the quilt to drag off the edge of the sewing table. Place a table to your left if necessary (or lower your ironing board to table height) to support the quilt. Place another table behind the machine to hold the length of the quilt as you feed it through the machine.

- -

Q My shoulders and neck get so tired when I am machine-quilting. Is there an easy remedy for this?

A The obvious one is to take frequent breaks, but even then you can still experience strain. One way to improve your posture is to tilt up the back of machine a bit so you can better see what you're doing. You can purchase a special table-top apparatus for this purpose, or use two rubber doorstops to lift the back of the machine off the table. An empty 3-ring, 3"-thick notebook binder will work too. Tuck the thin end under the back of the machine and slide it in far enough to tilt the machine forward. Here are a few other tips:

▶ Set a kitchen timer every 30 minutes to remind you to get up and stretch, roll your shoulders forward and then backward, and get a glass of water! A regular series of stretching exercises will keep you limber and balanced and help correct poor posture.

▶ Make sure the sewing machine is as close to the front edge of the table as possible and bring your chair close to the table so you can reach your work easily.

▶ Don't cross your legs and don't hunch or slump over your work. Keep your feet flat on the floor. Sitting up straight and raising your chest automatically repositions your shoulders and prevents hunching.

▶ Prevent the foot pedal and the sewing machine from slip-sliding away by placing custom-cut pieces of the nonstick rubber-like mesh that is sold to use in refrigerator vegetable drawers underneath. If your sewing room is carpeted, try a piece of carpet padding (designed to keep a rug in place on top of a carpet) under the foot pedal. A computer mouse pad works, too.

▶ Purchase a product like SewSlip to use when machine quilting. This Teflon-like white sheet has a sticky side that adheres to the bed of the machine and has a hole for the needle. The slippery surface cuts down on resistance so the fabric layers don't drag or hang up. That makes it easier to move the quilt sandwich as you stitch. Remove the sheet when you're finished, reapply it to its backing paper, roll up, and store in its tube until you need it the next time. I've also heard of quilters waxing the machine bed with butcher's wax to help quilts slide more easily as they work. Wax lightly and buff to a shine with a soft cloth if you want to try this method.

Q How do I prevent lint balls from getting caught on the quilt backing when I machine-quilt?

A Regularly clean out the interior of your sewing machine to remove stray threads and lint — after completing a project or more often if you are making large quilts. Use a small, soft brush; do not blow into the bobbin area, as the moisture from your breath can cause rusting. Don't use canned air either. It can blow lint further into the machine mechanism. Also, wipe off the needle periodically to remove microscopic lint buildup that can transfer into the bobbin case. Clean off any sticky buildup from temporary spray adhesive by wiping the needle with rubbing alcohol.

Q Is it okay to use nylon or polyester monofilament thread in my quilt?

A If the stitching needs to be truly invisible, then this thread is your only choice for quilting. It is strong and durable, but some say it may be too strong and will cut through cotton over time. Many quilters use it for invisible machine appliqué and for quilting because it seems to disappear into the fabric. If you are concerned about the longevity of your quilt, then whether or not to use it is up to you. Polyester monofilament thread can take a higher heat than the nylon version can.

Q Monofilament thread is difficult to see when threading the needle. Do you have any suggestions?

A To make threading easier, use a permanent marker to color the cut end of the thread so you can see it and place a white index card behind the needle. After clipping the thread, use a piece of blue masking tape to secure the thread end to the bed of the sewing machine so it won't "unthread" and you can find it easily when you're ready to sew.

- -

Q My monofilament thread keeps puddling off the spool and gets hung up. Any advice?

A Monofilament thread has a mind of its own. To prevent puddling, place the spool on a separate thread stand on the table behind the spool pin on your machine. The thread goes up through a loop that keeps it from reeling off as you sew, and sends it to your needle with the just the right amount of tension. These stands work best if you find a way to weight or anchor them in place so they don't get bumped out of position as you sew. A chunk of poster putty will do the trick.

- -

Q I've finished quilting and a stray thread that I missed is lying under a light-colored background block. How do I fix it?

A As careful as I am about clipping stray threads before making the quilt sandwich, this still happens to me, too. Occasionally the thread gremlin manages to sneak a piece between the layers while I'm layering and basting the quilt sandwich. On most quilting cottons, I've been able to "wiggle" the stray thread to the surface of the quilt by using the point of a large needle to move the fabric threads aside so that I can use a fine needle or pin to lift the offending thread through the quilt top and clip it off. Sometimes I'm lucky and the loose thread is not attached to the quilt so it comes out entirely. If the thread is attached to a seam allowance or trapped under quilting stitches, I gently tug to pull out as much thread as possible and clip close to the quilt surface. If there is more thread to release, I just repeat the process. It may not be possible to remove trapped threads that are caught in stipple quilting.

- -

Q **My quilted borders have a slight ripple and the quilt doesn't lie flat. How do I correct this?**

A If your quilt center is heavily quilted and the borders are not, it's not unusual to find a little rippling. You might want to add more quilting to the borders to help draw them in to match the quilted center. If that's not desirable, it's essential to remove the rippling. If steam pressing and blocking the quilt (*see page 369*) doesn't work, try easing out the fullness.

1. Machine-baste a scant ¼" from the quilt top's raw edges, beginning and ending the stitches at each raw edge and leaving long thread tails at each corner. *Do not pivot* at the corners.

2. Place the quilt top on a large flat surface, grasp the bobbin thread at one end of one edge and gently pull to "gather"

the edge a bit. Repeat at the opposite end. Adjust the excess fullness along the entire edge; repeat with the remaining edges.

3. Make sure that the edge of the quilt lies flat and the corners are true and square. Measure the opposite edges to make sure they are the same length before tying off the threads to secure the easing. You may want to steam-press the edges to help shrink out any obvious fullness.

Quilt-As-You-Go

You may want to try the quilt-as-you-go method for hand- or machine-quilted projects. Portability is its best asset; if you don't like manipulating large quilts under the needle, this may be just the answer for you.

Q What is quilt-as-you-go and how do you do it?

A This means that you finish each block and quilt it before you join all of the finished, quilted blocks to assemble the quilt top. You can hand-quilt as you go for easy portability. With this method, you quilt each block, strip of blocks, or wholecloth or unpieced strips before you join them to complete your quilt. The quilt is quilted piece by piece. It's a good choice if you prefer to work on smaller quilt sections rather than using a floor hoop or frame. For machine quilting, managing a single block or strip as you quilt by machine is easier than trying to move a large quilt sandwich under the sewing-machine needle.

This method requires extra backing fabric and batting for the seaming technique on the back of the quilt so make sure to purchase extra yardage if you plan to quilt as you go. First complete the block or strip assembly for your quilt and plan the arrangement and the quilting pattern. If your quilting pattern requires it, transfer the design to each block (*see page 258*). Quilting designs must end at least ¾" from the outer edges of the block to allow room for sewing the quilted blocks together. Quilt one block or strip at a time and then join them.

1. Cut the batting and the backing the same size as the block (or strip) and stack the layers with the backing face down, the block face up, and the batting in between. Hand-baste diagonally through the center in both directions and around the outer edges.

2. Quilt the block as desired, but do not quilt within ¾" of all raw edges. Go back and extend the quilting pattern after joining the blocks if necessary, but it's best to choose a quilting design that won't require completion after all the pieces are joined. For hand quilting, use a hoop that is slightly smaller than the block or baste scrap strips around the outer edges to extend the block so it will fit in the hoop. Layer and quilt each block or strip and then remove all basting stitches.

3. To join the quilted blocks in rows (or to join the quilted strips), place the two blocks right sides together and peel the backing and the batting out of the way. Stitch the blocks together by hand or machine, backstitching at each end of the seam. Press the seam open. Continue in this fashion until you have joined the blocks for one row of the quilt.

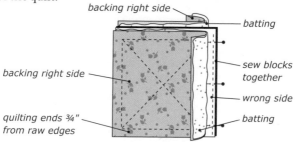

backing right side — *batting*

backing right side — *sew blocks together*

— *wrong side*

quilting ends ¾" *from raw edges* — *batting*

4. Flip the row of blocks over, fold the backing out of the way, and carefully trim the batting pieces so they butt perfectly for a smooth, flat finish. Use a catchstitch to splice the batting edges together (*see page 63*).

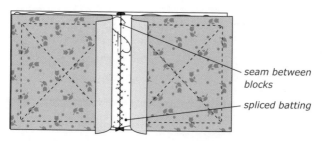

— *seam between blocks*

— *spliced batting*

337

5. Turn under ¼" along one backing square and slipstitch to the backing of the adjacent block. Be careful not to catch the front of the quilt in this stitching. Join completed block rows in the same fashion. Use the same method to join strips for strip quilts and finish the seams on the back.

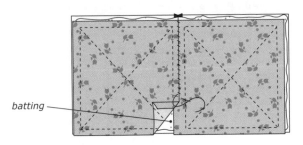

batting

Note: If your quilt has sashing strips (*see* Quilt-Top Assembly, *page 216*), you will need to adapt this method. *Block by Block, New Techniques for Machine Quilting and Assembly* by Beth Donaldson has very good directions for this variation.

DOUBLE UP

You can make a completely reversible quilt with blocks on both sides using this method. Substitute blocks for the backing squares and follow the directions above.

QUILT-AS-YOU-GO PATCHWORK

You can also quilt-as-you-go while you create patchwork blocks on a foundation. For this method, place an oversized piece of prewashed cotton flannel or thin batting on the wrong side of a backing square and baste the layers together. Cover the flannel with stitch-and-flip string piecing (*see* Foundation Piecing Methods, *page 159*). You can start at one corner of the block with strips placed on the diagonal or across the square, or with a strip or patch in the center and add pieces around it.

Log Cabin blocks can be made in this manner (*see pages 17 and 150*). Cut each log to the correct width and length, and then add them to the center square in a clockwise or counterclockwise fashion using the stitch-and-flip technique. When the batting and backing are covered with patches, trim it to the desired size and then sew the blocks together. This takes the place of stitching in the ditch of the seams after piecing the block.

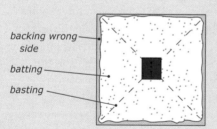

backing wrong side

batting

basting

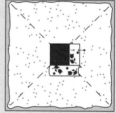

stitch, flip, and press

Tying a Quilt

Tying the quilt layers together is often used for baby quilts and comforter-style quilts with thick polyester batting that is difficult to maneuver under the needle for machine quilting. It's technically not quilting but may be an alternative to consider for quick finishing. You can assemble the layers with the lining method and then tie the layers, or you can make the quilt sandwich, tie the quilt, and then bind it traditionally.

- -

Q How do I tie a quilt?

A First decide whether you will bind the edges (*see page 346*) or sew the batting and backing to the quilt top like a lining (*see page 373*). If you plan to tie the quilt, it's still a good idea to use safety pins or hand basting to hold the layers together, whether it will be bound or lined. Decide whether you want the tie ends to form tufts on the surface or on the quilt backing and make the ties accordingly. Pearl cotton thread (#5) is an excellent choice for tying, but other heavy threads and lightweight yarns also may be used. Make sure that you can tie a secure knot in what you choose — avoid slippery threads and yarns.

1. Thread the needle with the chosen yarn or thread for the ties. Insert the needle through all layers from the side where you want the tufts, leaving a 2" tail of thread or yarn on the surface. Take a small stitch and bring the

needle back up through the layers. Tie a snug square knot — right over left and then left over right (or vice versa). Cut the thread or yarn, leaving a 2" tail.

2. Make a tie at each location as desired, spacing the ties no more than 3" or 4" apart. After completing all ties, trim them to an even length — at least ¾".

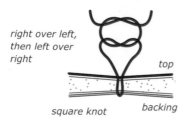

right over left, then left over right

top

square knot

backing

Note: For continuous tying, stitch from location to location, leaving the thread or yarn uncut. After stitching a number of the ties, stop, cut the thread halfway between the stitches, and then tie and trim.

- -

Q Is it possible to "tie" a quilt by machine?

A Yes, you can use machine-made bar tacks to form the "ties." There will be no tufts on the surface and the tacks can be almost invisible depending on the thread color you use. To make them disappear, choose a bobbin thread color to match the backing and a needle thread that will blend into the colors on the quilt top. Do not use monofilament thread for this method as it could cut the fabric layers; because this thread is wiry and slippery, it can also come undone. Try using top-stitching thread or polyester buttonhole twist for the ties if you want more obvious bar-tacks.

1. Thread the machine with the desired thread colors and attach the bar-tack foot if available. If not, use an open-toe appliqué foot or the zigzag foot.

2. Adjust the machine for a zigzagged bar-tack stitch (satin stitch) as directed in your machine manual. Test to determine the desired width and make note of it or save it in your computerized machine's memory file. Drop the feed dogs or cover them with an index card taped to the bed of the machine.

3. Set the stitch length to 0 and begin by stitching in place for a few stitches. Adjust to the desired bar-tack width. Take three or for stitches in place, one over the other. Return to stitch length 0 and take several stitches in place.

4. Without cutting the threads, move the quilt to next "tie" location and make a tie in the same manner.

5. After completing the stitches in an area of the quilt, remove the quilt from the machine and clip the top and bobbin threads between the tacking stitches close to the quilt surface. Return to the machine and continue in this manner until the quilt surface is tied as desired. Clip threads close to the quilt surface on each side, or draw them into the quilt layers with a needle.

Last But Not Least

Q How do I wash my finished quilt to remove the marks?

A If you prewashed the fabrics in your quilt before you made it and you know that the dyes won't run, you can wash it in the washing machine.

1. Put the quilt in the washing machine and set for the gentle cycle with cold water. Add a mild detergent that contains no brighteners. Orvus Paste is a good choice. Use only ⅛ cup. If possible, use a front-loading machine to avoid agitator damage.

2. Allow to agitate for 3 minutes and then let it soak for 10 minutes. Agitate again for 3 minutes.

3. Turn the knob to the spin cycle and run until most of the water is drained.

4. Run the rinse cycle, allowing the washer to agitate for 3 minutes and then drain most of the water.

5. Run the final spin and lift carefully from the machine. Hang to dry on a clothesline or tumble-dry in the dryer on a low setting.

- -

Q I have an old quilt that needs cleaning. Is there some way that I can wash it?

A Perhaps. Test first by making a mild washing solution with soap flakes. Dip a cotton swab in the solution and dampen each fabric in the quilt. If the swab picks up any color, don't wash the quilt! If no colors come off, *wash at your own risk.* Try the method below on a sunny day.

1. Cut a fiberglass screen large enough to cover the bottom and sides of your bathtub. Wrap the cut edges with fabric strips and baste in place.

2. Place the quilt on a large flat surface, lay the prepared screen on top, and use low suction on your vacuum cleaner to draw out surface dust on both sides of the quilt.

3. Fill the bathtub with 8" of warm water. Use the screen to gently immerse the quilt. Use your hands to gently force water into the quilt layers. Gently rock the quilt. Drain. *Caution:* If you see any color in the water, remove the quilt immediately and dry as directed in step 6.

4. Gently push the quilt to one side and refill the tub. Add ⅛ cup of mild detergent to a gallon of warm water and add to the tub. Gently rock the quilt. When the water is dirty, drain and repeat until water remains clear.

5. Fill tub with clear water. Rock, drain, and repeat as needed to remove soap. In the last rinse, use your hands to gently press out as much water as possible.

6. Arrange a large mattress pad or several terry towels on the lawn and a clean sheet in the shade. Use the screen to transfer the damp quilt to the pad or towels, and use your hands to press out additional moisture. Transfer the quilt to the clean sheet. Smooth out the quilt, square the corners, and cover with another sheet to protect it. Turn the quilt periodically. Store only when you know it is completely dry.

CHAPTER 12

Finishing the Quilt

Your quilt is quilted — but it's not quite finished. It's time to finish the edges with binding — the outer narrow fabric strip that frames it and covers the raw edges. There are several other edge-finishing options, depending on the desired finished effect and the way in which the quilt will be used. If you want to hang your finished quilt on the wall, you'll need to add a hanging sleeve. If you're planning to show your quilt in an exhibit, you will definitely need a hanging sleeve — even if it's a bed quilt. And, last but not least, it's nice to add a label to the back of the quilt to document your work for future generations.

Planning the Binding

The outer edges of the majority of quilts are finished with a narrow width of fabric that wraps the raw edges for a ravel-free finish. This is the binding. In addition to choosing the fabric for your quilt binding, you must answer these questions:

▶ Do I want the binding to "disappear" at the edges, create a more obvious frame, or really stand out in a contrasting color?

▶ How wide do I want the finished binding?

▶ Should the binding be single- or double-layer?

▶ Should I use straight-grain or bias-cut strips for the binding?

- -

Q **Should the binding fabric match the fabric at the outer edge of the quilt or can it be a different fabric?**

A If you don't want an obvious visual "frame" around the quilt, use the same fabric or one that is a close match in color and value (*see page 44*) to the outermost fabric in the finished quilt. For a beginner, using the same fabric is a sure thing. Many quilters use one of the fabrics used in the blocks or borders, or they match the binding to the backing fabric.

Bindings are usually made of a single fabric, but they can also be pieced to create a rainbow or scrappy edge finish (*see page 367*). If you're not sure what you want at the time you purchase fabrics for the blocks, you can purchase enough extra of one or more of the fabrics for the binding — or wait until

PASSING THE AUDITION

I don't choose binding fabric until the quilt is finished and I can "audition" binding options at my local quilt shop. I choose several fabrics that might work and test by placing one corner of the quilt on top of the bolt to simulate a corner of the binding beyond the quilt-top edge. Then I step back and squint to see if I like how it frames and finishes the quilt.

you've completed the quilt-top assembly to purchase the binding fabric. It can be a little risky to purchase fabrics for the quilt and then take more than six months to complete it, since color stories change twice each year and finding a fabric that coordinates with the quilt fabrics may be more difficult the longer you wait.

Q How wide should quilt binding be?

A Binding width is a quiltmaker's personal preference. The most commonly used finished widths are ¼", ⅜", or ½". However, the binding can be narrower or wider, depending on the desired finished effect. *Important:* If the outermost edges of your quilt have pieced borders or corner blocks, your finished binding should be ¼". A wider seam will "bite" into the patches at the outer edges of the blocks, nipping off points and destroying the pieced symmetry. If you want a wider finished binding, when you trim the excess batting and backing (*see* Attaching the Binding, *page 356*), leave enough beyond the quilt-top edge for the desired binding-width seam allowance.

Note: The seam allowance width does take away some of the border width — which won't make much difference visually if the outer border is wide or the binding is the same fabric or a close match to the border fabric. It will make a difference on quilts with narrow outer borders, so if you opt for a wider binding than specified in the pattern, in a contrasting color or a print that is not the same as the outer border, you may want to cut the outer border a bit wider to compensate.

- -

Q Why choose double-layer over single-layer binding — or vice versa?

A Single-layer binding is not as durable as double-layer. It also requires turning under one edge by hand during the finishing step — which can be tedious on large quilts. Reserve this finish for miniature quilts, wall hangings, and other small quilted projects that won't receive a lot of wear. Double-layer (French) binding, is cut twice as wide as single-layer binding and is folded in half so it already has a folded finished edge to sew to the back of the quilt after you sew the raw edges in place on the front — no extra turning required! Two layers wear longer than one along the edge of the quilt.

- -

Q Why choose bias binding over straight-cut? Is one better than the other?

A For wall quilts that won't get a lot of wear, straight-cut binding is a good choice. However, if the quilt is a lap quilt or one that will be used on a bed and will be laundered often, bias-cut binding is the better choice. When binding strips are cut along the crosswise or lengthwise grain, a continuous thread or two of the fabric lies along the folded outer edge of the quilt, which is always susceptible to wear. When the thread wears out, it's as though you slit the folded edge and a new binding will be necessary.

When binding is cut on the bias, the threads cross the folded edge at a 45-degree angle across the quilt edge. That means no one thread along the edge receives as much wear as do the single thread or two that lie along the edge in straight-cut binding.

Bias binding requires more yardage than straight-grain strips, so if your pattern calls for straight-grain strips, buy at least an extra ¼ to ½ yard to be sure you have enough for cutting on the bias.

Bias binding has built-in stretch, making it the only choice for a scalloped-edge quilt or one with rounded corners. The stretch factor means it can be eased around curved edges without puckers or pulls.

SEE ALSO: *Bias Binding Calculations, page 402, and Bias Strip Yield, page 403.*

Cutting the Binding

Q How wide should I cut the strips for the binding on my quilt?

A The first thing to be done is determine the desired finished width.

For single-layer binding: Multiply the desired finished width by 4 and cut the strips this wide. For example, the binding strip must be at least 1" wide for binding that finishes to ¼". I always add at least ⅛" extra to the determined cut width to allow for the thickness of the batting so that I am sure to have enough binding to turn under along the stitching line on the back of the quilt.

For double-layer binding: Multiply the desired finished width by 7. For binding that finishes to ¼", the strips should be at least 1¾" wide. I add an extra ⅛" or ¼" for "wiggle room" to accommodate the quilt thickness, so I would cut the strips 2" wide for ¼"-wide finished binding. The folded edge of my double-layer binding then sits at or just beyond the binding stitching line on the back of the quilt. For ⅜"-wide finished binding, I cut the strips 2½" wide.

- -

Q How do I know how many straight-grain binding strips to cut to fit my quilt?

A First, determine the distance around the quilt perimeter 2 x (L + W), and add 12" for sewing the strips together, mitering the corners, and joining the binding ends. (You will probably have a little extra binding when you finish — better than ending up a few inches short.) Divide this number by 40" — the average usable width of most quilting cottons after preshrinking. Round up to the nearest whole number. For example, if the quilt measures 100" around, cut three 40-inch-long strips. When sewn together, the resulting strip will be about 116" long — plenty of length for the quilt perimeter.

- -

Q How do I know how many bias strips to cut and how much fabric I'll need?

A First determine how long the binding needs to be following the directions in the previous question. Then read Bias Binding Calculations on page 402. *Note:* If the quilt has rounded corners, or is scalloped, measure around the outer edge following the curves of the quilt and add 12".

- -

Q Should I cut straight-grain strips along the fabric width or parallel to the selvage?

A If you are following a pattern in a book or a quilt pattern, you will probably find that the yardage is based on cutting strips across the grain — this is the most economical method for most quilt designs. Crosswise grain does have some inherent stretch, making it easy to handle, but you must take care not to overstretch crossgrain strips while sewing them to the quilt to avoid a pulled or puckered edge. You can also opt to cut the strips along the lengthwise grain and some patterns may require that to take best advantage of yardage requirements. However, the lengthwise threads in woven cotton have very little give and this could present problems.

Q How do I cut straight-grain binding strips?

A Determine the appropriate strip style (single- or double-layer) and cut width. Then refer to the directions for rotary cutting crossgrain strips for strip piecing on page 91. Always cut, never tear, fabric for the strips — the wispy threads that result along the torn edges are misleading and can affect sewing accuracy. Tearing narrow strips can also cause damaging "runs" in the strips, making them unusable.

Q I've cut all the straight-grain strips I need for the binding. What's next?

A They must be joined to form one long strip and then the strip must be prepared for sewing to the quilt edges. You'll need your rotary mat, cutter, and a small square ruler.

1. Sew all the strips together using bias seams. Place one strip face up on the mat and cross it with the second strip face down. Use the lines on your cutting mat to make sure they are arranged at right angles. Draw a diagonal stitching line from corner to corner.

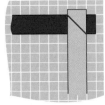

2. Stitch on the line. Trim the excess ¼" from the stitching and discard the cutaway. Press the seam open.

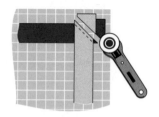

3. With the wrong side up, cut the left end at 45-degree angle and turn under and press ¼".

4. For double-layer binding, fold the strip in half lengthwise with wrong sides facing; press.

Q How do I cut bias strips for binding?

A For large quilts, try the continuous-bias cutting method on page 362. For smaller quilts, cut individual strips and join them with bias seams (*see previous question*) to create a strip about 12" longer than the quilt perimeter.

1. Straighten the cut edge of the fabric so that it is true and perpendicular to the selvage edge. Fold the fabric on the true 45-degree diagonal with the cut edge parallel to or even with the selvage; press. Place the rotary ruler on the fabric and trim away ¼" at the folded edge. Remove the cutaway triangle and set aside to use later if you need more strips. (*See illustration on next page.*)

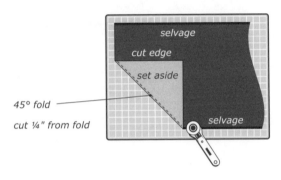

2. Using the cut edge as your guide, carefully rotary-cut bias strips of the desired width. Take care not to stretch the fabric or the strips.

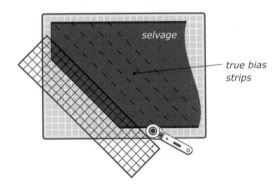

3. Cut all ends at the same angle, "truing" them to 45 degrees if necessary. The angles at each end of each strip should be parallel to each other — the strip should be a parallelogram. Some of the first strips you cut from the angled edge may be trapezoids rather than parallelograms — these will need trimming.

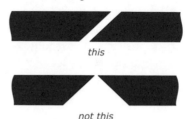

this

not this

4. Sew the angled ends together to make one long strip. Use ¼"-wide seam allowances and press the seams open. Prepare the strip for the binding method you are using — single- or double-layer (*see page 353*).

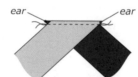

ear   *ear*

CUT THE RIGHT ANGLE

To make sure both bias ends are the correct angle for accurate sewing, stack one strip on top of the other, *with both of them right side up.* Trim one of them to match the other if necessary. This quick step eliminates the frustration of trying to sew opposite angles together!

Attaching the Binding

Q How do I actually sew the binding to the quilt?

A The classic binding method for borders with square or angled corners requires careful stitching and mitered corners. Before you attach the binding, machine-baste the quilt layers together a scant ¼" from the quilt-top raw edges through all layers to prevent shifting during stitching. Do not pivot at the corners. Instead, stitch from raw edge to raw edge and leave 6"-long thread tails at each edge. Stitch all edges in the same manner. (Pivoting at the corners can cause pulls and puckers.)

Next, trim the batting and backing even with the quilt-top edges and then check the quilt to make sure the opposite edges match in length. (*See* Do Be Square *on page 359.*)

Note: The steps shown here are for double-layer binding. To attach single-layer binding, ignore references to folding and pressing the binding strip. To attach it to the back of the quilt, turn under the raw edge with the fold along the stitching line and slipstitch in place.

For best results stitching through multiple layers (five), attach the walking foot or engage the even-feed feature, if available, on your machine. The cost of a walking foot is worth it if you use it only for attaching the binding.

If you want to add a hanging sleeve and catch it in the machine stitching when you add the binding, see page 376 now.

1. Somewhere a few inches above the lower corner on the right-hand edge of the quilt, position the turned end of the prepared binding with raw edges even. Pin the upper turned end in place and place a pin 2" below the lower turned end.

2. Begin stitching at the second pin and continue stitching to the seamline at the lower corner of the quilt — the width of the binding seam from the quilt edge. Backstitch carefully to lock the stitching. For example, if your binding will finish to ¼", use a ¼"-wide seam and stop stitching ¼" from the edge; for ⅜" finished binding, stitch and stop ⅜" from the edge. Clip the threads and remove the quilt from the machine.

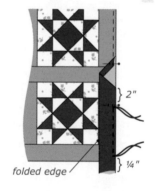

folded edge

} 2"

} ¼"

3. Place the quilt on a flat surface (not in your lap). Gently fold the binding back on itself at the corner to create a 45-degree-angle fold in the binding, intersecting the quilt corner precisely and making sure that the edge of the binding is aligned with the raw edge of the quilt. Pin in place.

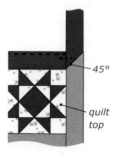

45°

quilt top

WALK ABOUT

I use my walking foot when applying binding. The distance from the needle to the edge of the foot is not quite ⅜" but due to the bulk of the quilt layers, the finished binding turns out to be about ⅜" wide. If I want narrower binding, I adjust the needle position one click to the right. Test on scrap layers of the fabric, batting, and binding and fine-tune the seam-width as desired.

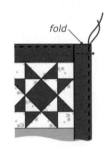

fold

4. Fold the binding back down onto the quilt with a straight fold at the upper edge of the corner and pin for an inch or so. Stitch, backstitching for added security, and continue to the end of the seam. Stop at the seamline and repeat steps 3 and 4. Continue around the seam in this manner until you reach the folded binding end where you started.

5. Lap the binding over the folded end and cut away the excess, leaving enough to tuck into the open end. Complete by stitching over a few of the stitches at the beginning before backstitching. Clip the threads.

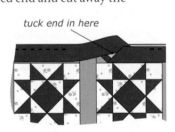

tuck end in here

6. Turn the binding over the quilt raw edge and slipstitch in place along or just below the stitching line. Miter the corners as you reach them. Slipstitch the mitered folds to the binding for a tidy finish at each corner, front and back.

quilt backing

DO BE SQUARE!

When quilt edges are trimmed and corners are square but one side is longer than its opposite side, even if only ⅛", the quilt is still not "square." Use the following method to "adjust" the longer edge to match the other.

1. Fold the quilt in half lengthwise to determine which edge is longer. Machine-baste a scant ¼" from the quilt top raw edge that is too long, beginning and ending the stitches at each raw edge and leaving long thread tails at each corner.

2. With the quilt top on a large flat surface, gently pull the bobbin thread at one end to "gather" the edge a bit. Gently slide the fullness along the edge of the quilt. Repeat at the opposite end. Adjust the excess fullness evenly along the edge and make sure it matches the length of the opposite edge. Check that the corners are true and square before tying off the threads to secure the easing. Steam-press.

3. Machine-stitch on top of the ease-stitching to secure and stabilize the adjusted edge.

Q If I tuck the binding layers into the end, won't there be a lump of fabric at the join?

A The binding will be slightly thicker at this point. If you don't like this, you can trim the ends and sew them together on the bias so the binding fits the edge without an overlap. It's a bit more challenging, but it's the best finish for show quilts and those that are in judged competitions. For this method, it is not necessary to cut the binding strip end on the bias or turn it under as previously shown for double-layer binding preparation (*see page 353*). It works for single- and double-layer binding.

1. When you sew the binding to the quilt edge, leave the first 6" of the binding unstitched. End the stitching 7" from the beginning stitches so you have two long tails of binding to facilitate the seaming. Pin the beginning and ending tails to the quilt top edge so they meet about half-way between the beginning and end of the stitching. Make a very short clip through all layers where they meet. Remove the pins.

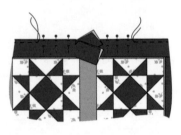

2. Open the ends of the folded binding strip and place them right sides together at right angles to each other so the clips are aligned with the strip edges; pin. Draw a stitching line on the diagonal from one corner to the opposite corner; stitch on the line, and remove the pins. (*For clarity, the illus-*

tration shows stitching next to the line.) Check to make sure
the binding fits the remaining unstitched edge of the quilt
before trimming the excess binding ¼" from the stitching.
Press the seam open (you can finger-press this one).

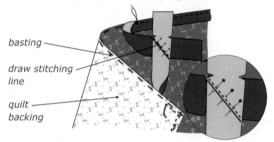

basting

draw stitching
line

quilt
backing

3. Refold the binding with wrong sides facing and raw edges
   even and complete the binding seam. Turn the binding to
   the back and sew the edges in place as shown in the previous question.

- -

Q Is it really necessary to sew binding to the quilt backing by hand? Can I do this step by machine?

A While many quiltmakers find the handwork required to
finish the binding a soothing and meditative process,
some prefer to finish this last step by machine. You probably
won't find a machine-stitched binding on an award-winning
quilt, but that doesn't mean you cannot or should not
machine-stitch yours in place. A machine-stitched binding is a
great option for pieces that will be used a lot — small quilts for

babies and kids, lap quilts, table runners, quilted pot holders, and other small projects, for example, including wall hangings.

If you plan to do the last step by machine, you must cut the binding strips a bit wider so that they extend past the binding seamline on the back of the quilt — for double-layer binding, cut the strips ¼" wider. You may want to hand-baste the binding in place on the back of the quilt to be sure it will be caught in the stitching along the binding on the front of the quilt (stitch in the ditch). Corners must be mitered and pinned smoothly in place for this finish, too.

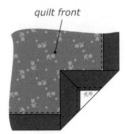

quilt front

Q How do I cut one continuous strip of bias from a piece of fabric?

A There are a few ways to do it; this is my favorite because I think it's the easiest.

1. Using rotary cutting tools, cut a large square of the binding fabric with straight-grain edges all around. (See the next question to determine the size of the square required for binding for the quilt you are making.) Place a straight pin at the center of each of two opposite edges and then cut the square in half diagonally to yield two large triangles, each with a bias edge.

2. Pin the resulting triangles together with pins matching and the bias-cut edges crossing each other. Stitch ¼" from

the raw edges — noting that a small
ear of fabric will extend at each end
of the seam where stitching intersects
the raw edges. Press the seam open to
reveal a bias parallelogram.

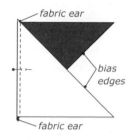

3. Use the rotary ruler and a sharp making pencil to draw cutting lines on
the wrong side, parallel to the long
bias edges of the resulting
parallelogram. Space them
the correct cutting width
for double-layer binding (or
single-layer if you prefer)
that will finish to the desired
finished binding width.

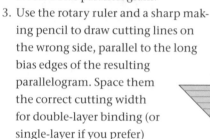

4. With right sides together and raw edges even, pin the
two short, angled edges together, offsetting the seam one
width of the binding strips drawn so there is a tail of fabric extending at each end of the seam (*See illustration on
next page*). It's a good idea to place a pin where each set of
lines meets to make sure they match when stitched so the
cutting line is continuous around the tube. Don't worry
— the tube that forms will not lie flat and will have a bit
of a twist in it (not shown in the illustration for the sake of
clarity). Adjust the machine for 15 to 18 stitches per inch.
Stitch ¼" from the raw edges and press the seam open.
Using dressmaker's shears, begin cutting at one fabric tail,
following the lines drawn around the tube. After cutting,

you'll have one long strip of bias with several short seams.

Note: You can slip the bias tube over the end of a narrow dressmaker's sleeve board to make it easier to cut the strip along the marked lines

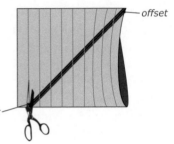

Q How do I determine the size square I need for continuous bias binding?

A You'll need a calculator with a square-root function. First, determine the distance around your quilt perimeter 2 × (L + W), and add 12". Also decide whether you want double-layer or single-layer binding (*see page 348*) and the required cut width for the desired finished width of the binding. Then use the following equations to determine the size of the square to use:

▶ Required strip length × bias-strip width = fabric area required

▶ Square root of fabric area = Required size of fabric square to cut for bias binding

---

SEE ALSO: *Bias Binding Calculations, page 402.*

Binding Variations

Q I plan to bind my quilt but want rounded rather than square corners. How do I do that?

A Rounded corners look best on a quilt with a wide outer border or a wide area of background fabric when there are no borders. They're particularly effective with appliquéd designs and with patchwork quilts with blocks that have curved rather than geometric elements. (Quilts with geometric blocks are generally more aesthetically pleasing with square corners.)

After completing the quilt top, use the edge of a round piece of dinnerware or a computer CD as your pattern to mark the trimming line at each corner and cut away the excess. Layer the shaped quilt top over the batting and backing rectangles (*see page 277*) and machine-baste together around the outer edges before trimming them even with the quilt-top outer edges. Apply the binding.

Note: To create a wavy scalloped edge, baste the quilt layers and then use the edge of a plate to mark alternating inner and outer curves. Scallop-marking tools are also available for traditional shaping.

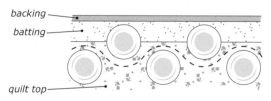

draw around plates or CDs to create wavy scallops

Q Are there any tricks for applying binding to traditional scalloped edges with inside points?

A You must use true-bias binding strips (*see page 353*) for the smoothest application on any curved edge. The "give" in the bias makes it easier to shape the binding strip around the curves.

Note: The following directions assume that the quilt is layered and quilted and the *scalloped edges are marked but not yet cut* around the outer edge of the quilt. It also assumes you are using double-layer binding (*see page 348*). For best results, attach a walking foot or engage the even-feed feature, if available on your machine.

1. Pin the quilt layers together along the marked curves, using long quilter's pins and making sure the layers are smooth and wrinkle-free. Machine-baste ¼" from the marked line. Do not trim away the excess fabric along the marked curves yet.

2. Beginning 2" below an inside corner of one scallop, pin and stitch the binding to the edge of the scallop. As you work, take care not to stretch the binding. Instead, *gently ease* it around the curve so that it is aligned with the scallop cutting line marked on the quilt top; pin in place. Pin only one scallop at a time.

3. Begin stitching 1" from the beginning of the binding strip and stop stitching at the first inside corner with the needle in the fabric layers. Raise the presser foot, clip the binding to the stitching (only if necessary), and pivot so you can begin the next scallop. On shallow scallops, clipping may

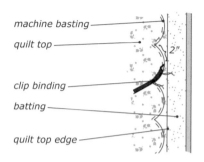

machine basting

quilt top

2"

clip binding

batting

quilt top edge

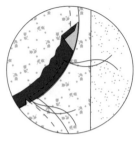

not be necessary. Stitch for about 1" from the pivot and then stop to pin and gently ease the binding to the next scallop. Stitch to the next inside corner.

4. Repeat this stop-and-start positioning and stitching method until you reach the end of the binding where you started. Join the ends using the method shown for seaming binding ends (*see page 360*).

5. Turn the binding to the back of the quilt and slipstitch in place along the folded edge. Make a neat fold at the inside corner when you reach it and tack the folded edge in place with a few stitches before moving on to the next scallop.

- -

Q Is there an easy way to make striped binding to match my quilt colors?

A You can strip-piece the colors and/or prints you want in your binding and then cut strips from the strip-pieced unit. Sew the strips together to make one long "striped" binding strip. This is a great way to use up scraps from the quilt or from your fabric stash. The "stripes" can be as wide or as narrow as you wish and can be straight or cut on the bias. For **straight-grain, striped binding strips** that will finish with the "stripes" perpendicular to the quilt edge:

1. Decide on the colors, the color rotation, and the desired width of the stripes. Cut strips of each color across the fabric width. The stripes can be the same width in each color or different widths — you're the designer!

2. Adjust the sewing machine for a shorter-than-normal stitch length. Sew the strips together in the desired color arrangement and press the seams open.

3. Use rotary-cutting tools to cut the binding strips of the desired width from the strip-pieced unit. Sew the pieces together to make one long strip.

For bias striped binding that will angle away from the quilt edge, join the strips in the desired order and cut the binding strips on the true 45-degree diagonal. Join them to make one long strip of the required length.

straight-grain rainbow binding   *bias-cut rainbow binding*

Solving Problems

Q How much fabric do I need to make binding for a quilt I've designed?

A If you're not following a pattern that specifies this, decide on the grainline (bias or straight), whether you want single- or double-layer binding, and the desired finished width. Then see Cutting the Binding on page 350 and Bias Binding Calculations on page 402.

- -

Q I'm ready to attach the binding but the border edges ripple a bit — the quilt doesn't lie flat. How do I correct this?

A If your quilt center is heavily quilted and the borders are not, it's not unusual to find a little rippling. It's essential to remove the rippling before applying the binding. First, try blocking the quilt as directed below (if you preshrunk your fabrics) or steam pressing — sometimes a little steam is all it takes to shrink out a little fullness. Easing the fullness out with machine basting (*see* Do Be Square! *on page 359*) is another method that may be necessary. Try blocking first.

1. Fill the washing machine tub with *cold* water and run the machine on the delicate cycle just long enough to get the layers damp all the way through. Then run the spin cycle for a few minutes to remove excess water.

2. Smooth the quilt out on a padded work surface for small quilts or on a carpet for large quilts (vacuum first).

3. Working on one corner at a time, gently pull the quilt into a "square" shape. Check the corner with a square ruler to make sure the adjacent edges form a true 90-degree angle. Anchor the edges to the work surface with T-pins. Square and anchor the next corner and then align the quilt edge between the corners with a long straight ruler or yardstick and anchor with pins. Space pins every 2" to 3". Continue in this fashion to square the remaining edges.

4. Allow to dry thoroughly before removing the pins.

- -

Q Why are there puckers in the finished binding on my quilt?

A Stitching through the layers at the quilt edge can be challenging, particularly with thicker batting. It's always a good idea to hand- or machine-baste the layers of the quilt together around the outer edge before attaching the binding. And, it's best to do this before you do any trimming (*see page 356*). Then, engage the even-feed system on your machine or attach a walking foot (*see page 73*) before stitching the binding in place to prevent puckering.

Note: A wide, medium-length zigzag stitch close to the outer raw edge will compact the layers, making them easier to handle, but you must take care not to stretch the fabric layers while stitching if you try this method. Use a walking foot for best results.

- -

Q I used bias binding, but now the bound edge won't lie flat. What happened?

A You probably stretched the binding as you sewed it in place. Even straight-grain strips have some give. If you stretch binding as you sew, it makes the binding shorter than the edge to which it is being sewn, and the finished quilt edge will not lie flat. If available, use an even-feed/walking foot (*see page 73*) or even-feed function on your machine to attach binding evenly without stretching it.

- -

Q How do I keep my binding from getting tangled and twisted while I sew it to the quilt? (My cat isn't any help with this!)

A Here is an easy way to corral your binding. Wrap the binding around your fingers into a loose coil or into a ball and tuck it into a gallon-size ziplock bag. When you are ready to apply it, partially open the bag and pull out the pressed end. Drop the bag on the floor by your feet or tape it to the edge of the sewing-machine table. The binding will feed from the bag as you sew.

Another idea: Cut a slit in the top of a clean, discarded butter tub or other inexpensive plastic storage container. Place the rolled binding inside, and feed the beginning end of the binding through the slit. Hold the tub in your lap or put it on the floor close to your feet. No more tangles, just even feeding!

- -

Q The rounded corners and scalloped edges of my quilt don't lie flat. What can I do to fix them? Pressing only makes wrinkles.

A Nothing, unless you are willing to remove the binding, make new binding and reapply it following the directions on pages 366–67. The next time you bind any edge with outward curves such as scallops, remember that you must ease the bias binding to fit around the curved edge — don't stretch it. Without the easing, it's impossible to align the cut edges, so the binding gets stretched and the finished edges will curve or cup under like yours did.

Optional Finishing Methods

Sometimes a flat edge is the best finish for a quilt, achieved with a lining method. It's particularly appropriate for art quilts, where the addition of a binding around the outer edge might interfere with the artistic design. This finish is often used on tied quilts (*see page 340*) or for a child's quilt or comforter. The lining method incorporates the batting with the front and back layers as you sew them together. Tied quilts may also be finished with binding if you have used a thinner batting. A knife-edge finish is necessary for quilts with irregular edges. You can use the excess backing fabric for a backing-to-front binding application.

Q How do you line a quilt?

A You will need batting and backing for this easy technique.

1. Cut the backing and the batting at least 2" larger all around than the quilt top. Working on a large, flat surface, center the quilt top on the oversize backing *with right sides facing.* Pin them together around the quilt-top raw edges, making sure that both layers are smooth and wrinkle-free.

2. Stitch the layers together ¼" from the raw edges, leaving an 8"-long opening for turning. Trim the backing even with the quilt-top edges.

3. Arrange the oversize batting on a flat surface and smooth out any wrinkles. Center the quilt top/backing unit on the batting with the wrong side of the quilt top against the batting and the wrong side of the backing facing you. Working from the center out, smooth the layers in place and pin together around all edges. The batting will extend beyond the quilt top/backing edges.

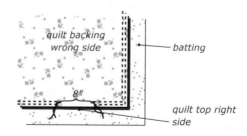

quilt backing
wrong side

batting

8"

quilt top right
side

4. With the backing facing you, stitch again, following the first stitching and leaving an opening. Trim the batting close to the stitching, taking care not to cut the quilt top or backing. In the opening area, trim the batting just inside the stitching line to eliminate bulk in the seam.
5. Turn the quilt right side out through the opening. Press as needed around the outer edges.
6. At the opening, fold the quilt-top seam allowance in over the batting edge. Turn under ¼" along the backing edge and pin in place. Hand-sew the backing to the quilt edge. At this point, you are ready to tie the layers together or to hand- or machine-quilt as desired.

SEE ALSO: *Tying a Quilt, pages 340–42.*

Q Can I fold excess backing over the quilt edge and use it for binding?

A This finishing method is often called "mock" binding. Since it's always a good idea to cut the quilt backing at least 2" to 4" larger than the quilt top on each edge (*see page 268*), you should have enough backing remaining to turn to the quilt front, saving time and eliminating the cost of a separate binding fabric. However, if it wears out and requires replacing, you will need to undo the stitching, trim the backing even with the quilt-top edges, and apply a traditional binding with a double-layer bias binding, which will wear much better. This may not be an issue in a wall quilt, but is something to consider when a quilt will be laundered a lot.

Q How do I use the backing to bind my quilt?

A It's easy. Here's how you do it:

1. Peel the backing out of the way and *trim only the batting* even with quilt-top edges.

2. Replace the backing and machine-baste ¼" from the quilt-top edge through all layers.

3. Trim the backing ¾" from the outer quilt edge (for a finished binding width of ⅜"). Fold the raw edge in to meet the quilt edge and press. Turn the folded edge over the quilt edge onto the quilt top, mitering the corners with folds made in alphabetical order (a–e) as shown in the illustration.

4. Trim away and discard the excess backing corners (f) before hand- or machine-stitching the "binding" to the quilt top.

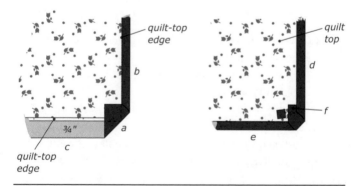

Adding a Hanging Sleeve

Q I'm finishing up a quilt that I'd like to hang on the wall. What's the best way to plan for this?

A You will need a hanging sleeve on the back of the quilt just below the binding. Quilts are hung on rods inserted through the hanging sleeve and then attached to the wall in a variety of ways. A fabric hanging sleeve is easy to make and attach during the quiltmaking process but can also be attached after the quilt is completed.

▶ You can use a dowel or a curtain rod to hang a quilt; the larger the quilt, the sturdier the rod must be.

▶ For small wall quilts, a curtain-sashing rod makes an inconspicuous mounting rod that is easy to hang.

▶ Café-curtain rods are available in a wide range of sizes and finishes and are an excellent choice as well. Other options include wooden yardsticks, lathe, or dowels.

- -

Q How do I make and attach a hanging sleeve before I attach the binding?

A Trim the batting and backing even with the quilt-top edges and then do the following:

1. Cut a 6"- to 9"-wide strip of fabric the length of the top edge of the quilt. The sleeve will finish to 2" shorter than the finished quilt edge and to just under half of the cut strip width. For small quilts that will be hung on small-diameter rods, you can cut the sleeve only 4½" to 6½" wide.

2. Turn under and press ½" at each short end of the hanging-sleeve strip. Turn and press again to make a ½"-wide double hem at each end; machine-stitch in place.

3. Fold the strip in half lengthwise *with wrong sides facing* and finger-press to make a light crease along the fold. Unfold the strip and turn one long edge in to the crease. Lightly crease the edge and then machine-baste ¼" from the creased edge to create a temporary ease pleat. Fold the pleated strip in half with wrong sides facing and press the lower folded edge. Avoid pressing the ease pleat.

raw edges

basted ease pleat

4. With raw edges aligned, center and pin the strip to the upper edge of the quilt. There should be room at each end of the sleeve to attach the binding without catching the sleeve in the stitching. Machine-baste ¼" from the raw edges. Attach the binding (*see page 356*).

5. Slipstitch the short edges and the lower edge of the sleeve to the quilt backing only. Catch only the underlayer of the sleeve at each end. Remove the basting stitches and press the sleeve. The released pleat adds ease to the front of the sleeve so the hanging rod takes the weight of the quilt.

Q How do I attach a hanging sleeve to a quilt that is already bound?

A To add a hanging sleeve to a finished quilt:

1. Complete steps 1 and 2 in the directions on previous page. Next, fold the strip in half lengthwise with *wrong sides facing* and long raw edges even; machine-stitch ¼" from the raw edges to make a tube. Machine-baste ¼" from the long folded edge to make the ease pleat.

2. Position the sleeve on your ironing board with the seam centered on the tube and press it open. The raw edges will be on the outside in the center of the resulting tube and the ease pleat will be on the other side of the tube.

3. With the seam against the backing, center the sleeve on the quilt back with one folded edge along the lower edge of the binding. Slipstitch the long edges in place and only the lower layer of the tube at the short edges. Release the basting and press the sleeve.

backing

Q Won't hanging a long quilt on the wall cause stress on the fabric and stitches over time?

A Yes, that can be a problem. If you plan to hang the quilt for long periods as part of your decorating scheme or in an exhibition, it's a good idea to make a hanging sleeve for the bottom edge, too — unless the quilt has an obvious one-way direction. The second sleeve allows you to hang the quilt from the opposite end periodically so the quilt takes the hanging stress from both ends. If the quilt is a one-way-only design, it would be best to take the quilt down every few months and allow it to rest for a few months before rehanging.

Labeling Your Quilt

Adding a label to the back of your quilt is a lovely touch that documents the maker for future generations. It is also a safety measure in case your quilt is lost or stolen.

Q How do I make and attach a quilt label?

A Adding a label requires a bit of fabric, a fine-point permanent marking pen, and a piece of freezer paper to stabilize the fabric for writing. Then follow the steps on the next page.

1. For the simplest label, place an 8½" × 11" rectangle of muslin, white, or off-white fabric (or a solid color that coordinates with the quilt backing) face up on the waxy side of a similarly-sized piece of freezer paper. Press with a dry iron at medium heat to temporarily attach the paper to the fabric. This size allows room to draw the desired finished size for your label, including a turn-under allowance. A 4" × 6" finished rectangle should be large enough.

2. To keep your writing neat, use an air-soluble temporary marking pen to draw lines on the fabric or draw them on the matte side of the freezer paper with a black pen so they will show through the paper and the fabric. Use the permanent-ink pen to write the desired information on the label. You may want to include any or all of the following:

▶ Quilt name
▶ Your name
▶ Your city and state (or your complete address if you want)
▶ Date of completion (month and date)
▶ Recipient's name (if a gift)
▶ Any other information appropriate to the particular quilt

3. Press the right side of the label to help set the ink. Trim to the desired size, allowing at least ¼" turn-under allowance all around. Peel away the freezer paper. Turn under the allowance and press. Position the label on the quilt back — the lower right corner is a good place — and pin. Slipstitch to the quilt, catching it to the backing only.

CHAPTER 13

Quilt Embellishments

After you've learned the basic techniques for patchwork and appliqué quilts, you may be ready to try many of the related textile techniques for embellishing your quilts. Featured in this chapter are a few of the most popular ones — yo-yos, prairie points, flat piping trim, and embroidery. Watch for other interesting ways to add texture and color to your work at quilt shows and at your favorite quilt shops. Classes and workshops with quilting pros who specialize in embellishments are always fun and a great way to expand your knowledge base and learn new ways to create your own signature quiltmaking style.

Prairie Points

Two of the most popular and classic embellishments, much beloved by quiltmakers worldwide, include small 3-D puffs and triangles made of fabric: prairie points and yo-yos. No quilting book would be complete without including them.

- -

Q What are prairie points?

A These are folded fabric triangles, often used to embellish the outer edges of a quilt. They can also be incorporated into patchwork blocks to add dimensional interest. For example, a small prairie point makes a fine beak for a chicken or duck. Adding prairie points to the seams in a pinwheel block adds interesting motion to the quilt surface.

Choose from two basic prairie-point styles, butting (see page 385) or overlapping them, or nesting them. They can be made from one fabric or an assortment of leftover scraps.

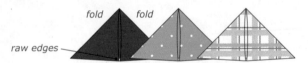

overlapping center-fold prairie points

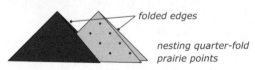

nesting quarter-fold prairie points

Q How do I make prairie points?

A First determine the size of square required to make points of the desired finished height — the distance from the seamline to the finished point (*see* Size Matters, *on the next page*). Multiply by two and then add ½" for seam allowances. For example, for a 1"-tall finished prairie point, measured from the seamline to the point, cut a 2½" square. Follow the diagrams below to fold and press the square to create the prairie-point style of your choice.

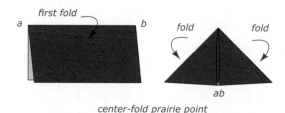

center-fold prairie point

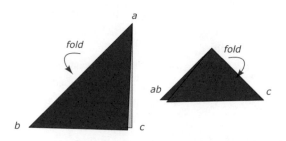

quarter-fold nesting prairie point

SIZE MATTERS

When planning a prairie-point-edge finish, choose a thin batting. Prairie points are four layers thick, adding more bulk to the seamline than binding would. Don't make prairie points much "taller" than 2½" from the seamline to the tip to prevent them from overpowering the quilt and getting too "floppy." Use a size that is proportionate to the finished overall size of the quilt. This may require some experimentation before you settle on the correct size for your quilt.

Q **How do I know how many prairie points I need to fit my quilt?**

A For butted (side-by-side) center-fold prairie points, calculate what you need, by multiplying the finished height of the prairie point × 2 and dividing that measurement into the finished measurement of the quilt edge (excluding the ¼" seam allowance at each end). Round up to the nearest whole number. For example, if the finished height is 2", and the long finished edge of the quilt is 75":

$$75 \div (2 \times 2) = 75 \div 4 = 18.75 = 19 \text{ prairie points required}$$
for each long edge.

Repeat to calculate the required number for the top and bottom edges.

Q How do I attach center-fold prairie points to a quilt so they butt into each other?

A Complete the quilting, making sure there is no stitching in the outermost 1" of the quilt at each edge. For some designs, you may need to go back and finish quilting to the outer edge after attaching the points.

1. Trim excess batting and backing even with the quilt edges. On the back of the quilt, fold the backing fabric back on itself and pin in place out of the way of the next stitching.

2. Arrange the prairie points on the quilt right side, overlapping the points as shown. When the seam is stitched ¼" from the quilt edge, the edges of the points touch. Baste in place, taking care not to catch the backing in the stitching. Trim the batting as close to the stitching as you can.

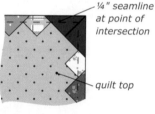

¼" seamline
at point of
intersection

quilt top

3. Flip the points so they extend from the quilt edge and the seam allowance rolls to the back. Press the seam as flat as possible all around the quilt edge.

4. On the back of the quilt, turn under the backing edges even with the stitching line and slipstitch in place.

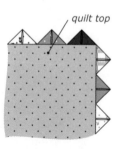

quilt top

center-fold butted
prairie points

Q How do I attach overlapped center-fold prairie points?

A You need approximately twice as many prairie points for this finish. Follow the directions for butted center-fold prairie points to prepare the quilt. Determine the size, cut the squares, fold, and press to make the points (*see page 383*). Arrange the first row of points with the lower-edge points touching point to point, and folds facedown. Add the alternating points in the same fashion. Pin to the quilt-top edge with the folded center against the quilt top and stitch ¼" from the raw edges. When you flip the points outward, they will overlap as shown with the folded edges of the points meeting at the center of the underlying triangles.

arrange with points meeting

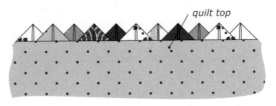

quilt top

overlapping center-fold prairie points

Q How do I attach nested prairie points?

A It takes more nested prairie points than butted ones to fill a quilt edge, but not as many as for overlapped, center-fold prairie points. Use the formula above to estimate the number required for each edge of the quilt, knowing that you may need a few to several more depending on how far the points nest into each other — on most quilts, a ¾" overlap is nice but you may need to adjust this for the size of your quilt. Begin by positioning one prairie point at the center of one edge, and add one at each end. Then add the remaining points, tucking one into the next and adjusting the spacing as evenly as possible. Baste in place. Follow the directions for butted prairie points to sew them in place and finish the backing.

BIND IT RIGHT

If prairie points are sewn to outer edges that will be bound, they will lie on the quilt rather than extend from the edge. Cut the binding strips for your quilt at least ¼" wider than normal to allow for the added thickness that must be encased in the seam around the outer edge of the quilt. Make a test sample if you're not sure what width is best for your quilt.

Yo-Yos

Quilters love to make these circular puffs (also called Suffolk puffs) for embellishing and making a full-size quilt — actually a topper that is placed over a spread or comforter. Perhaps they originated as a way to use up small scraps since each yo-yo requires only a small circle of fabric. Yo-yo quilts, pillow tops, and table runners — even vests and other wearables — are fun to make with this method and are especially good take-along projects after the circles are cut. Many quiltmakers use yo-yos as an embellishment. For example, add a button center and few embroidery stitches to make a whimsical flower.

- -

Q How do you make yo-yos?

A You'll need fabric scraps, template plastic, and a compass, plus needle, thread, and a thimble.

1. Decide on the desired finished diameter of the yo-yo and multiply by 2, then add ½" for the turn-under allowance. Use a compass to draw a circle template on template plastic or lightweight cardboard. Carefully cut out the template and trace around it on the wrong side of the fabric.

2. Cut out the fabric circles with sharp scissors. Thread a hand-sewing needle with quilting thread, buttonhole twist, or two strands of all-purpose sewing thread. Knot the end(s) securely.

3. Turn under ¼" around the outer edge of the circle and baste in place with long running stitches close to the folded edge for a yo-yo with a small hole in the center. For a larger hole, make short running stitches. When you reach the knot, tug on the thread to gather the folded edge into the center. It helps to put a finger in the center of the yo-yo and then draw up the gathers around it. Adjust the gathers, draw them snug, and take several stitches in place to secure the stitching. Use your hand to flatten the circle so the opening is in the center.

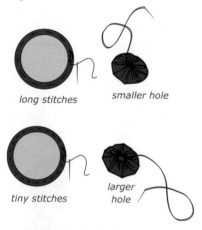

long stitches

smaller hole

tiny stitches

larger hole

Note: Rotary cutters specifically designed to make quick work of cutting yo-yo circles are available. You can also purchase the Clover Yo-Yo Maker, which is available in several sizes and also in some novelty shapes.

Q **How do you sew the yo-yos together make a yo-yo quilt?**

A Making a yo-yo quilt is pretty straightforward. The key is to have fun with the arrangement of colors and prints.

1. Arrange the yo-yos in rows in the desired pattern of colors and/or prints. To make this easy, use straight pins to attach them to a design wall (*see page 212*) row by row.

2. To join the yo-yos into rows, place two adjacent yo-yos together, gathered sides facing, and sew together with a few tiny whipstitches as shown in the illustration. Backstitch at the beginning and end and then open out the joined yo-yos. Add the remaining yo-yos in the row in the same manner. *Note:* If you prefer to sew by machine, use a small zigzag stitch (3mm wide and 1.5mm long) that spans the two edges to sew them together. Begin and end with stitching in place to lock the stitches. You may want to use monofilament thread for this task.

3. After sewing all the yo-yos together in each row, sew the rows together in the same manner.

whipstitch by hand or *zigzag by machine*

Piping and Edge Trims

You can accent quilt edges with flat or gathered trims or piping caught in the seams. Flat piping (without the cord used in traditional piping) is a popular way to add a precise, narrow line of color next to the quilt top or binding, or both.

- -

Q How do I make and add flat piping?

A Catching flat piping (sometimes called a flange) or other flat, ready-made trim in the seam between the quilt-top and the first border is a nice touch and it can disguise less-than-perfect points at the outer edges of blocks. For flat piping, choose a fabric in a color that contrasts nicely with the underlying fabric.

1. For flat piping that finishes to ¼" wide, cut 1"-wide straight-grain strips across the fabric width. Sew them together with bias seams (*see page 352*) to make enough to go around the quilt, adding an extra 10" so you're sure to have enough. Press the seams open.

2. Measure the quilt-top length through the center and cut two strips this length from the long piping strip. Fold in half lengthwise with wrong sides facing and press. Matching centers and ends, pin and then machine-baste the flat piping strips to opposite edges of the quilt top a scant ¼" from the raw edges. Ease the quilt to the strip if necessary.

3. Repeat step 2 to measure, cut, and baste flat piping strips to the remaining quilt-top edges. The piping will be caught in the seams permanently when you add the borders to the quilt top or bind the outer edges.

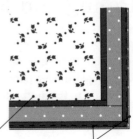

quilt top

flat piping along quilt top and basted to outer edge of border

---

Q Can I incorporate rickrack in the binding seam?

A Yes. Use ½"-wide rickrack and align the points with the outer edge of the quilt top. Note how the rickrack is arranged at the corners and where the points lie in relationship to the seamline. Baste in place and then apply binding. For a bolder statement, use wider rickrack, adjusting the seam-allowance width and the binding-strip width as needed. For miniature quilts, use very narrow rickrack. No matter which width you use, make sure the stitching falls just inside the rickrack edge as shown.

baste rickrack along inner curve of outer edge

Ribbon, lace, and other fancy trims are other options. Make a small test sample to determine the best placement and seam width before you sew the trim to the quilt.

Embroidery

It's fun to add embroidered accents to quilts — by hand or machine. Crazy quilt blocks (*see pages 16 and 160*) are often embellished with hand or machine embroidery.

- -

Q **I'm interested in adding some embroidered touches to my quilt. Any suggestions?**

A See page 394 for a selection of hand stitches that you might use to embellish your quilts. You can also consult a number of books for more on these and other embroidery-stitch options (see the Resources section). Silk-ribbon embroidery is another popular method for embellishing quilts.

- -

Q **Is there any way I can do embroidery on my quilt with my sewing machine?**

A You may be able to duplicate many basic embroidery stitches with built-in stitches on computerized machines. Remember, though, when substituting machine stitches for handstitching, be sure to back the quilt blocks with a tear-away embroidery stabilizer to prevent puckering while you stitch.

CLASSIC HAND-EMBROIDERY STITCHES

Backstitch

Featherstitch

Herringbone stitch

Buttonhole stitch

French Knot

Satin stitch

Chain stitch

Lazy Daisy stitch

Cross-stitch

Chevron stitch

Stem (outline) stitch

CHAPTER 14

Quilter's Math Made Easy

Unless you use only simple geometric shapes, designing and planning your own quilts requires lots of mathematical calculations. The information and charts in this chapter will help speed those calculations.

Yardage Facts and Figures

Q How do I allow for shrinkage when I'm buying a specified amount of fabric?

A Quilter's cotton fabrics shrink at varying rates — usually 1 to 3 percent, but sometimes as much as 5 percent. When calculating required yardage, it's a good idea to multiply the amount you actually need by 1.05 (which will add 5 percent more fabric) and round up to the nearest ¼ yard. Because fabric is always sold in yards and fractions of yards, to do these calculations you will need to convert from yards to inches, do the math, then convert your total back into yards. (*See* Converting Yards to Inches *and* Decimals to Fractions, *for help with this.*)

Let's try an example: Suppose you need ⅝ yard for the binding strips for your quilt.

⅝ yard = 22.5" × 1.05 = 23.625" = ⅔ yard

Note: For additional cutting insurance, add 3" for clean-up cuts. In the example shown, adding 3" would mean purchasing ¾ yard rather than the ⅝ yard originally calculated. That's a safe amount of fabric to purchase — you might have a little left to add to your stash, but having a little extra is better than running short. If you'd rather not do the math, adding at least ¼ yard to the calculated yardage will give you some insurance.

CONVERTING YARDS TO INCHES

Below are commonly cut yardage amounts, based on a 44/45"-wide cotton fabric before preshrinking.

Yards	Inches
1	36"
⅛	4½"
⅙	6"
¼	9"
⅓	12"
⅜	13½"
½	18"
⅝	22½"
⅔	24"
¾	27"
⅞	31½"

DECIMALS TO FRACTIONS

.125	=	⅛
.25	=	¼
.375	=	⅜
.50	=	½
.625	=	⅝
.75	=	¾
.875	=	⅞

Q **What's the advantage of using fat quarters for quilt-making?**

A The shape of the yardage allows for cutting several different shapes for quilts that don't require shapes in large multiples. They are particularly useful for scrap quilts. Often, using a fat quarter instead of a quarter-yard cut results in less waste and fewer scraps. If you cut a 2" × 40" strip and then cut only 10 squares from it, you'll have a leftover 2" × 20" strip and a 6" × 40" strip. If you need 8" squares, you can't cut them from the remaining 6" × 40" strip, so you will need additional yardage. On the other hand, if you cut two 2" × 20" strips from the fat quarter, you would have no strips left over after cutting 2" squares —

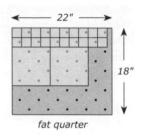

fat quarter

and there would still be room to cut two 8" squares — or place the remaining fabric in your stash to use for appliqués.

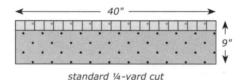

standard ¼-yard cut

Q **Is there an easy way to figure out how many squares I can get from the fat quarters in my stash?**

A Use the chart on the next page to get a general sense of how many squares of varying size you can cut from each fat quarter. As always, results may vary depending on the actual size of the cut and the shrinkage that occurs if you prewash the fabric.

SQUARE YIELD FROM 1 FAT QUARTER

This chart assumes a piece that measures 17" × 20" after preshrinking.

Size of squares	Number of squares
2"	80
2½"	48
2⅞"; 3"	30
3½"; 3⅞"; 4"	20
4½"; 4⅞"; 5"	12
5½"; 5⅞"	9
6"; 6½"	6
6⅞"–8"	4

Straight-Cut Binding Yardage

Q How do I figure out how much fabric I need to make straight-cut binding for my quilt?

A Divide the total length required (*see next page*) by 37" to determine the number of strips to cut across the fabric width. Since these strips are 40" or longer, using 37" allows enough yardage for bias joining seams (*see page 352*). Decide how wide to cut the binding strips for the desired finished width. Multiply the number of strips by the strip width and add 4" for shrinkage and clean-up cuts.

For square or rectangular quilts: Measure the length and the width of the quilt and multiply by 2. Add 12" to allow for joining the ends and mitering corners.

For scalloped-edge quilts: If quilt is scalloped and the scallops are all the same, measure one scallop and multiply by the number of them, then add 14".

For odd shapes: Measure the perimeter and add 14".

SEE ALSO: *Cutting the Binding, pages 350–55.*

Q How wide should I cut the strips to end up with binding the width I want for my quilt?

A The finished width of your quilt binding will depend on several factors: how wide you cut your strips, how small or large you make your seam allowance, and how thick your quilt batting is. You will need a wider binding strip for a quilt with thicker batting, even when the desired finished width of the binding is the same as it would be on a quilt with thin batting. The chart will help you determine how wide to cut your binding strips to get the finished binding width you want. See chapter 12 for more on measuring for, cutting, making, and attaching binding.

Note: Because I recommend double-layer binding in most cases, since it is more durable and is easier to sew (no turning under by hand!), the chart is for double-layer binding. See page 348 in chapter 12 for more information on single-layer binding.

Q How do I figure what I need for double-layer binding?

A Double-layer (French) binding is cut twice as wide as single-layer binding and is folded in half lengthwise with wrong sides together so it already has a folded finished edge to sew to the back of the quilt after you sew the raw edges in place on the front — no extra turning required! Two layers wear longer than one along the edge of the quilt. You can cut straight-grain or bias strips for binding — it's your choice. If your quilt has curved edges, you will need to cut the strips on the bias for sure, so that they will fit easily around the curves. (*See the chart below.*)

CUT WIDTHS FOR DOUBLE-LAYER BINDING

As a rule of thumb: 1 yard of 44"/45"-wide fabric (after preshrinking) will yield approximately 30 yards of 1¾"-wide bias, 16 yards of 2¾"-wide bias, or 14 yards of 3¾"-wide bias.

Finished Width (Seam Width)	Cut Width for Medium-Loft Batting	Cut Width for Low-Loft Batting
¼"	1¾"	1⅝"
⅜"	2¼"	2⅛"
½"	2¾"	2⅝"
⅝"	3¼"	3⅛"
¾"	3¾"	3⅝"
1"	4¾"	4⅝"

Bias Binding Calculations

Q Is there a way to determine how many binding strips I will get from a square of a given size?

A Here are some calculations that will help you determine how much binding you will need, and what size square will yield how much binding.

The example is for a quilt that measures 40" × 56" with medium-loft batting and a ⅜"-wide finished binding (which will require cut strips that are 2¼" wide); substitute your finished quilt dimensions. (You will need a calculator with a square-root function for the last step.)

1. First, calculate how much binding you will need:
   (Quilt length + Quilt width) × 2 + (10" for seam allowances, etc.) = inches of bias needed
   Example: (40" + 56") × 2 + (10") = 202" binding required

2. Next, determine how much fabric that binding represents:
   Cut-strip width x needed length in inches = fabric area needed
   Example: 2¼" × 202" = 454.5" (fabric area needed)

3. Use the calculator to determine the square root of the fabric area needed and round up to the nearest inch.
   Example: Square root of 454.5 = 21.31 = 22" square required for 202" strip of continuous-cut bias binding.

The box on the next page will provide more guidance and guidelines to help you figure out how much bias binding you can get from a given square of fabric.

BIAS STRIP YIELD

If you want to cut bias from a piece of fabric you have on hand, to figure out how much bias yardage you can cut from it, use the following calculation and example:

(Fabric length ÷ × width)	(Desired bias strip = cut width)	bias yardage
(15" × 15") ÷	2.5" =	bias strip yield
225" ÷	2.5" =	90" or 2.5 yards

Don't forget that you will lose some length with joining seams, whether you cut individual strips and sew them together or cut continuous bias strips from a square of fabric. Subtract 10" from the yield to allow for this and make sure you have enough.

Batting Facts and Figures

Q **How do I determine how much batting to buy for my quilt?**

A When calculating the batting size to purchase, be sure to add at least 2" extra at each edge beyond the finished size of the quilt top for small to medium quilts, and 4" extra on each edge for larger quilts. You will trim the excess after the quilting is completed.

For example: For a 56" × 64" quilt, the batting should be at least 60" × 68" (you're adding 4" to the dimensions to allow for

2" extra on each edge). To get this yardage, you would need a twin-size or double batting, if you are planning to buy your batting in prepackaged sizes. (*See chart below.*)

For a quilt top that measures 84" × 84", the batting should be least 92" × 92" (adding 8" to each dimension, which allows for 4" extra on each edge) so you would need to purchase a king-size batting, or use a queen-size and splice on an extra strip (*see page 63*).

Batting is also sold by the yard. Purchase the desired length if the type you want is available that way. Batting is often doubled and rolled onto the tube on which it is displayed, so be sure you know how wide it is before you order the required yardage.

Standard Batting Sizes	
Crib	45" × 60"
Twin	72" × 90"
Double	81" × 96"
Queen	90" × 108"
King	120" × 120"

Cutting Charts

Q **I'm making a patchwork quilt that requires a lot of squares and triangles. How do I figure out how large to cut them to get the finished results I want?**

A Use the illustrations at right as your guide to calculate the required cut size for the most commonly used geometric shapes. Many traditional patchwork blocks require quarter-square or half-square triangles added to the sides of a square.

Cutting them correctly ensures that the outer edges of the block are on the straight of grain (not on the bias) for piecing accuracy and edge stability. Cut sizes for commonly used half- and quarter-square triangles appear in the chart on page 406.

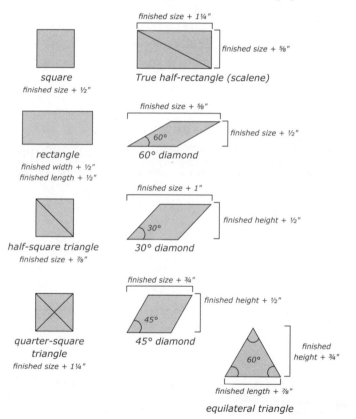

square
finished size + ½"

finished size + 1¼"
finished size + ⅝"

True half-rectangle (scalene)

rectangle
finished width + ½"
finished length + ½"

finished size + ⅝"
60°
finished size + ½"

60° diamond

half-square triangle
finished size + ⅞"

finished size + 1"
30°
finished height + ½"

30° diamond

quarter-square triangle
finished size + 1¼"

finished size + ¾"
45°
finished height + ½"

45° diamond

finished size + ¾"
60°
finished height + ¾"
finished length + ⅞"

equilateral triangle

405

Q I'm using a quilt pattern with half- and quarter-square triangles, but I want to change the block size. How large do I cut the squares that are then cut into triangles?

A Many traditional and new block designs feature these common triangle shapes. Refer to the chart below to determine how large to cut the squares so that the blocks will finish to the correct size for the desired finished block size.

CUTTING TRIANGLES FROM SQUARES

Finished Block Size	Cut Square for ½-Square Triangles	Cut Square for ¼-Square Triangles
3"	3⅞"	4¼"
3½"	4⅜"	4¾"
4"	4⅞"	5¼"
5"	5⅞"	6¼"
5½"	6⅜"	6¾"
6"	6⅞"	7¼"
6½"	7⅜"	7¾"
7"	7⅞"	8¼"
7½"	8⅜"	8¾"
8"	8⅞"	9¼
9"	9⅜"	9¾"
10"	10⅞"	11¼"
12"	12⅞"	13¼"

Q How do I know the width of a block that's set on point in a diagonal setting?

A Use the handy chart below for the most commonly used finished block sizes. To determine the diagonal for block sizes not listed, multiply the length of one finished side by 1.414 and round up to the nearest ⅛". For example to find the diagonal of 17":

17 × 1.414 = 24.038 or 24⅛ rounded to nearest ⅛" (*see* Decimals to Fractions, *page 397*).

DIAGONAL MEASUREMENTS OF BLOCKS

Block Size	Diagonal
2"	2⅞"
2½"	3½"
3"	4¼"
3½"	5"
4"	5⅝"
4½"	6⅜"
5"	7⅛"
5½"	7⅞"
6"	8½"
6½"	9¼"
7"	9⅞"
7½"	10⅝"
8"	11¼"
8½"	12⅛"

Block Size	Diagonal
9"	12¾"
9½"	13½"
10"	14⅛"
10½"	14⅞"
12"	17"
12½"	17¾"
14"	19⅞"
14½"	20½"
16"	22⅝"
16½"	23⅜"
18"	25½"
18½"	26¼"
20"	28¼"

$$\underset{\text{A}}{\text{Q}}$$ My quilt has a diagonal setting requiring half-square and quarter-square triangles. How do I cut these?

It's important to cut these triangles from the appropriate-size square, so that the edges that will lie along the outer edges of the quilt are on the straight grain to avoid stretching. To determine the correct size to cut them, use the chart on the next page.

Note: For best results when cutting side setting triangles for the outer edges of a quilt, add 2" to the square size given in the first column and cut the squares oversize before cutting them into quarter- or half-square triangles (*see page 93*). After assembling the quilt, trim away the excess to square up the quilt edges.

Quilt Size and Design Guidelines

$$\underset{\text{A}}{\text{Q}}$$ What size do I need to make my quilt to cover a standard mattress size?

There's nothing really standard about bed-quilt sizes if you are designing your own quilt or adapting someone else's design. See the chart on page 411 for standard mattress sizes. Some questions to consider are on page 410.

You can customize the quilt to fit your mattress precisely, with the desired drop from the edge of the bed partway or all the way to the floor.

CUTTING SETTING TRIANGLES FROM SQUARES

Find your block size. For side setting triangles, cut the square at the size given and then cut twice diagonally as shown in *Cutting Triangles* on page 93. The resulting triangles have straight-grain on the long edge.

For corner setting triangles, cut the square size given and cut once diagonally as shown on page 93 so the resulting triangles have straight grain on two adjacent edges.

Finished Block Size	Cut Square Size for Side Setting Triangles	Cut Square Size for Corner Setting Triangles
2"	4⅛"	2⅜"
3"	5½"	3"
4"	7"	3¾"
5"	8⅜"	4½"
6"	9¾"	5⅛"
7"	11¼"	5⅞"
8"	12⅝"	6⅝"
9"	14"	7¼"
10"	15½"	8"
12"	18¼"	9⅜"
14"	21⅛"	10⅞"
16"	23⅞"	12¼"
18"	26¾"	13⅝"
20"	29⅝"	15⅛"
24"	35¼"	17⅞"

▶ How much extra width is required to cover the mattress width, plus the "seam" where the mattress meets the box spring — the point where the dust ruffle drops?

▶ Should the blocks stop at the mattress edge, with the drops composed of borders?

▶ Is there a footboard and how will that affect how the finished quilt will look on the bed?

▶ Do I want the quilt to tuck under and cover pillows (which requires extra length)?

- -

Q Are there steps I can follow to plan a quilt to fit my bed?

A First, determine the mattress size; for example 60" × 80". Then, here's what you do:

1. Determine how far you want the quilt to drop from the side and bottom edges of the bed. Measure from the edge of the bed to the place where it meets the box spring and add at least 2" so the quilt will hang over this area. For a 9" drop, the finished drop width would be at least 11".

2. Add the drop to the *side and bottom edges* of the determined mattress size.

> **60" wide + (2 × 11" for side drops) = 82"**
>
> **80" + 11" (for bottom drop) = 82" wide × 81" long.**

In this case, you would probably make the quilt 82" square to allow for a finished quilt to use with pillow shams. For a quilt with a pillow tuck, add at least 12" to the length; if your pillows are extra plump or you like a deep tuck, add

16". For a queen-size bed, that would require a finished quilt length of at least 93".

3. Draw the outer finished dimensions for the quilt to scale on graph paper and then determine how many blocks of the desired size will fit, along with the border or borders of the desired width(s).

STANDARD MATTRESS SIZES

Note: Mattress depths are not standard. Some are only 9"; others with pillow tops may be as deep as 16". If you are planning your own quilt, you can design it to fit the mattress. If you are following the directions for a quilt in a book or pattern, you may need to adjust the design so the finished quilt top fits the mattress size.

Crib	23" × 46" or 28" × 52"
Toddler	30" × 57" or 30" × 75"
Youth	32" × 66"
Twin (Single)	39" × 75"
Long Twin	39" × 80" (common in college dorm rooms)
Double (Full)	54" × 75"
Queen	60" × 80"
Queen Waterbed	60" × 84"
King	76–78" × 80"
California King	72" × 84"
King Waterbed	72" × 84"

Reducing or Enlarging a Block Pattern

Q I'd like to make a quilt that's bigger than the one in a pattern. Is there a way to "blow up" the blocks in the pattern?

A When designing your own quilts, you may need to adjust the size of the block pattern you have to fit the planned layout.

REDUCING AND ENLARGING BLOCKS

		Desired Size (% to reduce or enlarge)					
	1"	2"	3"	4"	5"	6"	7"
1"	100	200	300	400	500	600	700
2"	50	100	150	200	250	300	350
3"	33	67	100	133	167	200	233
4"	25	50	75	100	125	150	175
5"	20	40	60	80	100	120	140
6"	17	33	50	67	83	100	117
7"	14	29	43	57	71	86	100
8"	13	25	38	50	63	75	88
9"	11	22	33	44	56	66	78
10"	10	20	30	40	50	60	70
12"	8	17	25	33	42	50	58
14"	7	14	21	29	36	43	50
16"	6	13	19	25	31	38	44

Original Size (leftmost vertical label)

Use the chart below to determine the enlargement or reduction required. Take the drawing or printed copy of your block to a copy machine. To use the chart, locate the original block size in the left column and then follow the horizontal row to the desired new size to find for the correct percent of increase or decrease. Set the percent on the photocopy machine and copy the block (or the actual block templates if you have them).

For example: If the original block is 6" square and you want a 4" square, you would reduce the original to 67 percent of its size.

Desired Size (% to reduce or enlarge)						
8"	9"	10"	11"	12"	14"	16"
800	900	1000	1100	1200	1400	1600
400	450	500	550	600	700	800
267	300	333	367	400	466	533
200	225	250	275	300	350	400
160	180	200	220	240	280	320
133	150	167	183	200	233	266
114	129	143	157	171	200	229
100	113	125	138	150	175	200
89	100	111	122	133	156	178
80	90	100	110	120	140	160
67	75	83	92	100	117	133
57	64	71	79	86	100	114
50	56	63	69	75	88	100

Q I can't find my block size on the chart. How can I figure out how much to reduce each block?

A The formula is pretty easy: To calculate block sizes not given in the chart, use the following equation:

Desired size ÷ Original Size = Enlargement %

For example, to **enlarge** a 4" block to a 12" block:

12" desired ÷ 4" original = 300% enlargement.

Or, to **reduce** a 12" block to an 8" block: 8" desired ÷ 12"

original = 33% reduction.

Decoding Needle Sizes

Sewing-machine needle thickness increases as the size number increases. As fabric weight and density increases, so should the needle size. For piecing most quilting cottons, use a size 80/12 Universal needle.

SEWING-MACHINE NEEDLE SIZES

American Size	8	9	10	11	12	14	16	18	19
European (mm)	60	65	70	75	80	90	100	110	120

Guide to the letters on needle packaging:

H–J: machine piecing

H–Q: machine quilting

H–E: quilting with decorative threads

MET: use with metallic and Mylar thread

Resources

Suggested Reading

There are hundreds of quilting reference books. Some are out of print but available at your local library or as used books from *www.powells. com, www.amazon.com, www.e-bay.com,* and other online sources for crafts and textiles books. Rare volumes often sell for much more than they did when new, but many are very affordable.

The following is just a small sampling of the books I use the most. They will take you steps beyond the content and answers in this small handbook. Some include step-by-step directions for quilts that you can make to develop your skills.

Barnes, Christine. *Color: The Quilter's Guide.* That Patchwork Place, 1997.

Brackman, Barbara. *Encyclopedia of Pieced Quilt Patterns.* American Quilter's Society, 1993.

Cleland, Lee. *Quilting Makes the Quilt.* That Patchwork Place, 1994.

Dietrich, Mimi. *Basic Quiltmaking Techniques for Hand Appliqué.* Martingale and Company, 1998.

———. *Happy Endings: Finishing the Edges of Your Quilt.* Martingale and Company, 2003.

Doak, Carol. *Show Me How to Paper Piece.* That Patchwork Place, 1997.

———. *Your First Quilt Book (or it should be!),* That Patchwork Place, 1997.

Emery, Linda Goodman. *A Treasury Of Quilting Designs,* American Quilter's Society, 1990.

Fons, Marianne and Liz Porter. *Quilter's Complete Guide.* Oxmoor House, 2001.

Hanson, Joan. *Sensational Settings: Over 80 Ways to Arrange Your Quilt Blocks.* Martingale and Company, 2004.

Hanson, Joan and Mary Hickey. *The Joy of Quilting.* That Patchwork Place, 2000.

Johnston, Ann. *The Quilter's Book of Design.* McGraw-Hill, 1999.

Kimball, Jeanna. *Loving Stitches: A Guide to Fine Hand Quilting,* Martingale and Company, 2003.

Lehman, Libby. *Threadplay, With Libby Lehman: Mastering Machine Embroidery Techniques.* That Patchwork Place, 1997.

Montano, Judith Baker. *Elegant Stitches.* C & T Publishing, 1995.

Noble, Maurine. *Machine Quilting Made Easy.* That Patchwork Place, 1994.

Soltys, Karen Costello, ed. *Fast & Fun Machine Quilting.* Rodale Press, 1997.

Thomas, Donna Lynn. *Shortcuts: A Concise Guide to Rotary Cutting.* That Patchwork Place, 1991.

Quilt Magazines

These are a few of the most popular American magazines for quilters. There are many others, including some from other countries.

American Patchwork & Quilting, www.allpeoplequilt.com
Fons & Porter's Love of Quilting, www.fonsandporter.com
Quilter's Newsletter, www.qnm.com
Quilter's World, www.quilters-world.com
Quilting Arts Magazine, www.quiltingarts.com

Quilting Resources

There are numerous resources for quiltmakers. Doing an online search will yield many more than the few included here.

Quilt History Resources

The Alliance for American Quilts, *www.centerforthequilt.org*
American Quilt Study Group, *www.americanquiltstudygroup.org*
International Quilt Study Center & Museum, *www.quiltstudy.org*

Quilt and Textile Museums

Some of the museums listed are quilt museums only; others offer a broader range of historic textiles, including quilts, in their collections.

American Quilt Study Group (Lincoln, NE)
    www.americanquiltstudygroup.org
American Textile History Museum (Lowell, MA) *www.athm.org*
Brooklyn Museum of Art (Brooklyn, NY) *www.brooklynmuseum.org*
Cooper-Hewitt National Design Museum (New York, NY)
    http://cooperhewitt.org
International Quilt Study Center & Museum (Lincoln, NE)
    www.quiltstudy.org
Lancaster Quilt & Textile Museum (Lancaster, PA)
    www.quiltandtextilemuseum.com
Los Angeles County Museum of Art (Los Angeles, CA)
    http://collectionsonline.lacma.org
Museum of Craft and Folk Art (San Francisco, CA) *www.mocfa.org*
Museum of the American Quilter's Society (Paducah, KY)
    www.quiltmuseum.org
New England Quilt Museum (Lowell, MA) *www.nequiltmuseum.org*
The People's Place Quilt Museum (Intercourse, PA)
    www.ppquiltmuseum.com
The Quilters Hall of Fame (Marion, IN) *www.quiltershalloffame.org*
Shelburne Museum (Shelburne, VT) *www.shelburnemuseum.org*
Smithsonian Institute (Washington, D. C.) *www.si.edu*
The Textile Museum (Washington, D. C.) *www.textilemuseum.com*

Noteworthy Quilt Fabric Companies

Below are a few of the most popular quilt fabric suppliers with Web site addresses. Although these manufacturers do not sell directly to consumers, they often offer quilting tips, free patterns, and previews of their new lines. Many other companies have Web sites.

Alexander Henry Fabrics Inc., *www.ahfabrics.com*
Andover Fabrics, *www.andoverfabrics.com*
Benartex, *www.benartex.com*
Cranston Village, *www.cranstonvillage.com*
FreeSpirit, *www.freespiritfabric.com*
Hoffman California Fabrics, *www.hoffmanfabrics.com*
Marcus Brothers Textiles, *www.marcusfabric.com*
Michael Miller Fabrics, *www.michaelmillerfabrics.com*
Moda Fabrics, *www.modafabrics.com*
P & B Textiles, *www.pbtex.com*
RJR Fabrics, *www.rjrfabrics.com*
Robert Kaufman Fabrics, *www.robertkaufman.com*

Quilting and Notions Catalogs
Shop online at these sites; many offer printed catalogs, too.

C & T Publishing, *www.ctpub.com,* books and the *3-in-1 Color Tool*
Clotilde's, *www.clotilde.com*
Connecting Threads, *www.connectingthreads.com*
Hancock's of Paducah, *www.hancocks-paducah.com*
Keepsake Quilting, *www.keepsakequilting.com*
Nancy's Notions, *www.nancysnotions.com*

Notable Quilt Shows
American Quilter's Society Exposition, *www.americanquilter.com*
International Quilt Festival, *www.quilts.com*
The National Quilting Association Quilt Show, *www.nqaquilts.org*
Quilt National, *www.quiltnational.com*
Quilters' Heritage Celebration, *www.qhconline.com*
Road to California Quilter's Conference and Showcase,
    www.road2ca.com
Sisters Outdoor Quilt Show, *www.stitchinpost.com*

Online Education

AllPeopleQuilt.com, *www.allpeoplequilt.com*
Quilt University, *www.quiltuniversity.com*
QuiltCampus, *www.quiltcampus.net*

Free Quilt Patterns on the Internet

About.com, *www.quilting.about.com*
Block Central, *www.blockcentral.com*
Free Appliqué, *www.freeapplique.com*
Free Quilt Patterns, *www.freequilt.com*
Quilter's Cache, *www.quilterscache.com*
Scrap Quilts, *www.scrapquilts.com*
World Wide Quilting Page, *www.quilt.com*

Quilt Membership Organizations

The Alliance for American Quilts, *www.centerforthequilt.org*
American Quilt Study Group, *http://americanquiltstudygroup.org*
American Quilter's Society, *www.americanquilter.com*
The Appliqué Society, *www.theappliquesociety.org*
Baltimore Appliqué Society, *www.baltimoreapplique.com*
Crazy Quilt Society, *www.crazyquilt.com*
Front Range Contemporary Quilters, *www.artquilters.org*
The National Quilting Association, *www.nqaquilts.org*
Professional Art Quilters Alliance-South, *www.artquiltersouth.org*
Studio Art Quilts Associates, *www.saqa.com*

Fabric Online

There are many Web sites that offer quilting fabric. Favorites include:
eQuilter.com, *www.equilter.com*
FabShop FabSearch, *www.fabshophop.com/fabsearch.asp*
Quiltshops.com, *www.quiltshops.com*

Index

Page numbers in *italics* refer to illustrations; page numbers in **bold** refer to charts.

how it works, 177–78
iron protection and cleaning,
182
fussy cutting, 123, 172, *172*

G

geometric shapes used in blocks,
20–21, *20–21*
cutting charts for, 404–5,
404–5
glue stick
freezer-paper appliqué, 193
water-soluble, 175
grainline, 35–36, *36,* 157, 185
graph paper, 22, 126, 212
grid method for cutting half-
square triangles, 137–39,
139
grid, designing on a, 22–23,
22–23

H

hand piecing, 107, 118–21,
119–20
joining seamed patches,
121, *121*
making templates for,
108–9, *109*
marking and cutting
patches, 110

hand quilting
basic stitch, 295–98, *296–97*
frames and hoops, *291,*
291–93
needles, 72, 293
quilter's knot, how to make,
295, *295*
stitching on a frame, 299, *299*
threads, 294–95
tools, 290–91
hand-basting the quilt sandwich, 281–82, 286, *286*
hand-sewing appliqué, 194, *194*
hanging sleeve, 345, 376–79,
377–78

I

interfacing, 149, 173
invisible machine appliqué. *See*
blindstitch
iron and ironing board, 75–76,
76
cleaning off fusible web, 182
ironing *vs.* pressing, 113

J

joining
blocks with angled seams,
147, *147*
triangles to squares or rectangles, 148, *148*